Praise for *Small Farm Republic*

"I have read at least 20 books a year for the past 25 years and *Small Farm Republic* is absolutely one of the very best that I have ever read. John Klar describes in great detail the fallacies of the current agricultural production model and the changes that need to be made for the sake of our natural resources and humanity. A must-read not only for those involved in all facets of agriculture but policymakers and consumers as well."
—GABE BROWN, regenerative rancher, author of *Dirt to Soil*

"John Klar does an excellent job in *Small Farm Republic* of trying to snap MAGA Republicans out of their political and economic delusions by encouraging them to focus on supporting the needs of small farms in promoting regenerative agriculture. He makes a strong case that Republicans could use support of small farms as a way to shift the party's identity toward improving the environment and reducing the dangers of climate change. In the process, he makes a refreshing case for conservative Republicans reclaiming their traditional role in the political mainstream."
—DAVID E. GUMPERT, author of
Life, Liberty and the Pursuit of Food Rights

"John Klar makes a compelling case for thoughtful Republicans to put aside their differences with Democrats on divisive political issues and to focus on solving the environmental, social, and economic problems caused by today's corporately controlled, industrial agri-food system. The same case could be made for thoughtful Democrats to join forces with Republications to demand government programs and policies that incentivize and support small-scale, regenerative family farms and locally controlled, community-based food systems. Current US farm and food policies are the work of both Democrats and Republicans, and it will take a bipartisan consumer-taxpayer revolution to change them. Klar's *Small Farm Republic* is a clarion call for the revolution to begin."
—JOHN IKERD, agricultural economist; professor emeritus, University of Missouri; author of *Small Farms Are Real Farms*

SMALL FARM REPUBLIC

Why Conservatives Must
Embrace Local Agriculture,
Reject Climate Alarmism, and
Lead an Environmental Revival

JOHN KLAR

FOREWORD BY JOEL SALATIN

CHELSEA GREEN PUBLISHING
White River Junction, Vermont
London, UK

Project Manager: Rebecca Springer
Editor: Ben Trollinger
Copy Editor: Bridget Manzella
Proofreader: Hope Clarke
Indexer: WordCo Indexing Services
Designer: Melissa Jacobson
Page Layout: Abrah Griggs

Printed in Canada.
First printing June 2023.
10 9 8 7 6 5 4 3 2 1   23 24 25 26 27

Our Commitment to Green Publishing
Chelsea Green sees publishing as a tool for cultural change and ecological stewardship. We strive to align our book manufacturing practices with our editorial mission
and to reduce the impact of our business enterprise in the environment. We print our
books using vegetable-based inks whenever possible. This book may cost slightly more
because it was printed on paper from responsibly managed forests, and we hope you'll
agree that it's worth it. *Small Farm Republic* was printed on paper supplied by Marquis
that is certified by the Forest Stewardship Council.

Library of Congress Cataloging-in-Publication Data is available
at https://lccn.loc.gov/2023014746.

ISBN 978-1-64502-219-0 (paperback)
ISBN 978-1-64502-220-6 (ebook)
ISBN 978-1-64502-221-3 (audiobook)

Chelsea Green Publishing
White River Junction, Vermont, USA
London, UK

www.chelseagreen.com

CONTENTS

FOREWORD

Conservative radio talk show host and former presidential candidate Pat Buchanan called me shortly after President Bill Clinton arrived in the White House. The media was abuzz about the French chef that Bill and Hillary hired; he made the audacious claim that he would seek "free-range" chicken for the first family's kitchen.

Conservatives hee-hawed over the idea, and Buchanan quickly sought out a free-range chicken farmer to savage. That would be me. Live on his national radio show, he asked, "What is the difference between your chickens and regular industry chickens?"

My immediate good-natured answer: "Ours don't do drugs."

Without flinching, he pursued: "Why does the industry give them drugs?"

Answer: "First, to make them grow faster . . ."

He cut me off: "What could possibly be wrong with making them grow faster?" Laughing at me, he hung up. End of interview; he got his laughs, made appropriate fun of an environmentalist wacko, and I'm sure his audience ate it up.

Apparently, he didn't realize cancer is a fast growth. But this interchange shows the classic conservative bias toward industrial hubris and the philosophical vulnerability John Klar desperately wants to both expose and defeat. I quit counting the number of media interviews I've done in which at some point the journalist asks: "Wait, you're a conservative Christian? How can you possibly be in favor of ecological stewardship?"

In another exchange, a prominent Libertarian visited our farm with his entourage and within a few minutes quipped, "Of course I'm an Earth Firster! Let's exploit the Earth and then move onto Mars." Though we agreed on many political issues like limited government and freedom of choice, I was speechless at this flippant and cavalier attitude toward our mutual ecological womb. Unfortunately, this kind of hubris is all too common among political conservatives in America, and it's time to root it out once and for all. Remember how Rush Limbaugh routinely played a sound effect of shooting monkeys in the jungle? What caring person laughs at something like that? It's hideous, obscene, condescending—pull out your thesaurus and add more descriptions that strike your fancy. But conservatives laughed and ate it up. For shame.

I shudder when conservatives defend Monsanto's genetically modified organisms (GMOs) as the answer to food insecurity. I cringe when Christians say, "It's all gonna burn anyway. Haven't you read Revelation? Use it up, man, what are you waiting for?" In the same breath, they say it all belongs to God. Pardon me, but if I were God and I made something beautiful like the Earth, I don't think I'd appreciate infertile frogs, three-legged salamanders, eagle eggs that won't hatch, and a dead zone the size of Rhode Island in the Gulf of Mexico. I'd call that a poor return on investment. And I'd blame humanity for the abuse.

Unfortunately, because liberal Democrats own the environmental movement, Republicans feel compelled to make fun and crack jokes about caring for trees and earthworms. The liberal–conservative feud in this arena is tragic for our nation, for the soil, for healing.

Klar is an avowed conservative and finds himself politically aligned with Republicans. But he's embarrassed by both parties' failure to understand the practical environmental, economic, and social contributions of small family farms and local food systems.

I share this frustration, which is why many years ago I created my own introductory moniker: Christian Libertarian environmentalist capitalist lunatic farmer. If liberal Democrats have a blind spot toward Big Government tyranny, epitomized in the Green New Deal, conservative Republicans have an equally blind spot toward entrepreneurial small farming and land stewardship. In fact, they have enshrined support for Big Ag into their political platform.

Quoting from the 2016 Republican Presidential Platform: "Modern practices and technologies supported by the Department of Agriculture have led to reduced erosion, improved water and air quality, increased wildlife habitat, all the while maintaining improved agricultural yield. This stewardship of the land benefits everyone." To quote Klar: "What balderdash!" He's right, of course. USDA policies and the Farm Bill subsidize everything that's environmentally degrading and stifle everything that's environmentally healthy.

In his inimical attorney style, Klar takes on climate change, GMOs, aging farmers, carbon credits, solar panels, food safety regulations, school lunches—you get the picture. For each problem that plagues our culture generally and agriculture specifically, he offers a simple solution: small farmers serving local food systems. If this book has a refrain, that's it. And it's like a breath of fresh air coming from a politically savvy (he ran for governor of Vermont in 2019) conservative.

Poking fun at organics, poking fun at free-range chickens, poking fun at ex-urban small farmers—none of these will curry any favor with an increasingly food-conscious voting public. Especially since Covid, millions of conservatives woke up to the fraud and lies of government experts. A GOP platform extolling the USDA as angelic virtue no longer works with voters aroused to the reality of corporate–government cronyism and corruption. The lies and tyranny perpetrated on the American public during Covid are bearing fruit in a conservative community that prides itself on loyalty to institutions. What if those big institutions are wrong? Many conservatives are asking this question for the first time. So are many Democrats.

Klar eviscerates both liberal and conservative agendas, but his clarion call is to conservatives to rediscover and then own the moral high ground. Noting that the Green New Deal advocates moving everyone to urban living, he calls such a plan "CAFO4US," an obvious play on Concentrated Animal Feeding Operations—which Republicans love and supposedly "green" Democrats despise. The hypocrisies, from both liberals and conservatives, that he highlights are both eye-opening in their precision and mind-boggling in their scope.

While I may disagree on some of Klar's policy recommendations regarding government involvement in solutions (I lean toward eliminating government intrusion and letting Adam Smith's "invisible hand" of the market take over), I deeply appreciate another conservative voice calling out Republicans for supporting policies that destroy not only land but also culture and human health. He dares Republicans to get off their chemical-industrial, anti-health, soil-degrading train and embrace a bottom-up, entrepreneurial solution: small farms serving local food needs.

In quantity, carbon footprint, security, soil building, energy use, nutrient density, cultural development, and economy—you name it—aggressive encouragement of small farm wins the policy debate over current USDA orthodoxy. I'm thrilled that John Klar put in the time and effort to wrestle with these issues in such a creative way. While Democrats add regulation upon regulation and agency upon agency, assuming that bigger government will create better farms and better food, the Republicans by and large go along with most of it. But they also make no secret of their love affair with ever-bigger centralized corporate industrialism. What all sides need to understand is that Big Government and small farms can't grow at the same time.

Like most prophetic writings, this book might not be purchased by its intended audience of conservatives. Democrats may buy it for their Republican friends. That's fine. The truth is that both sides have a lot to learn from this little tome. The truth is that small farms feed more of the world than large farms—we just don't see it in America. The truth is that animals on pasture build soil faster than forests. The truth is that local food systems produce better food, more securely and with less transportation costs, than large farms. The truth is that alternative energy schemes have massive externalized costs that their advocates refuse to acknowledge. The truth is that fake meat destroys more soil than grass-based livestock.

This book is prescient and timely. "Food liberty is necessary for any liberty at all." Amen, John Klar. Conservatives who embrace liberty and freedom can get on the right side of national health and food/farm integrity by embracing this prophetic treatise. You don't have to agree with every point of the sermon to appreciate the message. Wrestling toward truth is always worthwhile, and I challenge everyone to do that with *Small Farm Republic.*

JOEL SALATIN
Polyface Farm
Editor, *The Stockman Grass Farmer*

Introduction

Arriving in Port Royal, Kentucky, on a dry September morning, my wife, Jackie, and I passed through a sparsely populated landscape of rural decay. The crops and land were different from back home, but the dilapidated houses, beat-up old trucks, and poorly maintained roads reflected the same legacy of squalor and struggle experienced by dairy farms in Vermont. We were driving to see our daughter, Emily, graduate from boot camp at Fort Leonard Wood in Missouri, but first we decided to take a detour—a pilgrimage really.

Finally meeting our hero, Wendell Berry, in the flesh was surreal. I had exchanged letters with him over the years, but to actually walk the ground where he wrote so many inspiring and prophetic works was dreamlike.

In his poems, essays, and novels, Berry has spoken to the foundational importance of local agriculture and family farms for five decades. He centers his writing in community and the vital connection of human beings to land and nature. The duty to nurture land and community is dependent on soil and small-scale agriculture. As Berry has asserted in his life's work of writing and activism, severing these relationships results in alienation, dehumanization, and destruction. Technology and profiteering hasten that decline.

Tanya Berry greeted us on the porch of their modest home and ushered us into the kitchen where Wendell was wrapping up a chat with another visitor. The Berry kitchen included a wall shelf crammed with books, mostly agricultural titles. While I gawked at his library, Wendell addressed Jackie with attentive southern hospitality, asking her polite questions about our travels. He generously offered us a bag of organic popcorn—his previous guest had delivered a case, and Wendell was emphatic that he and Tanya surely couldn't eat it all. We accepted his gift and countered with some Vermont Liberty maple syrup that we had custom-bottled.

Seated at the couple's kitchen table in the historic Kentucky landholding from which Wendell has taught readers so much about food and agriculture, Jackie and I quickly gathered that the Berrys, both lifelong Democrats, were rather baffled that conservative Republicans like us would hold such passionate views on the subject of regenerative agriculture. And yet, the conversation plowed ahead. I wanted to know what specific agricultural policies Wendell believed would most help reverse the decline of family farms and sustainable agricultural traditions. He was emphatic in crediting the foundational teachings of Albert Howard, an English botanist and early pioneer of sustainable agriculture, and also referred me to his own book *The Art of Loading Brush*.

Yet that sense of awkward puzzlement seemed to persist as we talked. As I explained that I sought to present regenerative, sustainable agriculture as a *conservative* environmental agenda, both he and Tanya were mystified. At one point during our chat, after a brief silence, Wendell blurted, "But conservatives are the *enemies* of the environment! Mitch McConnell is the *enemy* of the environment!"

"Then Mitch McConnell is *my* enemy," I said. "There are many conservatives who care very much about the environment and who understand the vital importance of agriculture in its care. I speak for those people. The Republican Party desperately needs a credible, effective environmental policy to offer voters, and that's what I want to write a book about."

I mentioned that I felt uniquely positioned to address agriculture policy issues as I am both an attorney and a farmer. Wendell's attention seemed to prick up at my professional credentials and my earnest determination to oppose Mitch McConnell and stake ground for family farms. "I have been trying for fifty years to get Congress to pass a proper farming bill to support small farms," he said. My hero then gently but emphatically bumped his fist on the little round table. "You're a lawyer and a farmer! You must write this book! *You must write this book!*"

This is that book.

The Primacy of Small Farms

So how did I end up at Wendell's table? A decade earlier, in 2006, I had first happened upon his book *The Unsettling of America*, which details how Americans rapidly emigrated from rural to urban areas and the resultant destruction of community, ecosystem, and human health. *The Unsettling of America* was hugely influential for me. I had become independently aware of the dire threats to health, culture, and self-reliance created by industrial food dependency, and this book affirmed my own observations. Over the ensuing years, I struck up an occasional correspondence with Berry while studying his writings. He encouraged me when I engaged in open civil disobedience against Vermont's agriculture authorities to preserve on-farm slaughter traditions, a story recounted in greater detail in chapter 1.

The Berrys' apparent confusion that there might be Republicans who fervently support local agriculture or organic farming is understandable. The conception that all Republicans are enemies of the environment is widespread, just as the general idea that Democrats are its savior is also commonplace. Both are oversimplifications. Though Mitch McConnell has consistently advanced the interests of coal-mining corporations, Barack Obama similarly supported the interests of Monsanto. Wendell himself has clearly become disillusioned with Democrats. He pointedly criticizes the Green New Deal in *The Art of Loading Brush* and complained to us that neither party has stood up for the small farmer. A key point of this book is to forge a middle path that unites Americans from all political backgrounds in support of local agriculture. This includes shattering not just Republican faith in industrial agriculture, but Democrat delusions that renewable energy manufacturing initiatives are any better. Both destroy more than they nurture.

Republicans are increasingly disconnected from large swaths of the electorate who might embrace some conservative positions (for example, fiscal integrity) if not repulsed by the environmental deregulation platforms that currently comprise the bulk of GOP prescriptions for the planet. The sentiment that Republicans don't adequately care about the environment has been compounded by occasional political chants of "Burn, baby, burn!" by some groups in response to claims of climate change, a mantra implying that Americans should pump and use oil and other fossil fuels freely and without concern for environmental consequence. This book crafts a way forward that rejects the reckless call for unlimited consumption without embracing climate change theory. American conservatism must present a plan to truly benefit our ecosystem and communities and not alienate voters.

The American landscape today is cluttered with existential disasters. In addition to the Covid nightmare, Americans are told that humans will be destroyed imminently by climate change; that there is a right-wing extremist threat (or a left-wing extremist threat) that will destroy democracy; that China is out to destroy us; that the economy is destined to collapse. Movies and headlines prey on these fears, which citizens were once told was the only thing to fear.

The fragility of the food supply has now intruded into the public's catastrophe radar. Most Americans do not understand where the bulk of their food comes from and have for decades been falsely convinced that small-scale farming is a losing proposition. This disconnect between consumer and farmer has allowed industrial agricultural and food-processing behemoths to widen their influence at the expense of environmental and human health. "Consumers" do not perceive that they can do anything about this condition of industrial food dependency. This book seeks to narrow that gap and renew the bonds between not just diners and farmers, but humans and soil.

Henry Kissinger reportedly said (more than once), "Control oil and you control nations; control food and you control the people." Monsanto Corporation (now part of Bayer Global) and other massive corporate actors have increased their domination of Americans' food supply. They are fully aware of the profitability and power inherent in controlling food production and have very actively sought to wrest that power—and increasingly the land itself—from individual farmers.

The materialistic reductionism of the Industrial Era has steadily decimated small, local farms. Meanwhile satellite businesses and communities have been destroyed in the bargain. This deterioration in the name of "progress" has been aided and abetted by the lies that there is no money in farming and that farming is drudgery. These false beliefs are a primary hurdle to reversing agricultural destruction.

Another dangerous delusion is that cheap food is here to stay. American consumers must be disabused of the expectation that they are ever entitled to cheap food and asked to consider what happens to their quality of life *when*, not if, food inflation sets in. Access to clean water and nutritious, unadulterated food will play an increasingly important role in geopolitical disputes, and the inflation unfolding now will not abate even if hostilities in Ukraine do.

The plight of thousands of Dutch farmers being compelled to shut down their farms in the face of climate regulation hints at the potential impact of global policies to "save the planet" by consolidating food production while pushing renewable energy platforms. The Rockefellers, who launched Standard Oil, have switched to renewables; Bill Gates is buying up large swaths of farmland and patenting fake meats; the World Economic Forum and chemical companies claim that genetically modified organisms (GMOs) are necessary to save the planet from CO_2.[1] This Orwellian pretense of saving us through increased control and domination should be concerning for all humanity. Wendell Berry has warned us about all of this with a gripping image:

> The food industrialists have by now persuaded millions of consumers to prefer food that is already prepared. They will grow, deliver, and cook your food for you and (just like your mother) beg you to eat it. That they do not yet offer to insert it, pre-chewed, into our mouth is only because they have found no profitable way to do so. We may rest assured that they would be glad to find such a way. The ideal industrial food consumer would be strapped to a table with a tube running from the food factory directly into his or her stomach.[2]

Americans of all political persuasions are waking up to the dangers of industrial food, which erodes human health, the environment, local economies, communities, and culture. International conflicts expose a dire threat to national food *security* as well. China is purchasing farmland for a reason and already owns huge interests in US industrial food production. (Most Americans are unaware that Smithfield Foods is majority-owned by Chinese interests, controlling some 25 percent of the US pork industry.)

To make an analogy, cigarette manufacturers distributed massive shipments of free cigarettes to US soldiers in World War I, ensuring a captive (addicted) consumer base when they returned home. Doctors extolled the health benefits of tobacco, and famous athletes spoke of how much better they performed after a butt. It took decades and millions of preventable deaths before limits were put in place on the tobacco industry. Do

Americans actually *trust* food companies to be any more scrupulous? Are the regulatory agencies that failed to take action against tobacco companies now cracking down on Monsanto or properly studying chemical food additives, glyphosate, or antibiotics in food?

We need a hero to break us out of our industrial addictions, but the saviors of humanity are not technological miracle workers or billionaires: they are *farmers*. Small farmers are the antidote to the tyranny of the corporate hierarchies that dominate America's abhorrent food practices. Young, old, left wing, right wing, fat, skinny—who has the knowledge to save humanity from its plight when aging farmers are retiring without replacements, disappearing much like the 93 percent of heirloom vegetable strains that are lost forever?

Imagine if what has been spent at NASA had instead been invested to nurture local farm production. As awareness grows of the dangers of dependency on imported food and as food prices steadily increase, more Americans will come to understand that local food is vitally important, not just a quaint luxury only economic elites can afford. This book outlines how to make local food production viable as well as desirable—how to pare back the unfair regulatory and tax pressures that have artificially undermined the profitability of small farms in favor of destructive and unsustainable agricultural practices by monolithic corporations.

High energy prices are here to stay; cheap energy is no longer cheap. Low-cost transportation and production methods contributed to the destruction of the family farm, and the rise in energy and fertilizer prices will reward local producers who move back to the land. Local food can be profitable food. It can also be a vehicle for reversing the inhumane industrial treatment of animals, the decimation of soils by chemical applications and excessive tillage, and the accelerating drawdowns of precious underground water aquifers.

Republican Party platforms are deficient regarding environmental stewardship. However, there is a growing voice of common sense and reason within conservatism that must be heard and welcomed by an audience hungry for an informed strategy for Republicans to reclaim (or at least copilot) leadership in environmental policy. And that leadership must be premised on supporting local and regenerative agriculture in all its forms.

Republicans have shirked a leadership role when it comes to land stewardship. Democrats have formed a doomsday cult centered around climate and technocracy. However, there is common ground if we begin to support local and regenerative food economies that reverse the damage created by an industrial food system. To do this, the false dichotomy between organic and conventional farming must be bridged. It is necessary to articulate a definition of regenerative farming practices that is neither purist (organic) nor co-opted by industrialists as a veil for continued destruction. A nuanced approach values the least destructive options in both large- and small-scale production and generally favors local over distant food sources.

Republican intransigence on ecological issues has been hardened by the global warming debate, leaving conservatives to be viewed as enemies of environmental health. But conservatives are not enemies of their own children's health. Many simply need to better understand the importance of local farming. CO_2 emissions are hardly the sole measure of environmental degradation, though shifting to more regenerative and local agriculture will sequester carbon while reducing numerous chemical and fossil-fuel inputs in the bargain. One need not embrace the primacy of global warming to understand the importance of local food. The industrial food supply is polluting our ecosystem *regardless* of whether the planet is being warmed.

This book is "carbon neutral" in that, for conservatives' purposes, CO_2 is irrelevant to the small-farm, regenerative equation. Regenerative practices do restore soils and thus improve the sequestration of carbon, but that is ancillary to other benefits that we embrace: reduced water pollution, soil erosion, and chemicals in food; nurturing of rural culture and economies; decreased reliance on imported food; less risk of supply chain bottlenecking; and improved human health outcomes. Importantly, supporting local and regenerative agriculture serves as a legitimate *political* prescription for conservatives. Republicans can demonstrate credible environmental leadership by reforming agriculture policies while also combating the Democratic folly of renewable energy manufacturing that is a net destroyer of climate and human health.

Those of a liberal persuasion who support regenerative agriculture will support these same arguments and may also cite this work as authority before legislators. There are many conservatives who greatly value environmental stewardship and thirst for such a message, and many will be persuaded of the political, economic, and food-security benefits of improving that stewardship using local farming—without requiring commitment to global warming arguments. Conservatives often scoff at small-scale and organic agriculture as economically nonviable, but a fresh look is warranted.[3] Local farms are supportive of local economies, but also of community, culture, environmental stewardship, individual liberties, and national security. All of these benefits align with conservative values.

There is another asset in the local farm basket that should particularly appeal to conservative thinkers: "environmental politics." When intelligent observers like Rachel Carson, Wendell Berry, and Aldo Leopold cautioned Americans against profligate destruction via mindless consumption, they offered a very different prescription than the current techno-industrial provision of solar panels and electric vehicles (EVs). In contrast to those "renewable energy solutions," this book will prove how unhelpful, even counterproductive, such industrial panaceas are to reducing pollution by comparing them to the impacts of an increase in local agriculture. America's small farms produce food with less CO_2 emissions and fewer chemical inputs, and they transport food shorter distances. Solar panels and EVs generate huge amounts of CO_2 as well as air, water, and soil pollution, and these products are then transported over tremendous distances.

This book makes the case for these positions, as well as the benefits of these same farms to reboot rural economies, improve the nutritional quality and freshness of food while combatting food inflation, and serve as a national security against famine and dependency on foreign agriculture. The goal is to equip conservatives to talk common sense on tax and policy changes that will nurture small-scale farming across the nation, especially for young people. Many young people are already returning to the land, seeking an alternative to urban life.[4] Their success is imperative for America's future.[5] The federal government acknowledges this need and is increasingly considering policies to encourage and enable more young farmers to take the leap.[6] However, it is not the premise of this book that all humans must flee to remote rural subsistence farms—it is that the more people do so, the more all of society will benefit. The better informed about their food origins that urban residents become, the better equipped they will be to make decisions that preserve rather than destroy the air, water, and soil on which they still depend.[7] And the more small farms reappear on rural hillsides, the more healthy food will be available to sell for fair prices to urban eaters.

From Lawyer to Farmer John

When I was young, my mother, a single parent, raised our family on "affordable" junk food—Count Chocula or Frosted Flakes for breakfast; canned spinach and unchewable steak; frozen TV dinners. Despite that, I was lucky enough to experience rural life, both its virtues and struggles, firsthand. I'm told I was conceived in Vermont but I was born in Connecticut, making me a "flatlander" by birth, according to Vermont nativist traditions. I grew up in Connecticut but regularly stayed in Brookfield, Vermont, where my mother's family had farmed for six generations until bulk tank and other unaffordable regulatory requirements forced them out. I regularly visited Vermont dairy farms as a child because I had numerous great aunts and uncles who still dairied. All are gone now, but my connection to the land remained with me.

I was an outdoors type from an early age, and I loved to fish. I learned to backpack in an afterschool group in high school, taking excursions into the Connecticut and Massachusetts Appalachians. After a summer as a camp counselor in Casco, Maine, I ventured into New Hampshire's White Mountains and was hooked. I spent eight days alone crossing the range and became a White Mountain junkie.

This passion never left me. In fact, hiking in the wilderness was my "therapy" through college and law school. In 1982 I took a year off from college, disillusioned with my initial intention of studying chemical engineering at Rutgers University, to work at Yellowstone National Park's Old Faithful Inn as a line cook. Working for ten-hour days allowed me to hike into grizzly country on three-day weekends. I quit in late summer and bushwhacked my way through Yellowstone National Park, as well as Gallatin National Forest in nearby Montana. Even back then it was illegal to just live in the woods without permits, but it didn't matter much to me—I couldn't get enough.

I worked for a while in West Yellowstone, Montana, as a pizza cook, then hitchhiked home to Connecticut, working along the way. I returned to college and pursued a liberal arts degree at the University of Connecticut (UConn). I did well and was able to persuade my father to allow me to attend a study abroad program at the University of Essex in England. There I met and married my first wife and returned to the United States with my bride in 1985. I graduated from UConn in 1986 and then from UConn School of Law in 1989, with honors.

We were determined to return to England, and so my focus in law school was tax law and policy, qualifying me to work for an international public accountancy firm in Birmingham, U.K., following two years of tax practice in Hartford, Connecticut. My love of the outdoors persisted in England. I backpacked in Wales, Scotland, the Lake District, the Peak District, and elsewhere.

I returned to America in 1992 and hung out a shingle to practice as a litigator in Storrs, Connecticut. I developed an acumen for criminal law as that's what came in the door (along with divorce cases). I would go to the gym daily and took regular stress-relief ventures into the White Mountains, including winter forays up Mount Washington.

Hiking and nature had always been my church, but this became especially the case as a litigation attorney, a profession saturated with adversarial conflict and heightened stress levels. As a criminal defense attorney, I lived in a constant swirl of violent crimes, drug deals, drunk drivers, and aggressive prosecutors.

Worse was the family law practice—middle-class people getting divorced are far less rational than most criminal defendants. My cases included private investigators and adultery; allegations of adultery and child (or family pet) molestation; stolen bank accounts and unpaid child support. After a few years, I was in court almost every weekday, sometimes in several different jurisdictions. I might be in criminal court in the morning, then appear in a family matter before rushing to a probate hearing. My criminal caseload was substantial. I might have as many as eight clients in a single court visit before driving to yet another.

Hiking outdoors became a necessary respite now—without forays into the Whites, periodic visits to my family's backwoods farm, and winter jaunts up Mount Chocorua or Mount Washington, I could not have sustained my sanity. I always found something healing and transcendent in the forest that I never experienced elsewhere. This was my rebooting, my mindfulness, my foundation for mental health.

But sometimes nature can also bite back. In 1998, I was unknowingly infected with Lyme disease, and it crippled me. It manifested as fibromyalgia. When the muscle flares came, I could not even get off the floor, let alone go to the gym or hike mountains. I was thirty-four, bench-pressing 400 pounds, and then almost overnight I couldn't carry a bag of groceries. I worked eighty to ninety hours a week in a stressful occupation, as I had for years, and believed I had done this to myself from overwork and self-neglect.

Physical activity was crucial for my health. After my diagnosis, I attended a fibromyalgia support group, and every one of the people there was nearly crippled. Most were in a wheelchair or on crutches. I was horrified. I had to keep moving. The less I moved, the more I atrophied. But with too much stress or exercise, I was back on the floor in writhing pain such as I never knew could exist.

I was compelled to close my successful law practice, as the stress and long hours triggered my condition, and I could only work a few uncertain hours at a stretch. My first wife and I had divorced in 1993, and my second wife, Jackie, and I had a child on the way, plus a child each from previous marriages. Realizing just how deathly ill I was and not knowing how to endure economically or physically, I said to Jackie: "My entire life I have lived where the money was. I want to live where my heart is." After scouring the real estate options, we bought a 160-acre former dairy farm in a small town called Barton in Vermont's desolate but pristine Northeast Kingdom for $115,000. I'd never made a bale of hay, but Jackie is a horse woman as well as a registered nurse and had a lot of confidence.

Simply trying to learn how to husband animals and bale hay was challenging enough for a white-collar lawyer who was also a crappy mechanic and still suffering chronic muscle pain. I was compelled to improve those nonexistent mechanic skills, along with a host of hitherto unfamiliar abilities. I learned the hard way how to raise cows, buying newborn calves at a local commission sale, dairy castaways that often suffered disease or disability. We raised pigs, chickens, sheep, horses, and goats—each category its own education. We also constructed a raw-milk artisanal cheese house, together with a milking parlor where we milked both goats and cows. This required compliance with Vermont's detailed pasteurized milk ordinance (PMO) regulations. Jackie and I became quite a team at castrating piglets, docking lamb tails, delivering calves, and making our own butter and cheese. But our real education was in the growing awareness of where our food came from, along with all the economic and labor realities that entails.

This was all unplanned and unexpected, but we couldn't go back. I had embarked on a farming path almost solely because I needed to keep moving physically, and my heart was rooted in Vermont. Jackie, being a (crazy) horse person, was certainly enthusiastic. But I was in constant, agonizing pain. Shoveling manure and moving bales actually gave me relief. The transition to awareness of food quality, the challenges of profitability, and even how to care for a calf were ancillary to my need to find a physical rather than an intellectual occupation so that I could keep working in some capacity. There was never a business plan, just a desperate leap.

After a couple of years of farming in an effort to simply learn and make ends meet, Jackie prepared dinner one night and we came to a realization: *We had grown everything on our children's table from the ground!* Not just the vegetables, but the chicken, butter, and milk, too. We learned about the health benefits of raw (unprocessed, unpasteurized) milk; lacto-fermented and fresh-canned vegetables; grass-fed meats, whether fresh, brined, or smoked; and nutrient-rich fresh vegetables.

It wasn't merely the self-reliance that was infectious, it was the food *quality*. We had been conditioned to believe that homegrown foods were inferior to grocery-store wares. The opposite is the case. Home-raised chickens taste better; the animals are treated humanely; one knows what they were fed and how they were cared for. This is true across the board, from eggs to butter to cheese to ham steaks. We finally realized what real food was!

Another unexpected reward of our agricultural reorientation was the impact on our three children. All of them thrived in the harsh realities of farming, in a place where temperatures can plummet to -40°F and winters are about seven months long. Our children worked for what they had, without pay; valued things others took for granted; learned responsibility, frugality, initiative, and the creativity that is unique to farming; saw death and suffering firsthand; and worked harder as kids than most adults ever do. There is no better way to prepare children for life. We didn't always know this but are glad to share it widely now that we do.

Woven into this education was a stark contrast: a growing knowledge of the dangers of dependency on a food system that is fragile despite an illusion of plenty—untrustworthy, unhealthy, and harmful to land, water, human health, and community. Jackie and I likely would not have learned this had we remained in suburbia, but sometimes the truth is shocking. There is much in modern food that should not be ingested by humans, much horrific treatment of animals of which consumers are conveniently oblivious. The mega-companies that have consolidated the world's food production are about as trustworthy as the pharmaceutical industry—perhaps less so.

Another lesson I learned the hard way was about the government's control of farming through regulations. Suburbanites don't typically worry the government will pop in unexpectedly to inspect their homes for cleanliness. However, farmers are likely to experience routine inspections. This might seem like a good thing on its face, but it is often taken too far. In constructing our own milking parlor and cheese house, we experienced how counterproductive such bureaucratic red tape can be. One requirement was that we install a complete bathroom facility (including a septic system) in our barn, even though our home bathroom was merely seventy-five feet away from the cheese house and we had no employees. The costs of construction and compliance are one of the biggest reasons young people don't go into farming, along with the cost of much-needed animal processing facilities.

This education, too, was unforeseen but important. It is tragic that more young people do not migrate from the urban to the rural world to dig into the soil, and these regulations and economic factors are the biggest barriers. Many want to move "back to the land," but regulatory and financial hurdles are intimidating if not fatal to vulnerable newbies, especially because of the learning curve involved. Jackie and I were blessed to have learned these truths while we were still young. We have as a result become ardent small-farm advocates, not just as a way of life vital to restoring community and rural economies, but as a way of achieving human health. Healthier, local food production that also treats animals humanely and benefits rather than destroys the environment is the vital and only viable path forward for humanity. As related through these pages, backed up by current studies and scientific analysis, this regenerative agricultural path will also sequester more carbon than *all renewable technology projects combined* and unite Americans around that primary necessity we all share: nutritious and sustainable *local* food.

We sold the Barton farm in 2005. We had by this time constructed a raw-milk artisanal cheese house and milked goats and cows to make cheeses. We were fully certified to sell cheese, farrowed sows and sold piglets and pork, and had about 100 sheep. However, my health was still poor, and we could find little help to work on the farm. Our three kids helped us put up about 8,000 to 9,000 square hay bales yearly, but the long hours were not helping me, and the children were deprived of sports and other activities that we wanted to share with them. Years of taking strong antibiotics had failed to cure me of my Lyme disease. Also, I was convinced the real estate market would collapse with the mortgage industry. I still monitored money supply and saw that trillions of dollars were being poured into overpriced "derivatives" of mortgages issued to people with no assets or ability to repay them—a classic investment bubble. We rented a run-down house in Irasburg, Vermont, on another former dairy where we raised grass-fed beef and lamb for the next fourteen years.

In 2019, I was approached to run for Vermont governor against popular incumbent Phil Scott. I initially announced my run alongside a dozen Republican candidates for other offices, and we labeled ourselves the "Agripublicans." This was largely symbolic, but I gained a significant portion of the primary vote and recruited nearly forty other conservative candidates to run with me on a three-issue platform that included promoting local agriculture. Several of them became legislators. Chief among my policy proposals was the "2020 Vermont Farming Manifesto," which would help reverse the agricultural "unsettling" of Vermont and support both new and existing small farms using real estate and income tax incentives, streamlined regulatory structures, improved processing and distribution systems, and expanded marketing of Vermont foods. After the election, I decided to translate this farming platform into a book to advocate for such ideas nationally.

With the encouragement of many Vermonters, and also of Joel Salatin and Wendell Berry, that effort achieves fruition in these pages. This is not a wish list for an idyllic return-to-the-land fantasy, but a pragmatic analysis of the truly dire situation created by dependency on toxic agricultural and food-processing industries and concrete policy prescriptions—and a political strategy—to undertake the vital return of our nation to a sensible *local* agriculture. As an indictment against both the burn-baby-burn excesses of the Far Right and the only-Big-Brother-can-fix-it false utopianism of the Far Left, these proposals for an agrarian conservatism fashion an effective, workable alternative that draws farmers and consumers together in the problem-solving middle.

CHAPTER ONE

A Conservative Environmental Strategy

American conservatism desperately requires a viable environmental message for today's electorate, and no policy area will more serve to reduce environmental damage than regenerative farming and the local sourcing of food. By supporting small family farms and rural communities, Republicans can credibly offer a solution to numerous environmental problems without committing in any way to the "climate change" narrative or CO_2 limits. This reinforces traditional conservative values by nurturing community, rural culture, human health, economic growth, and national security. No compromise of values is required to endorse these agricultural practices, which are extremely popular with large swaths of voters.

Those on the political Left are already touting regenerative agriculture, organics, better food labeling, and other vitally important reversals of destructive industrial agriculture. Indeed, large livestock producers are shifting into genuinely grass-fed animal management operations. They increasingly understand the problems of water and soil depletion and are implementing no-till and low-till cropping techniques on a grand scale. But many Left-leaning voices prioritize "saving the planet from climate change" or "reducing carbon emissions" as their call to arms for agriculture. Regardless of the truth of these slogans, they alienate conservatives and fail to highlight concerns about human health, food security, and other associated problems that are equally, if not more, pressing.

Modern agriculture consumes massive amounts of fossil fuels, water, soil, and synthetic fertilizers derived from finite natural resources, all of which adversely impact the ecosystem and human health. Left-wing climate change activists have seized on the huge amounts of CO_2 generated by industrial farming methods, and they are moving to champion local and regenerative agriculture in order to curtail carbon emissions. Conservatives can claim this same back-to-the-local movement *without regard to carbon footprints*. Small-scale, local agriculture appeals to those on the left while also fitting well within the core conservative values of decentralized government, family, community, culture, and liberty through self-reliance.

The truths about our nation's agricultural system and its vulnerabilities demand effective responses from *both* parties, not fatuous pipe dreams of creating a new global social order that seeks to control humanity. The study of soil, food production and distribution, and the perils of industrial farming methods reveals the utter failure of the Green New Deal and its advocates to even begin to comprehend the problem.

The proposals of the Green New Deal will take America in the *wrong* direction environmentally and hasten our demise. The plan is merely a wish list of social justice platitudes envisioning technological and economic impossibilities: achieve net-zero greenhouse gas emissions and 100 percent clean, renewable energy; ensure prosperity, universal "family-sustaining wages," employment and paid vacations; guarantee universal access to healthy food; ensure everlasting clean air and water for all; eliminate cows while "supporting family farming."[1] This fantastic nirvana is to be achieved in one decade, employing the massive and corrupt federal government as the salvific vehicle. Humanity does not "Feed the World" with such schemes: the world is fed by supporting the *local*.

Attempting to expose the failed policies of "renewable energy" proposals rings empty with the electorate without positive alternatives to offer. Small, local farms are that alternative. Solar panels and electric cars do not address the dire soil erosion and water depletion being caused by large-scale agriculture, or the food inflation that will steadily increase as consumers learn the hard way—that is to say, financially—of the layers of fossil fuel and other industrial inputs necessary to the modern "miracle" of food production.

Increasingly, Americans want to know where their food comes from. But neither major political party has properly staked out this ground with credibility and commitment. The empty grocery store shelves and panicked stockpiling witnessed during the COVID-19 pandemic echoed hard times past. That crisis may have waned for now, but the Biden administration has hardly instilled confidence that ports and supply lines are secure, that Chinese-manufactured food is safe to eat, that corporate domination and pollution will be opposed, or that small farms will be nurtured as much as art projects, social justice agendas, and other partisan pet initiatives.

The Left is correct to advocate for small farms and increased local food production and distribution. And changes in agriculture policy that will reduce CO_2 offer in addition a panoply of non-CO_2, win-win planks for Republicans, who must take a strong and genuine lead in revitalizing America's family farms and rural communities. That is a winning prescription for the party, but also for liberal-minded Americans, the economy, and food security for future generations. It is radically inclusive.

A multitude of threats to the American food supply will intensify and converge in the near future. For many decades, Americans have lamented the disappearance of small family farms. But aside from the occasional symbolic rock-concert fundraiser, no real effort has been made to reverse the unfair regulatory pressures, bad policies, and corruptive subsidies that an ever-larger government and Big Ag have employed to systematically destroy those rural denizens upon whom our future depends. And now these same industrial voices call to eliminate meat from our food supply and to further compromise food production using unsustainable agricultural methods that also happen to be patented and chemical-dependent.

Small farms are the sole known hope to replace the gradual implosion of large-scale industrial farming. The clear truth of this seemingly bold claim will become more and more evident as the fissures in this fragile industrial system widen. Most dangerous of all is simply fuel price inflation and dependency on ever-more-costly fossil fuel resources. The industrial food system is utterly dependent on *cheap energy*. Without it, food will become increasingly expensive, plunging millions into poverty and seeding political turmoil and economic instability. Conservatives must take the helm with effective initiatives to support local food production and distribution, to lead Americans in both environmental stewardship *and* economic revitalization.

Food—both its availability and affordability—will become Americans' top concern, even above "the environment." Small farms and local food production are the cavalry that rescue neighbors from the vagaries of an unreliable and unhealthy corporate food supply. It is imperative that effective policies are implemented to expand this ever-shrinking sector called the "family farm" and that conservatives sincerely champion that mission. Those who understand food security and the looming threats of Big Ag are watching: this is a bipartisan recruiting ground for both parties, but especially for the GOP.

Conservatives nationally must learn what the regenerative and local farming movements are talking about in order to reap political, economic, cultural, and health benefits. Conservative values are not abandoned but *reinvigorated* by this effort. The Green New Deal proposes complete big-government domination to "save the planet from imminent destruction." Wendell Berry's contrasting admonition to all "parties" is that "it is foolish to complain about big government if we do not do everything we can to support strong local communities and strong community economies."[2]

Small and midsize farms are the fulcrum for a sensible farm policy that will attract voters enthusiastically to the conservative conservationist tent. Climate change activists favor grand technological solutions that enrich chosen special corporate interests in the renewable "industries"; working-class Americans instead want to be allowed to enjoy life and exercise personal responsibility. Writer and scientist Wes Jackson, a leading pioneer in sustainable agriculture and the development of perennial cropping, explains plainly the lines that will continue to define the future:

> The "human cleverness" folk are of a very different stripe from the "nature's wisdom" people. As I see it, the cultural battle to come has little to do with the traditional differences between Democrat and Republican, liberal and conservative. If we are lucky, it will be a conflict between the human cleverness folk and the nature's wisdom advocates. Of course, we have to exercise human cleverness and take advantage of nature's wisdom.[3]

Conservatives can woo swing voters and "walkaways" without sacrificing one whit on policy or values. Smart small-farm policy is universally positive in times of economic and social instability. It also focuses on narrow but vital agricultural policy rather than overbroad "grand designs."[4] The challenge then is to champion the most important cause of modern humanity—sustainable, healthy food production. Lacking a credible environmental policy plan is the death knell for the American GOP. It may be that the party can struggle along on anti-Marxist rhetoric, economic stimulus, and other traditional party planks. However, environmental deterioration, food quality and scarcity issues, and the decline of rural communities will all continue to worsen unless one of the two parties becomes a *true* leader in the effort to reverse these industrial pressures.

Under the contentious leadership of Democratic Socialist Representative Alexandria Ocasio-Cortez, Democrats have paid token acknowledgment to the need for more local, regenerative agriculture. The Green New Deal incorporates a single three-word policy item: "Support family farms." This is not policy, but a platitudinal continuation of the decades-long, blind idiocy exhibited by *both* parties regarding the vital importance of local agriculture. Meanwhile, global opportunists and the European Union are implementing a foolish top-down plan that will destroy agriculture, as is being seen in the Netherlands. Thousands of small farms are being eliminated, along with their livestock and efficient food production, in a bid to, among other things, preserve habitat for wild birds.[5] Americans are increasingly waking up to these truths: conservatives must join and lead that chorus.[6]

Will America's Republican Party champion policies that phase out billion-dollar subsidies to soil-depleting and environmentally damaging agricultural practices, including ethanol production and corn and soy monocultures? Republicans cannot claim to be the saviors of small-town America and court Big Ag at the same time. It is not the premise of this book that all large farming should be eliminated or even that organic methods should be favored over local; instead I advocate for a balanced transition. Gargantuan subsidies for Big Ag have for decades ensured the steady decline of local family farms and the communities they nurture, as well as soil and water health, food security, food quality, and the economy. They must be pared back to reverse these destructive pressures, and that cannot be accomplished overnight.

If conservatives do not act to lead American agriculture in the correct direction, so-called progressives will lead it in the absolutely *wrong* one—toward unbounded government power and expansion, using technological and industrial "controls" of pollution and carbon dioxide that will *dramatically accelerate the emissions of both*. The so-called "Green New Deal," and the salvific calls for limitless globalist or federal power to control all aspects of food production and distribution, will neither reduce pollution nor improve food security. Even *if* the Green New Deal were effective to redress environmental harms, it would come at the cost of the very nation—of American constitutional ideals and sovereignty.

Writer Kirkpatrick Sale, a longtime advocate for smaller government, explains that the Green New Deal seeks to thrust America toward an ineluctable global subjugation. He said that "its uncontrollable enormousness—its very non-human scale—becomes a matter for justifiable alarm."[7] Like the failed "Green Revolution" that ushered in volumes of cheap food in the short term but destroyed human and environmental health (and family farms) over the long term, the proposals of the Green New Deal seek to further expand the dominance of huge industrial interests to "save the world" with short-term "solutions" that are *worse* than inaction.[8]

Solar panels and EVs are net contributors of numerous toxins, a fact ignored in the blind drive to isolate the carbon culprit: they do not reduce but instead *accelerate* pollution. Both industries demand immense fossil fuel and other resource inputs and generate externalized pollution that is deliberately excluded from assessment by those advocating solar panels and EVs as "efficient." In contrast, a policy platform geared toward identifying and responding to the specific issues of agrarian pollution will garner consensus at the local level, boost domestic rather than foreign economic growth, and rapidly reduce industrial pollution while weaning us off fossil fuels.

Proposed in these pages is a policy list deliberately and narrowly crafted to be effective. It will appeal to millions of Americans who perhaps do not identify as liberal or conservative but merely as conservationists. The particular challenge for conservatives is to share this winning prescription with voters, to prove that their hesitation to accept dire warnings about a warming planet does not equate to a careless disregard for soil erosion, water depletion, toxic-chemical contamination, local economies, international food politics, or future food security. Conservatives must take up these causes with zeal. Once they do so, the number one weakness of the Republican Party platform will be cured overnight and instead become its number one strength!

The time is past due for politicians to take advice from those who understand the soil and the production of food—farmers and soil scientists, for starters. Modern society's extremely risky disconnect from the land upon which all life depends has increased to catastrophic proportions, demanding humility and a "return to the local."[9] Old-fashioned farmer common sense must prevail over a corporatist plan to save the world by manufacturing solar panels and EVs at taxpayer expense.[10]

Identifying goals that will garner consensus, that confine themselves to workable (local) rather than fantastical (technological) solutions, and which everyday Americans can see will benefit them, their communities, and local farm families—that is the subject of this book. This win-win-win political/economic/environmental strategy requires giving up nothing except massive, unconscionable federal subsidies for destructive monocultures. The challenge for the Republican Party and its candidates is to get informed, organized, and up to speed on these ideas—and connect with voters—and in turn impact the ecosystem and food markets as soon as is practical. Nothing succeeds like success, and the policies proposed herein for small farms will do more to help the environment than all renewable energy fantasies combined.

There is one thing conservatives must abandon: the "Burn, baby, burn!" mantra. Many if not most conservatives do not actually embrace that slogan, itself popular more for the agitation it inflicts on political opponents than a real belief system. To the extent some conservatives actually do embrace an idea that idiotic, they must be disabused before they destroy themselves, their heirs, and the political Right all in one fell swoop.

This should be an easy sell to American conservatives while opening the political tent to those who object to Big Government and understand the primacy of individual behaviors in responding to environmental threats.[11] Republicans have an opportunity to offer voters effective policies they can understand. Environmental policy built on agriculture demonstrates wisdom and foresight—food inflation will only increase, and these policies constitute an economic, as much as an environmental, strategy.

A Regenerative Politics

Where the Left screams "carbon," the Right must softly say "local agriculture." Conservatives can and must lead a bipartisan push to restore regenerative practices and local food security. There is no requirement for conservatives to hate GMOs or embrace organics: when food is transported vast distances (including from China, Chile, or other exotic origins), the energy consumed amplifies the energy inputs of production. Thus, local conventionally grown food may create *less* chemical pollution and/or energy consumption than distant regenerative or organic alternatives. Consumers must become more aware of where their food comes from and be trusted to make wise choices for themselves. It is not possible or desirable to end all industrial agriculture overnight—millions would perish.[12] The transition being proposed is a reversal of decades of bad policy, and this cannot be achieved abruptly.

A "regenerative politics" proposes impactful solutions to the (man-made) problems that have plagued small family farms for a century. It aims a very focused set of policies at a specific goal—advancing local, regenerative, pollution-reducing agricultural methods. These are policies that are *workable*—within, rather than beyond, the human scale. This contrasts with the grand top-down bureaucratic prescriptions of the Green New Deal emphasizing traditional conservative values.[13]

Not only must a reversion to more sustainable agricultural methods be undertaken transitionally and locally, it can be done without tackling every ecological problem. Expanding localized food production does not purport to address environmental issues caused by jet-fueled vacations, prolific lawn-mowing, or downhill skiing.[14] Americans can easily distinguish between proposals that empower them to act locally and personally versus those that lead them to abdicate their personal responsibility to the omnipotent state and await big-tech salvation from above. As the late U.K. conservative Roger Scruton wrote, "State solutions create a structure of arcane and impersonal directives, which encourage people to evade them by whatever means they can."[15]

With food prices sure to continue escalating, supporting the economically productive expansion of affordable, healthy, and local food will attract tremendous popular appeal. Even now there is bitter resentment among poorer and lower-middle-class Americans against rising taxes and electricity rates siphoned off to subsidize electric cars, mini-splits, and solar panels that only their wealthier neighbors can afford. This, too, is the reverse of what is called for economically as well as environmentally.[16] No single area can do more for the environment than reforming agriculture policies and practices.

COVID-19 spawned a rush of immigrants from city to country, including many who wish to learn to grow their own food, whether for survival, health, or emotional therapy. The rebuilding and repopulation of rural America has already begun, to the great benefit of those who live in cities as well as the country. This is a healthy development that Americans of all walks of life can experience and appreciate.

For more than half a century, numerous writers have chronicled the tragic demise of the American family farm—its causes as well as its consequences. As small family farms have vanished in the face of so-called progress, so, too, have local economies, jobs, businesses, communities, and cultures. When the dairy farms perish, soon the feed dealer closes, and then the equipment seller, the veterinarian, the carpenters and sawmills, then the schools and general stores—and all the rural families and economic production associated with them. We must work to reverse that process. Small local farms, usually family-owned, do more than just grow food and enrich soils. They are the backbone of our culture, families, and rural economies.

This may be compared to an old joke: "What do you get when you play a country song backward?" Answer: "You get your truck back, you get your dog back, you get your job back, you get your wife back." Let us imagine what it looks like to play the sad tale of the death of rural America *backward*—once the farmers are back, the communities and businesses who existed in symbiotic dependence with them can also return.[17] It is axiomatic to farmers, who know that "empty barns house no swallows."

Conservatives Must Lead

Embracing small-scale, local agrarianism is an about-face (a repentance?) from decades of industrial and technological dominance of American agriculture. Farming and food have always been profitable, but large economic interests and an illusion of endless "progress" warped food production unnaturally into a system that favored the most destructive of agricultural management practices. This has been achieved at the expense of small farmers and their families, but also of their arable lands, their communities, their economic viability, their artisanal knowledge, their agri-*culture*.

Small farms have been economically disadvantaged by subsidies and regulations that favor large operators. This is neither a free market nor an accurate representation of the true profitability of farming. American farm policy has artificially cheapened food through subsidies of unhealthy products. Leveling that economic playing field using transitional support for new and entrepreneurial small-scale farms will procure benefits favorable to family, community, and rural culture; increase food security; significantly improve human and animal health, with attendant savings of human life as well as healthcare costs and lost economic activity; nurture struggling rural economies; reverse soil erosion; rebuild water aquifers; reduce risks of flood, drought, and disease; sequester more CO_2 than all Green New Deal proposals combined; and foster a truly popular political strategy that will gain trust for conservatives seeking credibility on environmental policy.

That list of benefits is hardly exhaustive or exaggerated. The full appreciation of the simple truths offered by a truly regenerative, local-farm policy package is merely the perspective of the informed steward of the land—the astute farmer. This view is different from the corporate, profit-motivated, short-sighted creed that has dominated America's political-agricultural landscape like a clumsy strip-mining venture. As Libertarian farmer Joel Salatin writes:

> Folks, the worldview of the locally-based, community-imbedded, environmentally-enhancive, nutrient-dense farmer is as different from the worldview of globalist, mega-corporate, industrialized food elitists as East is from West. . . . Valuing farmers is the cornerstone of environmental protection.[18]

Federal subsidies of crops such as soy, corn, and wheat have supported the nation's largest farms and have indirectly enriched the chemical companies and manufacturers of GMO technologies upon which monoculture crops depend. These methods deplete soils by killing the microbial life in soils, which also accelerates water runoff, reduces mineral content, and creates a cycle of chemical dependency in place of natural growth cycles. This has disadvantaged the small farmer economically by artificially lowering the retail costs of food manufactured from soy, wheat, and corn. It's not that local, organic food is "too expensive"—it's that mass-produced, processed, industrial food has been made cheap by ill-advised subsidization. Those subsidies have been as dangerous and market-perverting to agriculture as the current support of solar and wind power are to both the energy sector and ecosystems—they create inefficient and dangerous dependencies, especially on cheap fossil fuels.[19] Removing wheat, corn, and soy subsidies would increase the cost of high-fructose corn syrup and many other products *without* a government sin tax, and more healthy local alternatives would quickly become cost competitive and more economically viable.[20] A gradual policy change would not necessarily translate to higher commodity prices for corn, since elimination of subsidies would also reduce the amount of corn purchased for ethanol production, which artificially spikes prices. It is unconscionable to subsidize corn, and thus high-fructose syrup production, and then tax people for eating the stuff because it's cheap.

Policies that expand regenerative agriculture methods and local farming take one chunk of the environmental problem at a time—they do not tackle jets, plastic bottles, cellular phones, or NASCAR racing, all of which impact the ecosystem negatively. The goal is to merely support rather than discourage small- and medium-sized local farms and reward regenerative practices for large as well as small agricultural producers. Taxes can be lowered; gas- and diesel-powered vehicles retained. This can also be done beneficially—independently of what China or Russia choose as future paths—a much easier sell to Americans. There is no call to abandon industrial methods overnight, only to wean off that dependency while gradually restoring soil health compromised by the historical dominance of Big Ag.

The cultural division in America today has long simmered. The country mouse and city mouse have interacted in various, sometimes conflicting, ways since agriculture enabled urbanization many thousands of years ago. But that urban center ignores its own peril when it undermines the periphery upon which it depends. Americans watched Hillary Clinton denounce swaths of their neighbors as deplorables. Bill Gates and others attack cows and rural livelihoods in a citified stupor. Political candidates of every stripe are deaf, dumb, and blind to these blistering political winds if they fail to perceive the pivotal importance for future elections of being responsive to the common voter and the real need for local food.[21]

It is time conservatives stood up and defined themselves as sensible (credible) environmental stewards.[22] Local family farms and rural culture are *popular* for good reasons. British author Chris Smaje argues that a local food "movement" is in the works and overdue and that such a transition boasts "a long history of peasant activism geared to recapturing the garden to draw from."[23] Smaje favors a populist agrarian uprising that would bolster sustainable farming.[24]

The broader implications of increased self-reliant farming is that this counters the policy inertia of the "climate change agenda." Americans can transcend identity politics by focusing on shared practical local livelihoods and thereby reaffirm what Smaje calls a "politics of emotional identity" at the national level. Americans view small local farms positively and are appreciating them more each day. Most people are anxiously navigating nosebleed gasoline prices and persistent food, housing, and healthcare inflation. The worse these inflationary pressures, the more relevant and sensible—and popular—local agricultural supports will become.

Rather than sit back and say, "Look at what a failure the Green New Deal is! Let's burn, baby, burn!" American conservatism must seize the agrarian day, propose policies that will elate rural and urban Americans alike, and promise more local, affordable food availability, *sustainably*. (As inflation soars, distant food becomes expensive food, however produced.) These policies also reduce erosion, toxic chemical applications, fossil fuel use, and carbon dioxide emissions.

The conservative environmental political path is agrarian. It is of both the extreme Left and the Mitch McConnell Right that Wendell Berry observes:

> It is, at any rate, impossible for highly credentialed profession-
> als and academics to appraise justly the intelligence of a good

farmer. They are too ignorant for that. You might as well send a bird dog to judge the competence of a neurologist.[25]

Conservatives can straight-facedly proclaim with Smaje that "our safest course . . . involves rejecting grand solutionism and creating local autonomies as best we can."[26] Climate change activists on the Left have presented to Americans in the Green New Deal a plan that reflects a profound ignorance of agricultural challenges and that *won't work* to address pollution. Conservatives must join with moderate and independent voters to embrace environmental policies that reverse or reduce ecological damage from industrialism, in the primary area in which effective responses can be quickly fashioned. This is a promise that *will work*, while securing liberties, economic prosperity for rural and urban America, and food quality and human health *for all*. This is the promise of a Small Farm Republic.

CHAPTER TWO

Reclaiming a Republican Legacy

Soil is making a comeback in pop culture.
—JOSH TICKELL, *Kiss the Ground*

This book advocates for a specific policy strategy for Republicans that will broadly appeal "across the aisle" to traditionalist Democrats, Libertarians, and Independents. Proponents of policies supportive of small-scale, local farms who are Democrats might be called "a Conservative's liberal." Conversely, let our nation's Democrats come to view similarly wise-minded conservatives as "a Democrat's conservative." There is no shame in it for either side.

This ability to sincerely seek and model genuine bipartisan consensus is the political backbone of a regenerative politics for a Republican establishment lost at sea on the issue of environmental leadership. Republicans may not be able to reconcile critical race theory to Judeo-Christian constitutionalism, transgender hormone therapy for teenagers with parental rights, bloated federal budgets with fiscal prudence. Included in the list of policies on which conservatives cannot compromise with liberals are many environmental initiatives, such as promotion of solar panels, nuclear power, and electric vehicles. But conservatives *can* agree on sustainable, local agricultural initiatives without compromising their core values. This presents a rare political island of positive consensus.

The political tides are shifting on the environment. Where the national Republican Party once led the nation in environmental remediation, it can do so again. The only thing from which the GOP must wean itself to accomplish a historic shift in environmental leadership is its commitments to mega-subsidies that benefit industrial corporate interests. Voters will quickly see whether there is sincerity in the GOP based on that issue alone.

President Richard Nixon is properly credited with invigorating a strong conservative environmental consciousness in America. Though remembered more for Watergate and the Vietnam War, Nixon also pushed an expensive, ambitious pollution-fighting agenda to Congress, which later resulted in the creation of the Environmental Protection Agency. That heritage should inspire today's Republican Party to reflect on its legacy and reimagine itself taking that helm once again. The problem, as in many policy areas, is to take that initiative without either aping the Left's scientific and policy errors or abandoning traditional conservative values.

The most substantial early contribution to our nation's collective environmental awareness began with Teddy Roosevelt and the founding of the National Parks system, in collaboration with the incredible passions and intellect of naturalist John Muir. But that conservation effort was undermined by the post–World War II advent of chemical pollution of the land, air, and water. The rapid technological advances of a war economy quickly found new applications in domestic and international agriculture. This transfer of technologies increased crop yields and agricultural production, not just in the United States but in developing nations as well. This shift came to be known as the "Green Revolution."

But things started dying . . . especially birds. Reports grew of thousands of birds suddenly dropping dead from the sky, and the decline of some endangered birds like the nation's symbol of might, the bald eagle, raised alarms. Describing the disappearance of songbirds in her ominously titled 1962 bestseller *Silent Spring*, chemist Rachel Carson attributed the die-offs to widespread applications of toxic chemicals, especially the pesticide DDT. A movement began. Richard Nixon sensed its importance and responded with political wisdom—he led the charge to redress the ills of dangerous chemical agents in the nation's food supply and ecosystem.[1]

Watergate stained this legacy. Additionally, the subsequent Republican shift toward distrust of the growing massive federal bureaucratic behemoth of regulations, agencies, and attendant economic liabilities was not without justification. Many regulations remain too stringent. Agriculture and food processing regulations have long choked local sustainable agriculture.

Wendell Berry wrote sharply of sanitation rules in Kentucky that benefitted large corporate interests while destroying local food producers—in 1978![2] Those who dismiss conservative complaints about overregulation are unaware how much these stifling regulations too often compromise rather than enhance human and environmental health.[3]

And so the Republican establishment began to distrust the environmental movement it had once championed. Some on the Left characterize this negatively, but there were sound reasons for conservatives to balk as federal environmental bureaucratic overreach often outpaced science or ignored economic and ancillary environmental impacts of overly ambitious technocratic policies.[4] Yet the environmental awareness that undergirded the Nixon GOP's acceptance of Rachel Carson's clarion call is present now for that same party to endorse *wise* environmental policies to advance measures supportive of a small/local agricultural producer model to displace industrial dependency.

Credible policy analysis demands that conservatives must embrace local agriculture. Copious scientific evidence establishes that soil erosion, water loss, and human and animal health can all be improved with regenerative, small-scale farming.[5] It is a no-brainer for informed conservatives to advocate for soil health and decry the evils of monoculture cropping. The policy proposals presented in these pages include the elimination of environmental and health regulations that are counterproductive or that weaken local economies and food security. Conservatives can comfortably support policies that nurture small farms, regenerate soils and water supplies, improve food security and quality, and restore local communities and families.

Republican intransigence to federal regulatory overreach has been highly justified when applied to food "safety" rules that run small producers out of the market while making food *less safe*. Similar skepticism is understandable when directed toward solar panels and EVs that accelerate *both* pollution *and* carbon dioxide generation while favoring special monied interests at the expense of both equity and ecosystem. Elevating farmers and common sense as "stakeholders" at the policy table to displace elitist university technocrats is a vital shift if Americans are to reverse the destruction of their lands and soils. As Wendell Berry, Aldo Leopold, and many other great (nonpartisan) intellects have alerted us for decades, it is the university elites and so-called experts who have herded family farmers into urban wage slavery and industrial dependency! Many current laws are anathema to food security, family farms, soil and animal health, and the ecosystem. Conservatives must *liberate* America from ill-considered food safety laws.

The Left seeks to "own" the environment as *its* issue, but it is a falsehood to claim that conservatives care solely about "the economy." In fact it is the Left that foolhardily disregards the connection between economic stability and environmental stewardship. Starving people don't care about CO_2.

Liberal pundits with supposed expertise on environmental issues lambast Republicans while they themselves serve Big Ag at the expense of family farms. Weaponizing every issue for maximum ideological propaganda, many on the Left divisively portray conservatives as climate-haters and themselves as the sole saviors of the Earth.[6]

This effort to pigeonhole conservatives is fallacious: conservatives *do* care—and are smart enough to understand the issues. Conservatives must outflank liberal extremism on the environment and join with moderate Democrats who understand that local solutions are required to address our shared global predicament. There is integrity in the Republican forthrightness that economic growth is relevant, and important, both to Americans and their ability to counter ecosystem degradation. There is no integrity in advancing monied economic interests in the "renewables industry" under the false pretense that the world is being thereby "saved." It is very much *not*.

Rather than claiming credit for increasing environmental awareness, Al Gore and the Democrats should be faulted for killing environmental progress and activism by stalling the world over carbon dioxide. It was the quick-shift folly of *An Inconvenient Truth* that uncoupled the train of environmental cooperation and fashioned the existential red-herring rift that sows contention still today. As Kristin Ohlson wrote in her book *The Soil Will Save Us*:

> Al Gore stepped into the political vacuum but, say prominent pro-environment Republicans, did so in such a partisan

way that it was easy for conservatives to scorn anything he championed. Given that most farmers and ranchers are deeply conservative, environmental activists maintain friendly ties with them by choosing their words carefully.[7]

The hyper-politicization of carbon dioxide as a source of global warming and climate change is a distraction, regardless of whether CO_2 is warming the planet. It is not unreasonable to suspect that consuming 90 million barrels of petroleum per day, plus other stored energy sources such as wood, coal, natural gas, and nuclear power, may warm the planet. But Gore's overhyped book marked a tectonic shift in the political focus of the entire environmental effort *away* from industrial toxins, Superfund sites, and dead bald eagles, toward the more esoteric, hard to prove, and *unimportant* warming issue.

How can this be dismissed as unimportant? Because humans (and all life, from microbes to whales) are in a crisis of *pollution by chemicals*, and there was widespread agreement on that before the Gore histrionics. Now there are some 3,000 new chemicals created yearly, with more than *80,000 man-made compounds* unleashed on the environment (and human biology) in the last 150 years. But instead of pursuing a campaign to regulate those toxins, the entire world shifted to the cult of carbon. This is a tragedy for which Al Gore has not yet taken credit.

If humanity were to target chemical pollution, it would sweep away carbon dioxide in the bargain—fossil fuels generate carcinogenic toxins *whether or not* their carbon dioxide is villainous. As the world dithers over speculative "ranges" of potential warming by CO_2, less effort has been devoted to policing chemicals, even as whole new dangers (for example, PFOAS, phthalates, and a myriad of potential endocrine disruptors) are discovered, and fertility rates are plummeting while cancer rates spike. But let's dither some more about carbon, shall we? Industry is rushing to *increase* the amount of novel chemicals created, and toxic pollutants generated, in the push to manufacture EVs, heat pumps, windmills, and solar panels as faux solutions to carbon dioxide "pollution"?

Who has benefitted from the shift to an emphasis on carbon, if not Big Oil, Big Ag, manufacturing industries, and the other polluters who have now been released from intense oversight as a bevy of opportunists smell money to be made from "renewables"? The foibles of Ronald Reagan and acid rain pale in comparison to this magnificent failure.[8] Those who pat themselves on the back for their glorious accomplishments are deluded, clothes-less emperors—carbon dioxide Ponzies.[9]

Republicans must no longer stand by and allow this tyranny of bad science and bad policy to dominate Americans. All the GOP has to do is advocate for small and local agriculture and be willing to put their political mouths *above* where the money is—let the Dems take campaign contributions and dine with lobbyists from Monsanto, Cargill, and the rest. The GOP will have no credibility to expose the failures of Democrats unless it repents its own failings here.

This is a simple action for Republicans, and the purge of guilt will be immediate. Instead of labeling all conservatives as Earth-haters, attention must be shifted toward the bogus claims of renewable energy and the Green New Boondoggle. The moment that door is opened, the house of cards from which the Green New Deal is constructed will collapse. The false hope of climate activists must be replaced with positive conservative prescriptions to conserve small-scale family farms throughout rural America.[10]

The current liberal prescription for salvation from pending climate catastrophe can be summarized simply: only technology can avert the end of the world—technologies that *accelerate* CO_2 and toxic pollution generation! This is not just overly simplistic and techno-mystical, it also ignores agriculture and farming as either cause of or solution to ecosystem degradation! Those who have exalted themselves as the "experts" on "climate change" are in fact shills for big corporate interests or (more sadly) just pathetically egotistical academics who have no clue where that plastic-wrapped Styrofoam tray of meat comes from.

The reversal of the alleged Republican reversal[11] on environmental policy includes *conquering* the false condemnation of conservatives as uncaring while exposing the ineffective posturing behind extremist, big-government, big-tech fixes such as the Green New Deal and Build Back Better. Success on this one issue will greatly improve the national GOP's public image, attracting Americans to examine additional conservative tenets that will improve their lives, that respect tradition and culture in a time of looting and chaos, and that offer economic growth, fiscal integrity, and preservation of personal rights. But more, it is an area of common political as well as cultural ground for moderate Democrats and Republicans to unite in a time when the nation is so tragically at odds.

In this regard, Republicans cannot credibly condemn Democrat ineptitude on the environment without viable proposals of their own. The prevailing public opinion that conservatives are do-nothings on environmental preservation can only be countered with demonstrable evidence to the contrary. The issue must be grabbed by its thorny horns. Credibility is easily gained for small-farm policies—they are understandable, scientifically reinforced, and backed by decades of conservationist wisdom that favors this path and condemns big-fix techno-utopianism.

While conservatives get serious about realistic environmental policies on a local scale and unite with similarly minded Democrats, Far Left "progressives" will doubtless continue to expound grand utopian visions to "eliminate all fossil fuels from agriculture,"[12] without a shred of policy, or even *possibility*. If so, the Far Left will remain hopelessly embroiled "in a kind of climate-change arms race, competing to see who could be most serious, and most ambitious, about the threat they universally declared as 'existential.'"[13] The *only* viable path forward is bipartisan: sensible Democrats will welcome conservative awakening to the crucial importance of regenerative local agriculture.

Many on the Left chafe at what they regard as foot-dragging by the Right on environmental issues, when actually the sides merely differ in ideas about *how* to address our shared problems. The Far Left demands everyone in the world see the "simplicity" of their global technological "fix" without critical reflection or discussion.[14] Yet "the science" now unequivocally proves the tremendous and numerous positive impacts of sustainable, local farming and also the multitude of insurmountable problems with "renewable technologies" manufactured via huge energy (CO_2) and resource inputs. The Green New Deal is the most ambitious rebuilding of America's social, economic, and political structures ever proposed, and it cannot withstand even a short and messy debate, let alone an extended critical analysis.

A "local and regenerative farming" environmental policy is an infinitely preferable alternative. Embracing local agricultural business and sustainable agricultural practices is also a potent bipartisan *political* policy because it directly opposes the draconian plans of the Green New Tyrants.

The Farce of the Green New Deal

For decades, the Left has argued that conservative foot-dragging on expensive big-government efforts to regulate the environment have caused dangerous delays in effective climate response. But the Green New Deal takes the world *backward* environmentally, increasing carbon dioxide emissions and pollution generated during manufacturing, transport, and disposal of favored renewable energy products. And it proposes to do so by funding huge manufacturing industries concurrently with an alarming expansion of federal powers.

Focusing on local agriculture compels accountability for this failure as food and energy prices soar worldwide. Americans increasingly see the elitist disconnect (on both sides of the political aisle) that threatens their health and security. As David Wallace-Wells wrote in his book *The Uninhabitable Earth*:

> The growing hypocrisy of the truly empowered—corporations, nations, political leaders—illustrates a far more concerning possibility, all the more alarming for being so familiar from other realms of politics: that climate talk could become not a spur to change but an alibi, a cover, for inaction and irresponsibility, the world's most powerful uniting in a chorus of double-talk that produces little beyond the song.[15]

That is precisely what the smokescreen of climate change has been—a cynical power grab by politicians and big-tech giants alike. It is inevitable that this truth will emerge in time, but America cannot afford to waste more time! Food inflation will increase steadily, and agriculture remains the number one cause of pollution. Sensible agricultural policies that nurture regenerative practices and local food production also augment food security, soil and water preservation, economic expansion, and rural revitalization, while greatly reducing fossil fuel use and sequestering astronomical quantities of carbon in soils. They also cushion food prices.

The choices offered as ecological solutions are not just between techno-logical versus old-school or even big government versus local authority—the choices are between individual autonomy and a one-world domi-nation.[16] A "big picture" utopianism is intrinsic to the Green New Deal. Unabashed global domination is woven into its every fiber, even as actual functional responses to environmental remediation are bleached out. Tom Philpott, food and agriculture reporter for *Mother Jones*, proclaims that "We have reached the limits of 'market-as-movement' to transform the food system," and gushes exuberantly about exactly these weaknesses.[17]

Promising the sky and the moon, with no plans for ladders—that is the Green New Deal. Philpott praises the new economy that will "eliminate pollution and greenhouse gas emissions from the agricultural sector," while leaving aside economics (or farming ability) in optimistic confidence that the perfect solution will be crafted under the nebulous—if dubious—goals of the Green New Delusion:

> [The Green New Deal is] bluntly agnostic on what policies
> should be put in place to achieve these goals. . . . Filling in the
> blanks of what specific legislation is to come out of the deal is
> left up to the public—including to social movements.[18]

Urban "social movements" restructured farming and now seek to print infinite money. It is a sure failure and reflects utter disconnect from how farms, and soil, function. Soil erosion doesn't respond to social justice movements; it adheres to a different discipline entirely. But since when are sweeping laws enacted with zero actual policies? Will a social movement eliminate monoculture subsidies and grow clean food? This is absolute fantasy. Reversing soil deterioration can only be achieved by dramatic, tar-geted policies, not dithering "agnosticism," a synonym for "carte blanche."

The true environmental response required—small-scale farming, particularly using rotational grazing that moves animals around pastures rather than confining them in buildings and using equipment to bring feed to them—is notably absent from these big-idea prescriptions. Mr. Philpott ironically calls these big-government efforts toward total agri-cultural domination "a genuine grassroots political movement," but what could be more "grassroots" than subsidizing local family farms, regenerative agricultural practices, and soil-building, rotational, grass-based animal husbandry? The entire "science" of sequestering carbon in soils is bound directly to the growth of that very thing—the roots of grasses (see chapters 3 and 4), not the expansion of quasi-fascist federal control.

Populism and Cooperation

The path forward for the nation must be bipartisan, and food quality and availability will increasingly form the basis of across-the-aisle cooperation and humility that will bond Americans of diverse backgrounds into cohesive agreement on at least one thing: the primacy of a nations' food supply to serve the people. Bipartisan support for regenerative and local agricultural policies is a virtual certainty. In order for the Republican establishment to seek consensus with a hostile Left, it must first establish consensus within its own ranks and then recruit like-minded Democrats who need not abandon their own party to join forces for the benefits shared by all. Conservatives united powerfully together to advance such policies will unleash immense political energy and galvanize Americans in the face of roiling domestic sociopolitical conflict.

Unlike the increasing distance between progressive Democrats and their traditional middle-class base, Republicans have moved more to that center. The renewables "industry" is an environmentally destructive, unsustainable, dead-end scam. Regenerative politics is a solution people can clearly see and easily understand, and it doesn't require eliminating private property ownership, seeding runaway food inflation, or destroying the nation's currency.

CHAPTER THREE

A Regenerative Farm Policy

*No other natural process steadily removes such vast amounts
of carbon dioxide from the atmosphere as photosynthesis,
and no human scheme to remove it can do so on such a vast
scale with any guarantee of safety or without great expense.*

—KRISTIN OHLSON, *The Soil Will Save Us*

Skepticism about the ability of small, local farms to "feed the world" is to be expected. But that very goal—"to feed the world"—is the dubious claim repeated dully by the agriculture industrialists to justify the continued *bleeding* of the world. It is not the goal of regenerative and local agriculture policy prescriptions to feed the world from the *top*, but from the *bottom*. The goal is to "feed the local"—the world will follow, while it heals from the scars of industrial rapaciousness. And while improving food quality and freshness and human health, these policies will at the same time reverse the environmental destruction that also can only be achieved at that same local level. A one-world government cannot save the planet environmentally.

The false logic is that there are only two choices: absolute industrially processed food fabrication (we are nearly there) versus a pseudo-Amish migration of all humans back to an idyllic agrarianism that never existed. A proper agricultural policy perspective dismantles this harmful division. Human food production causes a range of environmental impacts that include not just carbon dioxide emissions and energy consumption, but toxic chemical inputs, water depletion, and soil erosion—a myriad of consequences of food choices that vary depending on the method of production, crop variety, geographical location, shifting weather patterns, processing and packaging methods, and distribution.

For example, some so-called expert analysis asserts that there is a "water equivalency" to foods consumed and that the amount of water consumed in the growing and processing of various foodstuffs can be "measured" and summarized in a simplistic chart. This is useful information. Almonds are indeed a water-use offender, for instance, and greater individual awareness of that fact might incline some consumers to shift to peanuts instead. But consider "scientific" sources that claim that a six-ounce serving of hamburger consumes sixty-five gallons of water in production. Even if that were an accurate assessment of confinement-raised, grain-fed beef (which would also vary depending on geographic area, drought conditions, and so on), it is an absurd slander against grass-fed, rotationally grazed cows. The latter may well use *no* net water whatsoever and even *improve* water quality while preventing water runoff through grazing and soil-feeding manure, enriching soil health, sequestering carbon, and avoiding factory-farmed grains entirely. To equate the two products is absurd folly and explains the ignorance of condemning all beef production, as some politicians and academics do.

To effectively calculate the environmental cost of food choices, American consumers and policymakers must assess inputs and outputs on a spectrum of impacts. The debates over organics, labeling, and GMOs have obfuscated and delayed effective action. Local conventional (that is, *not* organic) produce is likely to use less energy and generate less CO_2 than organically grown food transported long distances—the energy, chemical pollutants, and CO_2 of transportation count as environmental costs. Local farms always improve freshness, reliability, and trust, but they also reduce pollution from transportation.[1] Similarly, organic vegetables raised on farmland that draws water from endangered underground aquifers carries a much larger water liability than conventional vegetables grown in the wet Northeast.

No one can accurately calculate all the vicissitudes of the various considerations of food origin and production methods. But to reduce all foods to a calorie-like measure of environmental damage is to avoid understanding their impact properly. Further, it is unrealistic to propose that all industrial agricultural production could or even should be abruptly halted. A nation dependent on this system would starve as precipitously as a heroin addict in withdrawal. Indeed, modern food consumption bears an eerie similarity to a synthetic opioid addiction en masse. Just like cigarette manufacturers who worked to make their products even more addictive (and deadly) while advertising them as the opposite, industrial food manufacturers and their high-paid lobbyists and political allies have conspired to peddle their Earth-destroying wares as Earth-saving. It is a truly Orwellian, dystopian fallacy that requires an organic, populist awakening to counter it.

A truly effective regenerative and local policy toolkit will create a level playing field for local farms and reduce the amount of food produced by mega-farms whose monocultures are dependent on destructive chemical inputs. It is neither an "all-organic" nor an "all-local" model but sensibly weighs pros and cons of each. This transition will involve a deeper under-standing of soil, supply lines, food security and healthfulness, and other vitally important considerations being ignored by the Green New Deal.[2] As America will see, these are not trivial matters. The nation's future economic and social stability depends on getting this balanced transition right.

In defining "best practices" for an agriculture that is not purist organics but instead assesses the complex interaction of transportation, processing, and production inputs, a more blended and realistic approach is required. Reducing and in some cases eliminating chemical pesticide and fertilizer applications is necessary, but our aspirations must not be overly zealous. Purist models often view agriculture in an input-narrowed vacuum, ignor-ing, for instance, that massive amounts of CO_2 and chemical inputs can be conserved in large-scale operations that still employ chemical inputs such as synthetic fertilizers when they shift to no-till or reduced-till practices or shift away from GMO corn or soy monocultures. It is imperative that large industrial producers are incentivized to reduce pollution and rebuild soils in viable ways. Overnight conversion to 100 percent organic is simply not pos-sible without calamity—witness the travesty of Sri Lanka and other nations that precipitously eliminated synthetic fertilizer and other chemical inputs.[3] And to the extent that converting chemical-drenched industrial soils back to nutrient-rich health can be achieved, it is a process that takes years.

As used in this book, the term "regenerative agriculture," refers to pro-duction methods that shift toward ecologically sustainable perennial crops; rotational grazing and reduced reliance on confinement feed methods for livestock; reducing tillable acreage or employing no-till or reduced-tilling practices; increased use of manures replacing synthetic fertilizers; and controlling or reducing soil erosion and water waste. These methods are distinct from the additional benefits of localizing production to curtail transportation, processing, and other inputs, and of downsizing scale. The redirection of American agriculture toward regenerative practices is not one-size-fits-all, and efforts to unilaterally compel compliance seed resistance and conflict instead of healthier crops.

This definition broadly encompasses a greater range of desired agricultural improvements, not limited to organic purism, itself a controversial and distractive exercise. These practices have application to immense tracts of land in industrial agriculture, not just small, local operations. But regenerative farming by itself does not address the large environmental costs of transport. Thus corn grown in tilled acreage and used locally could well inflict less total environmental impact than no-till corn grown 2,500 miles distant. A blended agricultural perspective weighs energy and pollution inputs in concert with other measures of environmental impact.

The foundation for all sensible agriculture policies is soil health. Regenerative practices are *an* important tool to improve the health of soil, which sequesters vast amounts of carbon that ultimately becomes the energy for the plants upon which we and our livestock dine. No amount of technology can re-create the balance of nature that fed humans before the Green Revolution of technology and industrial fertilizers. Though chemists and engineers can fashion amazing short-term "improvements" to bolster agricultural production, they cannot manufacture soil, water, essential minerals or the churning biological activity that thrives in that miraculous life-source we pejoratively call "dirt."

Americans are beginning to realize that food production is much more complex than simply pouring chemicals onto an inanimate substrate. It is quite the opposite. Animals and decay are central to the natural process, and pastures rotationally grazed with livestock are the pinnacle of soil health and carbon sequestration. Increasingly, people are coming to understand that the soil itself contains a "microbiome," much like the human gut, and it requires a cycle of living organisms that are anything but inanimate.

Histrionic slanders against cows abound, yet cows are a primary source of manure to reduce dependence on synthetic fertilizers manufactured from fossil fuels. But cows offer much more than that. When bucolic bovines munch on pasture directly rather than be confined to feedlots, they stimulate grass regrowth and the sequestration of carbon in the soil. Microbial life is nurtured, increasing soil productivity. Plants take up more phosphorus and micronutrients, reducing erosion and water runoff. This is an entirely different process from tilling, spraying, and harvesting through the use of fossil fuels and chemicals while the cows are confined in a concrete barn. It is also far more effective in sequestering carbon than letting trees grow, as Kristin Ohlson observes in *The Soil Will Save Us*: "When you graze and let the plants recover, they pulse carbon and moisture into the soil. . . . Trees don't do the same thing. That's why grasslands are so important to carbon recycling."[4]

American society has become so infatuated with gadgets that it falsely believes that the same technologies that created increased crop yields of the Green Revolution through mechanization can somehow substitute for the miraculous soil-building abilities of the great herds of bison slaughtered to conquer Native peoples. Yet the *opposite* is the case: soils are dying, water is disappearing, people are being sickened. Industrial agriculture is in its death throes and is taking the ecosystem to the grave in this Faustian rip-off.[5]

Destruction of our nurturing ecosystem is hardly inevitable, but it is a problem hardly appreciated. The stakes really are that high, which is a double blessing for regenerative and local agriculture: there actually is hope for improved circumstances, and conservation-minded conservatives and liberals alike need surrender nothing whatsoever ideologically to embrace shared solutions. However, most Democratic and Republican politicians are utterly oblivious of the need for this shift, as exhibited by endless cow-bashing and calls for yet more large-scale industrial production. In truth, cows are by far the primary resource to *rescue* humanity from its plight. Yet the Green New Deal and Bill Gates seek to eventually *ban* cows and eliminate healthy meat from our children's diets, replaced with plants that are produced using destructive, polluting, and unsustainable agricultural methods!

The EPA estimates that 11 percent of US greenhouse gas emissions in 2020 were caused by agriculture, of which 12 percent is attributable to "manure management."[6] The analysis of these gasses is imprecise, but the global agricultural contribution is estimated at 15 percent.[7] There is no question that shifting cows and other industrially raised animals away from inhumane confinement operations to smaller-scale or rotational-grazing systems will dramatically reduce greenhouse gas production while improving animal, human, and soil health. Massive manure pits that often result in horrific environmental and human disasters can be converted from Superfund-like liabilities into soil-enriching assets.

Local and regenerative farming practices reverse the climate and soil crises, reverse water depletion, and turn around the economic and cultural decline of rural communities. They reduce harms to human health from chemicals, preservatives, early harvesting (which deprives produce of vital nutrients), antibiotics, hormones, pathogens, nutrient deficiency, and so on; lessen inhumane treatment of animals during life and slaughter; and mitigate negative consequences of globalization, including related threats to national security. They also reduce American dependency on immense industrial producers and processors, ports, distributors, and retailers for food while building public trust in Republicans to offer sincere and effective solutions to observable environmental harms. These require a national reversal—by both political parties—of America's historic travesty of subsidizing cheap, destructive industrial agricultural production of monocultures that are sickening Americans while slowly toxifying and wasting essential soils and water.

Once the step is accomplished for modern "consumers" to appreciate healthy, lively soils as the key to agricultural, environmental, and human health, the second step can be made: valuing cows and other ruminants as the cornerstone of soil and microbial—and thus human and environmental —health. Maligning cows for the bad acts of industrial feed operations is an astonishing slander promulgated and perpetuated by blame-shifting special interests. Urbanites have been conditioned to see cows as enemies, but the culprit is those who treat cows badly: bovines are the victims, being yet further victimized.

Increasingly, learned agricultural voices are being heard above the vegan herd, to explain that one can't grow organic vegetables without enormous quantities of healthy, earthy poop. This poop cannot be procured by any means other than the methodical mastication, then contemplative "rumination" (digestive processes in the four bovine stomachs), which occasions a side effect called "cow flatulence."

Paying due respect to the cows upon whom we depend for life, Diana Rodgers and Robb Wolf explain in their book *Sacred Cow: Why Well-Raised Meat Is Good for You and Good for the Planet* that grass-fed, rotationally grazed meats contain healthy fats essential for human health and that vegan alternatives are likely *more* environmentally destructive than cattle farming. Ruminants comprise an integral link in sustainable agriculture, and converting industrial meat production to rotational, grass-based methodology is the *best single tool* to mitigate climate change.[8]

A diet and farming system primarily dependent on the subsidized industrial production of corn, soy, and other massive one-species crops (monocultures, whether or not genetically modified) is ecologically devastating and creates widespread human illness.[9] The Green New Deal proposes to mandate exactly this increased centralization, to dictate what foods citizens are permitted to eat, and to curb meat consumption of all kinds, including for children. It also proposes (as Stan Cox, a particularly ardent proponent advocates) to adopt a fantastical idiocy by the International Panel on Climate Change (IPCC): "The IPCC recommended . . . replacing annual grain crops with perennial grains that are under development."[10] That's a great plan, except that "under development" means these perennial alternatives cannot replace current food needs overnight. Local, animal-based husbandry is the solution.

Let us listen not to disconnected academics funded by farm-stifling corporate oligopolies, but instead to experienced regenerative and small-scale farmers. They work the land, understand profitability, soil health, and input streams, and are the stewards rather than exploiters of local communities, farm animals, and the land. Generally, the smaller and more hand-tended the farm, the higher the yield per acre and the quality of the food produced.[11]

A cursory examination of America's industrial-agriculture predicament exposes the fragility of the unprecedented "bigness" in food production coupled with increasing dependency on the federal government. This is like a nightmarish, bureaucratic *Andromeda Strain*,[12] and it will grow ever larger until it devours itself into oblivion, like a mighty dragon eating its own tail.[13]

Unifying and politically strengthening the "real food community" is the backbone of America's rescue from industrial food dependency. Expanding public awareness of food-related issues presents an opportunity for both parties to educate voters about these high-priority problems. As food prices soar, people will pay increasing attention to the spiking input costs, wage and land-price inflation, health risks, and vulnerable processing and shipping systems that have previously provided cheap food but are failing under these pressures—just like the soils and water supplies upon which our nation's farming depends are failing.

There is no single area that will do more to protect the environment than will a regenerative, local shift in American agriculture. This transition is an attractive political environmental platform for Republicans because it offers numerous additional positive impacts in addition to its environmental benefits, without embracing climate change or carbon dioxide measurements as yardstick. This is a reaffirmation of conservative values, demonstrating a genuine desire to responsibly steward finite resources.

Not all conservatives will enthusiastically embrace these proposals, but a great many already do. They are joined by growing numbers of informed Democrats, swing-voting Libertarians, and Independents who favor viable environmental balance over politicizing rhetoric. During Covid, many Americans were justifiably concerned about food safety, availability, and affordability. This issue will skyrocket in priority for people of all political persuasions well beyond 2023.

If that dreadful day comes when groceries gobble 25 or 30 percent of the average American family's budget, partisan loyalties will yield to the practicality of sustenance. Currently, neither party offers any viable policies to redress what will likely be the greatest cost-of-living crisis to strike Americans since the Great Depression. The Biden administration warns of future food inflation but has done nothing to combat it! Conservationists of all political dimensions must boldly advance a barrage of agricultural policies that will benefit *all* Americans by supporting local agriculture and small farms and methods of production that reduce energy and chemical inputs, employ less tilling and transportation, and conserve water and soils.

CHAPTER FOUR

Escaping the Carbon Cult

If only 11 percent of the world's cropland—land that is typically not in use—improved its community of soil microorganisms [sufficiently], the amount of carbon sequestered in the soil would offset all our current emissions of carbon dioxide. The growing understanding of the link between global warming and soil carbon is revolutionizing the environmental movement.

—**KRISTIN OHLSON**, *The Soil Will Save Us*

If America's political-environmental landscape suddenly time-machined back to the mid-1970s when the focus was on chemicals rather than carbon, carbon dioxide would be scientifically and politically irrelevant. If the "climate changing" contributions of industrial agriculture, the nation's chief offender in greenhouse gas emissions, were instead assessed in terms of the nasty chemicals used in the manufacture and application of pesticides, herbicides, fertilizers, fungicides, and insecticides and the pollution discharged from endless tractor and equipment operations to plant and harvest the tainted crops, then both ends of the political spectrum would largely agree that those substances are unsavory for human, animal, and ecosystem health. Add glyphosate, GMOs, antibiotics, hormones, and food-additive chemicals, and a growing consensus develops that these layers of unhealthy contamination of foods, water, soils, and humans must be urgently addressed.

Every agricultural practice blamed for generating carbon dioxide also generates some combination of the pollutants mentioned above. Conservatives can readily agree with liberals that, regardless of the impact on CO_2 emissions, reducing fossil fuel consumption through increased efficiency is always environmentally wise and economically beneficial, soil erosion is an extremely serious threat to be countered, and pumping vital underground water supplies to evaporate in the desert sun through wasteful irrigation of crops is a long-term folly.

Supporting these positive aspects of regenerative farming does not require conversion to the CO_2 doomsday cult. Instead, it will seed enthusiastic conservative support for agriculture policies that liberals assert will also reduce carbon dioxide generation. Returning grazing animals to the land sequesters massive amounts of CO_2 without turning on a tractor—regardless of whether that sequestration reverses anthropogenic impacts on planetary climate. Increased CO_2 in the soil enhances crop yields dramatically. Liberals and conservatives can embrace shared goals whether or not they share motives: everybody wins!

Self-styled "lunatic farmer" Joel Salatin notes that grass "is more efficacious at sequestering carbon than forests."[1] He is correct. Yet many proposals on the table would (and already are) allowing valuable pastures and croplands to grow back into forests when they are better employed for both carbon sequestration and food production as grasslands or for local cropping. The most efficient solar panel is a healthy blade of grass, and no technology will ever improve on that. Grass and plants absorb and convert the sun's energy directly into foods edible by animals or humans; cows and other livestock convert grasses inedible to humans into solar-generated healthy meats while rebuilding soils with manure and urea, improving water and nutrient retention in the bargain.[2]

Conservatives will likely express healthy skepticism that America can replace industrial food dependency with local farms.[3] Yet every morsel of food created by these alternative (traditional) methods will reduce CO_2—and chemical pollution as well as soil and water depletion—and build resilient local food security. And that's all while displaying to the American voters a conservative environmental agenda that is viable in stark contrast to the Green New Deal. Moreover, sequestering carbon in soil is a positive benefit regardless of climate change; plants thrive in carbon-rich soils, and healthy soils resist erosion. Republicans can embrace these plans that sequester carbon.[4]

There are three stages in the life of waste: generation, recycling, and disposal. The best path is to simply not generate poisonous chemical and other wastes. Once used, waste and pollution are reduced if materials can be recycled. Then, whatever is left gets landfilled, or dumped in the ocean, or flushed. In the 1980s, America realized its landfills were filling up fast—and leaking. Superfund legislation focused on containing and preventing the perpetuation of landfills and waste sites that had essentially become underground leachate generators.

This path of toxification is not confined to agriculture but includes iPhones, TVs, lawnmowers, cars, ski trips, and flights to Aruba. Americans of the modern age are *consumers*, and nearly *everything* they do (unless Amish!) generates harmful chemical byproducts that do not simply evaporate harmlessly. The landfill problem remains unsolved; recyclables are backed up in mountainous storage heaps, unprocessed; humans are generating new forms of pollution at ever-faster rates.

Most Americans are unaware that new chemicals can be added to foods with zero proof that they are safe. American laws and policy embrace the opposite methodology regarding chemicals—companies feed Americans whatever they wish, *unless and until it is proven harmful*. This involves tens of thousands of chemicals, recklessly released despite the past record of DDT, PCBs, dioxin, acid rain, and the warnings of Rachel Carson. As food-rights activist Vandana Shiva explains, "If we introduce into the environment chemicals with which we have not evolved, we must regard them as guilty until proven innocent."[5] Instead, federal regulatory structures purporting to protect consumers are more often joined at the hip with corporate actors and "large stakeholders." The USDA and FDA are similarly aligned: both provide lucrative revolving doors for corporate executives with careers that careen between Big Government and Big Agriculture.

Shall Americans label all conservatives as the sole polluting scapegoats, or instead share ownership of our communal sins? The idea of linking pollution to its source—holding businesses and individuals environmentally accountable for the toxins they generate—has been expounded for decades and has positively influenced a host of important policies. Paying a small fee for every gallon of house paint, for instance, was a way to link the cost of that pollution directly to its consumption. Superfund legislation made corporate manufacturers strictly liable for pollution sourced from their premises, making them financially responsible to ensure its safe handling and disposal without requiring proof of corporate negligence.

Today, the largest share of pollution costs remains "externalized"—passed on as a liability borne by the ecosystem and society, without accountability from those generating it. This invites yet more waste. Consider the long-term economic and environmental costs when China dumps toxic waste into the ocean, while America and other nations process waste responsibly. The environmental costs of Chinese dumping are thereby passed on to the future, and to the world, but those costs are then exponentially *higher* because it is more costly to extract pollution from the ocean than when it is properly disposed of on land—indeed, it is essentially impossible. To accurately track such externalized costs, American consumers would have to reflect on how many of the Chinese-manufactured products that they consume generate chemical and other pollution that ends up in the ocean. If you want to be certain your consumption is not evil toward the environment (or personal health), the first rule should be, buy *nothing* from China.

A full discussion of tracing externalized costs of production and consumption merits its own book. But readers who perceive the complex challenges of tracing pollutants back to their manufacturing (or forward to their consuming) sources will immediately grasp how backward and deleterious EVs, heat pumps, and solar panels are to the ecosystem, a topic taken up in detail in chapter 11. In all the glowing adulation of so-called "renewable" technologies, externalized costs have been very deliberately excluded from the equation, benefitting large manufacturers and political opportunists at the expense of both human and environmental health. These technologies are assessed in a vacuum in which *only* CO_2 and energy use *after manufacturing* are measured. This is absurd and grotesquely dishonest: just like has been done for decades in industrial agriculture.[6] All of them also possess limited periods of life, and so they themselves must eventually be disposed of and "renewed" again by yet more polluting manufacturing. These very real environmental impacts are also bypassed as inconvenient truths.

Increasingly, environmental groups are alerting the world that many solar panels are produced in China using horrific extraction and manufacturing techniques that destroy ecosystems and cultures, often employing equally horrific working conditions that equate to modern slavery and even deliberate genocide. Advocates for "clean energy" exclude from analysis the true costs of those shiny solar panels shipped in bulk containers from China. Coal-fueled manufacturing of solar panels uses massive amounts of energy and unleashes astounding amounts of water, air, and soil pollution. Mining of lithium and other metals and inputs requires mind-boggling quantities of fossil fuels and creates toxic effluents and waste products that spew into land, water, and air, and the open-pit mines leave disfiguring scars on the landscape visible from space. These costs are excluded from a product's "carbon footprint" when it is fraudulently peddled: "Look, this solar panel will use less energy and emit less CO_2 over twenty years than the grid-derived power from a natural gas plant." Yes, it may, but only so long as the energy use and pollution generated in its manufacture, shipping, installation, and eventual disposal are all conveniently *excluded from the equation.*

Solar panels are an environmental crisis unto themselves, as are electric cars. What is the energy and chemical footprint of manufacturing all those new cars, batteries, and charging stations as well as their eventual disposal? Meanwhile, the electric grid cannot function on solar alone, and residential rooftop applications are by far the most inefficient and expensive (and thus most profitable) implementations of solar power. To compound these environmental injuries with yet greater insult, all this is accomplished by regressively subsidizing these inefficient technologies using the electric bills and taxes of low-income people.

The most important first step in addressing pollution—whether personally or internationally—is accurately accounting for externalized pollution costs. But this is the last step that the renewable energy industry wishes to employ for analysis. Corporate interests seek to subvert real change with a profitable illusion of change. A proper holistic environmental focus invites critical analysis of the true environmental costs of the manufacturing or growing of products (including food), especially agricultural inputs. The tension will always be there: profit-seeking industrialists assuring consumers their products are safe; consumers dying of cancer from products touted as harmless. Whether from China or Monsanto, this is an adversarial system, and our children's food is in the balance. Caveat emptor (buyer beware) is even more important today than in the days of unregulated miracle-cure salesmen.

The degree of chemical contamination in America's food supply is terrifying. Rachel Carson loudly sounded that gong in 1962; her predictions and concerns have been proven true many times over (see chapter 12). When will humans listen? Do Americans enjoy being lied to so that they can hide in ignorance while they wolf down a toxic Twinkie? The moral choices being made are not confined to corporate boardrooms—food choices and healthy, informed diets are the province of personal responsibility and always will be. These issues are of much greater priority when the government and corporate America are conspiring to benefit financially at the expense of human and environmental health, as has been the case in American agriculture for eighty years or more.

Rather than strive to eliminate all chemicals from the entire world with the sweep of an ideological pen, a shift to local food production using less destructive means focuses on the area where the most dramatic and urgent problems reside, and thus where the most effective and immediate responses can be crafted: large-scale agriculture. By reducing the application of polluting, unsustainable, synthetic fertilizers, we can allow nature and cow poop to do better work, cleanly.[7]

The simple solutions of localized and regenerative agriculture—to reduce chemical fertilizer application and move cows back onto land—will yield a torrent of controversy and corporate complaint. Half a trillion dollars annually in global subsidies for agricultural industry will tend to do that. But this is the beginning of an essential conversation about how to unite Americans to support agricultural policies that are universally beneficial, regardless of whether carbon dioxide is a climate culprit. Let us please set the Gore-led red herring of global warming on the political shelf long enough to resurrect the consensus that toxic chemicals are universally bad.

CHAPTER FIVE

The Soil of a Nation

The soil is the great connector of lives, the source and destination of all.

—WENDELL BERRY, *The Art of the Commonplace*

I n contrast to climate alarmist claims that only novel technologies and all-powerful government can rescue humankind from the destruction of the world's ecosystems (a destruction *created* by the industrial technologies of the last 170 years, aided and abetted by the federal government), no single shift could more quickly benefit the climate than regenerative agricultural practices and more localized food production. As the Chinese philosopher Confucius humbly remarked, "For all Man's supposed accomplishments, his continued existence is completely dependent upon six inches of topsoil and the fact that it rains."[1]

That ancient observation is now imprinting itself forcefully on the world. The brief, destructive 100-year blip of industrialized agriculture has decimated soils and water, especially in the United States, the techno-leader of innovation. Soils are not mere lifeless substrates to which may be added a mixture of supplements to explode endless productivity. This itself is a modern, reductionist perspective that erases from view the true centrality of soils in not just human food production, but the very chain of life.

One of America's truly gifted teachers of environmental wisdom was conservationist and ecologist Aldo Leopold, whose 1949 book *A Sand County Almanac* advocated a land ethic that foreshadowed much of modern environmentalism. Leopold cautioned the world about the vital importance of healthy soils nearly 100 years ago.[2] The marvels of modern technology created synthetic fertilizers, but the technological awareness at the time regarding soil microbes was somewhat less marvelous. Their use was understandable, as synthetic fertilizers offer plentiful short-term productivity gains, while costs such as water pollution from runoff, decreased nutrient content, deteriorating microbial activity, and soil erosion are long-term impacts that eventually compromise productivity but were not immediately apparent. Over time those costs have become clearer as soil science has improved.[3]

Science has only recently begun to comprehend the delicate balance of the human microbiome. The same applies to the soil microbes that fuel the ecological circle of life. What is increasingly evident is that both of these balances become disrupted by chemical interference, including bursts of unnatural fertilizers in soil and chemicals in food that kill important bacteria in the human gut. The answer is found in marvels greater than human machines—in the cycle of photosynthesis, healthy herbivores, and in the vibrant microbial life of soil that nurtures all.[4]

There is great cause for hope in these soil discoveries. By learning how we are slowly killing ourselves and our planet with unnatural chemical augmentations (not carbon dioxide, a staple of the life cycle), we can take action to alter our perilous course. In awareness of our worsening plight, we simultaneously discover the natural remedy: dynamic, carefully stewarded microbial life. Science teaches us that there can be more than ten invisible tons of microbes on a single acre of well-tended earth.[5]

Spraying concentrated nitrogen, phosphorus, and potassium fertilizers (or herbicides, fungicides, and pesticides) on these microbes kills them outright or seismically disrupts their natural life balance. Perceiving the surface of the land as a writhing, roiling explosion of life helps humans understand why chemicals are bad and how feeding soils naturally is beneficial. The converse is already widely understood: to kill malicious unseen microbes, we spray them with Lysol or deadly chemicals. Reciprocally, if dangerous microbes are percolated in environments they prefer (such as with salmonella or *E. coli* hatched in confined, immunocompromised grain-fed animals), then they thrive. Americans must comprehend the 99 percent of health-protecting, life-creating bacteria as clearly as the 1 percent they fear.[6]

Burn-baby-burn Republicans in particular must embrace a humbler appreciation of the dire urgency to heed more soil-conscious farming voices. There is disagreement on whether carbon dioxide levels impact the climate; there is no questioning the foundational necessity of soil health or that America is losing its topsoil at alarming rates.

Referring to industrially produced foods, Shiva warns that for "every pound of red meat, poultry, eggs, and milk produced, farm fields lose about five pounds of irreplaceable topsoil."[7] Tom Philpott's 2020 exposé *Perilous Bounty: The Looming Collapse of American Farming and How We Can Prevent It* documents the alarming magnitude of soils already lost, claiming that at least half of the nation's topsoil has leached away.[8]

The problem of soil erosion is so severe and has worsened instead of improved for so many decades that America has essentially dumped much of its most fertile soils into rivers that carry it to the ocean—perhaps even raising sea levels, so great is the waste.[9] The soil loss is on a huge scale. Some 92 million acres of land seeded to corn each year in the United States loses an average of 5.8 tons of topsoil per acre annually.[10] Whether or not melting ice caps are bloating the world's oceans, the technological marvels of a clumsy-minded humanity are steadily refilling them with the soils of the continents.

The only feasible path to displace synthetic fertilizer applications is the same as in Confucius's time: spread manure liberally. Returning animals to the land converts manures that have become polluting liabilities into reinvested assets. Cows and other livestock offer humanity hope and are the chief saviors of the planet.[11] Farming communities for millennia understood that which has eluded our techno-mystical, postmodern folly. Decoupling from that industrial flow of chemicals onto the land means also reducing the use of machinery run on fossil fuels. The resulting reduction in carbon dioxide emissions is then joined by the positive increase in CO_2 sequestered in improving soils.[12]

Reduced tilling and "no-till" agriculture have increased in use, but often this is accompanied by heavier yet applications of chemical fertilizers to maintain productivity. The long-term problems of plowing up land and disrupting the soil's "microbiome" are what have occupied Wes Jackson and the work of The Land Institute for many decades: "Till agriculture is a global disease. . . . Unless the disease is checked, the human race will wilt like any other crop."[13]

Mismanagement of agricultural lands has destroyed productivity throughout history, and the result is usually gradual desertification as water is not efficiently retained by ever-thinner layers of anemic soil. The particularly aggressive ability of modern technological "innovations" to destroy soil was noted early on by British agrarian pioneer Albert Howard, who wrote: "In Great Britain itself real farming has already been given up except on the best lands. The loss of fertility all over the world is indicated by the growing menace of soil erosion."[14] What Howard referred to as "real farming" had already largely vanished in England a century ago. Remaining American pockets of rural agriculture must be celebrated and nurtured rather than extinguished via corporate-regulatory fiat and ignorant anti-cow propaganda.

Another aspect of food production intimately connected to soil health is nutrient depletion. All animal life requires certain essential elements and minerals to survive, and there are only finite quantities of these in soils. Perpetually extracting vegetable products from land steadily saps these trace nutrients from soils, leading to depleted nutrient levels in industrial food harvests. This nutrient drainage is particularly severe in energy-intensive crops like soy and corn. The combined problems of soil loss and declining soil health caused by industrial methods create a vicious cycle of destruction in order to maintain yields. It is a Faustian bargain, swapping short-term material profits in exchange for eventual collapse.[15]

Soil degradation by chemical applications accelerates erosion, which facilitates more rapid water loss, shedding yet more nutrients and soil, and so on. The magnificent dark world of soil life essentially collapses. This is a product not only of the volume of chemical applications, tilling, or other disruptions, but their frequency. Much like chemical compromise of the human biome, over time this disrupts the soil's microbial capacity to integrate even natural supplements.[16]

Many of America's croplands have been under these strains for decades and are vulnerable to ever-more-rapid deterioration if industrial abuses of the land persist. The longer there is delay, the more disruptive (to prices, markets, and cultures) will be the transition. And the longer soils endure such abuse, the longer it takes to reclaim and rebuild them. One day it may be too late, repeating the Great Dust Bowl on a grand scale, irrevocably converting huge swaths of once-fertile farmland to unproductive desert.

Conservatives must vocally advocate for policies to improve soil health. In doing so, they can confidently offer a nod to CO_2 sequestration in soils as an additional justification for a full about-face in America's agricultural landscape—literally and politically. CO_2 in soils increases fertility and soil health. Conservatives can also see that organic versus conventional farming methods are not just about human health. They are also about soil health. Carbon sequestration in food-producing soils produces more food by nurturing the processes that help life flourish regardless of whether the "grounded" CO_2 impacts climate change.

Regenerative soil practices are far and away the leader of the sequestration pack. Americans must better appreciate the primacy of soil health as the steward of carbon dioxide.[17] In order to sequester carbon, soil must be vibrant with bacterial and other living activity. This also is the most sustainable and productive way to make nutritious plants grow. Carbon is pivotal in the entire cycle and available without the help of Monsanto and others. This process thrives using manures and natural soil augmentation, not factory-manufactured and industrially applied synthetic fertilizer "products."[18]

This ancient, fascinating microbial cycle is all tightly woven together and works tirelessly without human technological interference. Working soils require continuous replenishment—a feeding of organic supplements. And when it comes to improving soil health with organic matter, the king of the pile is manure. This is especially true where *replacing* synthetic applications is desired. Poop is the preferred path. As David Montgomery writes in *Growing a Revolution: Bringing Our Soil Back to Life*, "Manure that we currently treat as waste could, once again, meet as much as a third of global fertilizer needs."[19]

Historically, humans recycled their own wastes as compost. It is popularly remembered that Native Americans planted fish heads and entrails in hills of corn. Modern man has created a supplemental augmentation that has failed miserably, and the best interim cure is the cow manure that will disappear if the ill-considered plan to eliminate meat from human diets takes effect. Until some genius scientist develops not synthetic meat (derived from soybeans raised in a toxic monoculture) but a proper, nature-fooling synthetic cow turd, there will be no relief from our steady societal self-destruction.[20]

The economic and cultural destruction of family farms has been no accident, nor has it simply been a by-product of "progress." On the contrary, as farmers who once dominated the nation's countryside (and legislatures) were pushed out by ambitious, urban, white-collar "experts," ever-larger corporate actors have been able to manipulate tax laws, regulations, and subsidies to eradicate those small farms for the expansion of large-scale agricultural (and chemical-industrial) interests. Universities are largely funded by business interests who don't value soil fertility. This has channeled research and development into exactly the wrong researching and developing.

In the greater battle, this Goliath has lost to the soil of David.[21] The abuse of land and humans (and cows and other livestock) cannot endure without collapse.[22] A forward-looking regenerative/local agricultural reversal does not propose to eliminate industrial farming, but calls to widely incentivize research and development for, and implementation of, regenerative practices capable of large-scale application. This is the opposite of the Green New Deal, which strives to transform the entire agricultural system abruptly but does not offer a single policy proposal as to how this impossible fantasy will be achieved. Will Republicans and Democrats credit American voters with the intellects to discern the difference?

There is no downside for conservatives to embrace regenerative, local, and organic farming practices. On the contrary, as David Montgomery shows, "increasing soil organic matter increases crop yields."[23] This also improves food security and nutrition, increases rather than depletes healthy soils, reduces fossil fuel use and tilling, augments water retention and conservation, and reduces pollution runoff. It also incorporates more carbon dioxide into the soil than all the renewable boondoggle fantasies combined, and then some.[24]

There is no more vital effort to improve America's environmental future than restoring local agriculture.[25] Understanding the persistent decline of small farms as a corporate-industrial conspiracy that threatens human and environmental health as well as national security and rural communities, it becomes clear why small farms can't survive and will soon be extinct—the deck has been consistently stacked against them. Let American conservatives rejoice in taking the lead to solve this terrible loss to our nation and in seeking out like-minded Democrats! There is no need to switch political parties to join as allies in this common populist cause.

It is time for the US Congress and those within it who possess the character, insight, and mettle to challenge this industrial juggernaut and join together in a loud voice and say, "Listen to the farmers! They know more about food than federal ag committees co-opted by corporate boardrooms!"[26] Our nation's true warriors for a healthy future are not wearing suits in a courtroom on behalf of wildlife NGOs. They more likely wear blue jeans or Carhartts and a torn flannel shirt.

The return of animals (and humans) to the land in stewardship must be exalted above the lulling lies of the "renewable technology" sirens. Renewable energy technologies need not be abandoned, but they are being pursued in lieu of, and even priority over, food production and soil conservation. This is a threat to our nation.[27]

This is the quandary in which America has placed herself. The Green New Deal *accelerates* the release of carbon dioxide and dangerous toxins by subsidizing "renewable" manufacturing industries that use coal and other fossil fuels, while increasing agricultural impacts by converting human diets to industrial monocultures, which will *increase* the release of CO_2 and the use of synthetic fertilizers. The fastest and easiest "truly green" way to replenish soils is a bovine "back-to-the-land movement"—a politics that advocates for and rewards regenerative and organic agricultural practices but also increases local production to reduce transportation impacts, regardless of whether the product is conventional or organic.

CHAPTER SIX

The Looming Water Crisis

Over the next three decades, water demand from the global food system is expected to increase by about 50 percent, from cities and industry by 50 to 70 percent, and from energy by 85 percent. . . . Water efficiency is as pressing a problem, and as important a puzzle to solve, as energy efficiency.

—DAVID WALLACE-WELLS, *The Uninhabitable Earth*

Increasing water shortages, and the contamination of rivers, lakes, and oceans, motivate voters of all political flavors to an increasing environmental awareness separate from either CO_2 or pollution concerns. Clean, plentiful water is something conservatives can all agree is a high priority, and no single policy area can more quickly remediate water depletion and contamination than de-industrializing American agriculture. The Green New Deal purports to address (but instead aggravates) carbon dioxide levels while ignoring issues of water scarcity, particularly aquifer depletion. In deliberate contrast, the policies advocated in this book largely deemphasize the importance of atmospheric carbon dioxide levels while actively and sustainably remediating water depletion.

The dominance of Big Ag in the post–World War II explosion of industrial growth created new sources and degrees of toxins and environmental damages. Many voices had been ignored prior to Rachel Carson's *Silent Spring*, warning not of man-made poisons but of man-made drought and erosion. In 1923, well before the Dust Bowl that loomed over Americans during the Great Depression, Aldo Leopold alerted the world to the agricultural dilemma still unresolved 100 years later:

Farms and waters must be considered together. . . . The outstanding fact that we can never change is that we have roughly
twenty million acres of water-producing or mountain area
and fifty million acres of area waiting for water. Most of the
latter is tillable. But, it takes say four feet of water per year to
till it, whereas less than two feet falls on the mountains, of
which only a very small percent runs off in streams in usable
form. Therefore, if we impounded all the non-flood runoff
and had no evaporation (both impossibilities), we should still
have scores of times more land than water to till it.[1]

A century on, despite improvements in irrigation technology, Leopold's
words are proven true. Steady increases in tillable acreage, "incentivized"
by senseless programs like subsidized corn/ethanol production, have
outpaced efficiency improvements in per-acre water usage. It is not rocket
science to realize this is unsustainable in the truest meaning of the word.[2]
As global populations grow, so too does the global water crisis as industrial,
residential, and agricultural demands swell.[3]

Consumers' economic buying power has risen steadily. The manufacture and eventual disposal of foodstuffs and consumer goods has transformed citizens of increasingly wealthy, formerly "developing" countries
to "progress" into proper Western consumers. As a result, the problem of
water scarcity will most certainly intensify in the near future.[4]

The USDA reports that irrigation accounted for 42 percent of the
nation's total freshwater withdrawals in 2015, to irrigate what in 2017 was
determined to be 58 million acres.[5] Despite improved water-pumping
and irrigation technologies, the net water used in agriculture continues to
deplete these priceless reserves.[6]

But the practice is unsustainable. A national and international water crisis
is upon us. Both the overuse and pollution of our groundwater is largely attributable to monocultures. Disgraceful ethanol production policy continues to
incentivize the use of weak and sloped soils for corn, which, along with soy,
requires extremely high applications of water-polluting synthetic fertilizers.[7]

The tragedy of the commons compounds the problem. Incremental,
modest increases in use of common water supplies collectively destroy the

resource. Additionally, the moral hazard of "externalized" costs again rears its ugly head. Neither producers nor consumers generally have to pay their fair share of the water costs associated with the products they grow and eat.[8] The root problem is not water or even food—it is massive subsidies to chemical companies like Monsanto, paid through the peasant-like labors of rural farmers, which require water-intensive methods of production of a grand, unsustainable magnitude. The end result has been depleted soils and aquifers, the destruction of family farms, and the consolidation of agriculture into larger and larger "industrial" operations.[9]

Our nation's entire food supply depends on the Ogallala Aquifer alone, which supports one-sixth of the *world's* grain production. But this mighty aquifer is no match for the massive drawdowns by a rapacious industrialism. For many decades this aquifer has been unable to recharge to keep pace with withdrawals. Much like fossil fuels, these are ancient reserves, irreplaceable without a dramatic reversal in industrial practices. The short-sighted irrigation infrastructure created to extract this vital Ice Age resource sucks about eight times more water from the ground than natural forces can restore. According to Timothy Egan, "The aquifer is declining at a rate of 1.1 million acre-feet a day—that is, a million acres, filled to a depth of one foot with water."[10] This abuse has accelerated since Egan's 2006 observation:

> And while the aquifer is losing that foot of water, it's barely being refilled. In most of western Kansas, less than one inch of water seeps underground to recharge the aquifer each year. The declines were especially dire in southwest Kansas, where average water levels fell by 2.17 feet last year. That's the region's biggest drop since 2013, up from a 1.25-foot decline in 2020 and a 0.8-foot decline in 2019."[11]

This unsustainable water dependence is a huge vulnerability. A substantial portion of America's produce is raised in California's San Joaquin Valley, which is utterly dependent on unsustainable groundwater withdrawals.[12] The unavoidable droughts of our future are California's problem, and also the nation's. Mark Bittman warns that California's "chronic water issues may be resolved only by literally reducing the land used for intensive agriculture by half."[13] Reduced winter precipitation has weakened traditional snowpack supplies of water in the artificially verdant Imperial Valley as well, which together with nearby Yuma County in Arizona grows more than half of all American winter vegetable production. This water is supplied by Rocky Mountain snowfall, which has declined more than 40 percent since 1982 and is expected to drop by another 30 percent by the middle of the century.[14]

The Central Valley contains some 75 percent of California's irrigated land—17 percent of the nation's. It produces a quarter of America's food, including 40 percent of nuts and fruits, on just 1 percent of US farmland. Some 20 percent of all the water pumped from aquifers in the country are sucked from the aquifers of this valley alone.[15] The Central Valley is a natural structural depression and sinking fast: in "large swaths of the region, the land is sinking at rates of up to eleven inches per year as underground water vanishes."[16]

Another productive but vulnerable agricultural region is the Salinas Valley, also known as "the salad bowl of the world." In addition to the usual water-gorging industrial suspects, the aquifers that supply this region face an additional threat: as irrigation depletes underground reservoirs, salty, farm-destroying seawater seeps in. The Salinas Valley grows some 150 specialty crops and exports nearly 400 billion pounds of produce each year.[17]

The relatively recent fanatical obsession with carbon dioxide ignores these problems while exalting technological "progress" as the techno-mystical solution. But there is no techno-industrial solution to the physical disruption and extermination of healthy soil microbiomes and vital aquifers that has been in high gear for a century. As climate "warriors" advocate for maniacal anarchism as environmental policy, they ignore this water problem that has inflicted so much damage to the nation's breadbasket in the Central Valley. Industrial tilling methods continue to do the greatest harm.[18] Alternatives must be reduced in scale and incorporate manure and livestock to replace synthetics and tilling. Shifting farming back to other geographical areas of the nation is an imperative. Increased localized production, especially in more water-rich regions, is America's farming future.

Tilling the ground disrupts plant roots and releases massive amounts of stored carbon; spraying that ground with synthetic fertilizers wipes out trillions of living organisms that hold soil together and perpetuate its health and expansion. Decades of this process have weakened soils and increased runoff. California's Central Valley has been decimated. Josh Tickell notes in *Kiss the Ground*: "Its soils are eroding, which means food growers require ever more water."[19] The reason growers require more water is not merely the reduction in volume of soil, but *weakened soil health*. Sickly soils do not retain anywhere near as much water as do those teaming with life, what is called "effective rainfall." As Kristin Ohlson explains in *The Soil Will Save Us*: "If there isn't effective rainfall . . . then total rainfall doesn't matter much."[20]

Little discussed in this age of raging California forest fires devouring residential hillsides is the unprecedented vulnerability to flood created by modern agricultural practices in the region. The Great Flood of 1862 is likely the worst natural disaster ever to strike that massive state, but destruction on that scale would be exponentially worse today. The horrible flood of 1862 is largely lost to Americans' collective memory despite killing fully a quarter of California's livestock while inundating the state with rivers of muck from landslides that wiped out entire towns. A similar event would today cause an estimated $1 trillion or more in damages. Climate scientists argue that there is a doubled risk of an even greater precipitation event in the relatively near future, but even if climate change is less severe than claimed by alarmists, the threat remains very real.

One popularized study named this potential event an "ARkStorm."[21] In an ironic twist, the name is not a reference to a biblical deluge in which people flock into arks but to an "atmospheric river" of air that transports large amounts of water vapor that can suddenly translate into *feet*, not inches, of rainfall. An updated study from 2022 has forecast an even greater risk, dubbed "ARkStorm 2.0," that suggests a repeat of the Flood of 1862 could be far worse than previously estimated.[22] The geological record reflects that these storms occur in the California region every century or two, but that changes in regional weather patterns exacerbate the risks today. People generally view drought, earthquakes, and wildfires as the great risks of California, but the dramatic increase in population since the Great Flood (of 1862, not Noah) make this threat exponentially more profound than even a split in the San Andreas Fault. And the risk is not California's alone, since the nation depends on that state (and neighboring Arizona, which would also be impacted) for such a huge proportion of its food supply.

The first ARkStorm study concluded that a Great Flood recurrence would be too sudden to make it possible to evacuate the estimated five to ten million impacted residents. The 2022 study estimates a 50 percent likelihood such a storm will recur by 2060, that it could be far more severe, and that it will be the largest natural disaster in world history. But the San Joaquin Valley has subsided nearly thirty feet in elevation since the last great California flood, ensuring yet another amplifier of impact on food production in the national salad bowl.

Regardless of when, or even whether, a cataclysmic storm recurs in the West, Americans concerned with food security will understand that diversifying agricultural networks rather than increasing the current highly concentrated agri-dependency on one tiny, highly vulnerable region that is alternately drying up or drowning out is of great national interest. Add to this the escalating costs and threats of trucking or otherwise transporting all that produce to the East Coast, and there is a vital urgency to this regenerative and local agrarian mission.

The solutions to these longstanding problems will not be achieved rapidly, but if action is not taken, the ecosystem will decline, food price inflation will escalate, and food shortages in America will need to be counterbalanced with dubious foreign purchases. The Green New Deal offers zero prescriptions for our encroaching water problems. Greenhouse gas reduction is a completely different issue from water conservation.

The proposals in this book to prioritize local and regenerative agriculture will delay or even reverse water loss and rebuild underground aquifers by reducing drawdowns, especially for animal feed grains and livestock. The quickest way to cut overall water use is to convert animal-raising operations to grain-free, rotational-grazing systems wherever feasible and to incentivize agricultural development in areas that do not require mechanical irrigation from underground aquifers.

Local, deindustrialized agricultural methods, particularly in animal husbandry, are more efficient in water usage. As Chris Smaje writes in

A Small Farm Future, such practices "often generate more product per unit of water input, despite poorer access to water overall."[23] Cows are the ruminants who can "save humanity" by replacing the bison herds that once acted as net soil-creators. As documented by Nicolette Hahn Niman in *Defending Beef*, "well-managed grazing does not cause water pollution."[24]

Grass-fed animals are the *only* viable alternative to industrial agriculture. Recycling currently wasted animal manures could replace fully one-half of synthetic (corporate) fertilizers, while restoring healthier soils, reducing erosion, decreasing pollution runoff, and *increasing* water supplies. The answer is not to eliminate cows but to eliminate artificial chemical soil inputs—which only cows can do.

This must be contrasted with confinement feeding operations and any animal husbandry dependent on feed derived from industrial agriculture and monocultures. Water-polluting inputs are trucked huge distances as feed for cows. Research shows that grazing animals cause pastures to sequester much more carbon dioxide, retain more water, and *decrease* phosphorus and other runoff. The animals take up phosphorus from the grasses, which in turn absorb yet more phosphorus from the soil in regrowth. It is the excessive input of phosphorus that has caused the pollution, not cows; cows are the best vehicle to clean up the mess that the *industrial grain* caused due to artificial synthetic fertilizers and excess phosphorus applications.

Manure from cows can potentially contaminate groundwater, but grass-fed cows don't carry as many deadly pathogens (for example, *E. coli*) as those excreted by factory-farmed, health-compromised, CAFO-raised, grain-fed animals. Cows should of course be fenced out of surface waters. Risks to human health are near zero for pasture-managed cows, and multiple benefits are provided. The king of those benefits is manure, which feeds and rebuilds soil. Joel Salatin relates the fundamental importance of compost (especially composted manure) in *You Can Farm*:

> One pound of organic matter holds four pounds of water. Not only does it allow water to penetrate faster, but the total holding capacity is greatly increased when organic matter is higher. This has everything to do with floods, erosion, drought

tolerance and capillary action, as well as aeration, root penetration and cation exchange capacity.[25]

In addition to cows, the array of available regenerative agricultural options coupled with increasing local, diversified agricultural operations will conserve water and prevent its contamination. Reduced tilling and soil compaction permit soils to retain and hold more water. Eliminating microbe-killing applications of synthetic fertilizers protects waterways from runoff pollutants while enriching soils to retain more water. Shifting production to water-rich regions (albeit with shorter growing seasons or other limitations that must be weighed) will reduce the water siphoned off from precious finite aquifers.

The Left's Green New Deal offers *no* solutions to these profound threats to America's water supplies. Conservatives must raise a conservationist voice in chorus with informed Democrats and Independents to preserve fresh water for all Americans, including residential but especially agricultural uses. Americans are squandering limited, vitally important water resources at an unacceptable rate. And that folly is being *subsidized* by taxpayers and encouraged by government regulations and production policies, to profit Big Business.

Conservatives must stand up to safeguard future supplies of fresh water. Agriculture is the best place to begin to conserve and rebuild this most precious of needs. The Green New Deal was fashioned by Manure Deniers who fail to recognize that healthy, organic cow manure is the hope of the future—including for water preservation. Local, small-scale farms implementing regenerative best practices where feasible are the top direction for water sanity. Thousands of young would-be farmers are ready and willing to undertake the task. The task of public policy must be to encourage them and urgently ensure their success.

CHAPTER SEVEN

A Matter of National (and Local) Security

If a man continues long in direct and absolute dependence on the government for the necessities of life, he ceases to be a citizen and becomes a slave.

—WENDELL BERRY, *The Long-Legged House*

In modern parlance, "food security" has been, like so many terms, morphed into a novel socio-ideological definition that refers almost exclusively to wealth disparity and the ability of poor Americans to secure affordable or healthy food. Yet the availability of healthy food is an issue of security for Americans of all races and classes—the very wealthy are equally capable of starvation and poor dietary choices. America's industrial agricultural system has rapidly unlocked nature's wealth but has created a deadly dependency that was never worth the price.

History instructs that an army marches on its stomach. Surely the American government is aware of the strategic importance of food for our nation, both internationally and domestically. After all, the federal government transferred oversight of the nation's Department of Agriculture to the Department of Homeland Security after 9/11. The still-extant USA PATRIOT Act and its Orwellian progeny provide that the US military can grab every cow, chicken, and generator it requires any time a national emergency is declared.

As to the right to self-defense—and to Second Amendment protections against tyrants—those are meaningless platitudes when there is no food. Gun owners will quickly trade their weapons for hamburgers when their grandkids are crying in hunger. Food is the pillar upon which survival depends.

In order to ensure food security, the United States must prioritize support of small-scale rural farming with meaningful policies, including subsidies.

The Green New Deal seeks to plunge America into the most centralized, omnipotent government behemoth in human history. And by extension, the GND will ensnare other countries around the globe since it benefits large multinational corporations and the globalist agenda to influence climate by regulating global food production. Alternatively, increasing local and regenerative farming production averts that suicidal plunge and will liberate America from Chinese food dependency and global domination rather than escalate those dangers. China and Europe may continue to destroy their soils and water using the toxic industrial methods they learned from America, but we can move on, with no down side. America's shift to sustainable agriculture need not depend on the actions of foreign powers or their people, or be governed by the World Economic Forum or other global players seeking to strengthen central control of food production and distribution. The American people and their future health and economic stability depend on it.

Monsanto and other corporate behemoths of Big Ag have plied the United States and other governments for decades to aid in increasing their monopolistic power. One need not believe this was a calculated conspiracy to see that it has in fact occurred and is a dangerous plight for those who say they value liberty. Particularly, securing patents on seeds (with the active support of the Obama administration) opened the door to an unprecedented authoritarian tyranny. Those who own the seed, control food production.[1] Most American heirloom vegetable varieties are gone forever, replaced with a narrow range of biologically vulnerable (if not potentially harmful) genetically modified or overly specialized seed varieties.

A global cabal of food producers and processors has an increasingly tight grip on food supplies. Four major corporate players now control 75 percent of the meat Americans eat.[2] The entire agricultural production, processing, and distribution system is dangerously reliant on fossil fuels and government control. Wendell Berry warns that our "agriculture, potentially capable of a large measure of independence, is absolutely dependent on petroleum, on the oil companies, and on the vagaries of politics."[3] As Joel Salatin explains: "A nation that can't feed itself is vulnerable. So is a state. So is a community. And so is a household. The ability of a locality to withstand shocks, whether they be economic, environmental, or societal, is the measure of its strength."[4]

This local versus global tension regarding economics, politics, culture, and environmentalism converges forcefully in agriculture. The situation has become much more dire than when Wendell Berry prophesied in 1969 that we must take control of the environment or destroy ourselves along with it.[5] We have *not* responsibly taken control of ourselves or our environment but have instead surrendered their governance to ever-larger business interests and an ever-expanding state and federal bureaucracy.

While Democrats dither over utopian fantasies to ensure everyone gets a "fair share" of food, increasing industrial destruction and dependency promise to *starve* everyone equally. Responding to the environmental crisis with carbon credits, sequestration boondoggles, and "renewable energy" frauds that *accelerate* our fast-growing plight threatens our future with greater and more widespread suffering than has ever been witnessed by humanity. This result follows from a modern ignorance of *food security*.

The solution to this disaster is to reverse the process. Yet the Green New Deal and its academic and bureaucratic prophets seek to instead *expand* supranational powers to create another great wave of polluting, techno-industrial "solutions," gussied up as world-saving "renewable energy," which benefit the very few over the short term at the expense of natural resources and environmental stewardship. The soil, well-tended, is renewable; solar panels destroy the Earth in their making and burial and "renew" nothing. The "world" is fed—and healed—solely on the human-to-human, community-nurturing, *local* level.

This local antidote to global problems is the opposite of the grand, deluded visions of the Green New Deal. The cure to globalism is found in a local sobriety absent from higher spheres of public influence—that wise self-sufficiency of the recent agrarian past that understands it is the "progress" toward the large and cheap that has destroyed that vital "local."[6]

"Urban self-reliance" is an oxymoronic impossibility, though inner-city allotments and rooftop gardening are fantastic supplements to local health and food security in densely populated areas. Nutrients and natural resources flow steadily from rural farmland to urban consumers, where nearly half are wastefully discarded. Urban populations export art and entertainment, manufactured goods, and computer algorithms, but from an ecological measure they also export consumer goods designed for planned obsolescence; sewage, noisome rivers, leachate and other toxic effluents; truckloads of solid waste staining rural landscapes with unnatural mountains of stench; income, sales, and real estate taxes; and health department regulations.

History suggests the Roman empire deteriorated in part because of a breakdown of societal connection between the rich city and the food-producing countryside upon which it depended.[7] The friction between city and country has existed since agrarian methods permitted the existence of things called towns, but the dependency of the center upon its periphery has never changed. In today's America, not merely urban and suburban, but even the vast majority of rural populations are dependent on industrially grown, processed, and distributed food.

The urban dominance of American political and social life has swollen to fill the void that was created as small farms and farm communities declined. Thousands of rural American towns resemble burned-out shells with little hope of economic revitalization. Like Romans, America's urbanites and suburbanites have taken their food for granted, along with the communities that grow it. It is quite possible that much or all of rural America will struggle with food shortages or runaway price inflation in the near future; it is quite impossible that urban centers will not.

The COVID-19 pandemic highlighted this rural–urban divide, resulting in a pronounced upsurge in purchases of rural homes. Supply chain disruptions related to the pandemic exposed quickly the frail urban dependency on rural food sources and how suddenly a large urban center could devolve into barbaric chaos. This revealed vulnerabilities not usually noticed and of which the United States is uniquely susceptible: societal breakdown, food riots, and widespread panic.[8]

The ability of large populations to live collectively in urban concentrations has been magnified by the incredible power of stored energy sourced from fossil fuels. As the relative cost of these fuels escalates, the reverse pressure will occur. The insightful writer Chris Smaje has cast this in apocalyptic terms, arguing that people must move *out* of cities and back into rural living to avert disaster:

And if it's impossible to trim [the energy and pollution costs of eating] back to a sustainable level, that may suggest a need to re-sort human populations more sustainably across agricultural space. . . . It seems likely that the coming years will see a major re-sorting along these lines due to climate change, energy descent, water stress and economic crisis, generally from cities to countryside, from coasts to interiors and from lower latitudes to higher latitudes. The potential for human conflict in this process is high.[9]

This is precisely the opposite prescription for humanity counseled by the purveyors of the Green New Deal, who advocate concentrating humans tightly into urban centers, like "CAFOs 4 Us." The entire premise of Wendell Berry's iconic 1977 treatise *The Unsettling of America* was that the government, corporate, and university pressures to herd humanity into urban clusters was not only the great destroyer of farms and farming communities, but also of humans themselves. Modern claims to save the planet court doom when they advocate for yet more of this corralling of humans into concrete jungles. The Rockefeller-funded Transportation Climate Initiative is shamelessly premised on the assertion that this is the answer to human destruction, when in fact it is the final chapter in a horror tale of industrial Armageddon.

Food security for America is threatened from a myriad of directions, including the failure of industrial agriculture itself. There are *no* voices arguing that monocultures and industrial agricultural methods are sustainable or healthy—even Monsanto and large corporations recognize the primacy of regenerative practices for the future. A plethora of potential calamities threaten America's industrial food supply.

For one thing, this system is highly specialized, concentrating production in a tiny, vulnerable area. As Tom Philpott chronicles in *Perilous Bounty*: "The United States has two dominant food-producing regions . . . and both are in a state of palpable and accelerating ecological decline."[10] This overdependence on a tiny, environmentally abused geographic area is just one of many frightening vulnerabilities of America's food supply. Americans must consider the various risks that could disrupt this long-distance food dependency. To draw a comparison, climate change assessments recognize that perfect prediction is impossible, but seek to present a range or spectrum of potential future possibilities. Computer models forecast only potential likelihoods that the world's climate will dramatically alter due to greenhouse gas emissions and a range of other degrees of potential damage accompanied by varied, and constantly varying, percentages of risk. Similar analyses of famine or crop failure are less common and less studied, and there does not appear to be an Intergovernmental Panel on Chemical Pollution and Distribution to mirror the Intergovernmental Panel on Climate Change whose findings are so widely and unquestioningly invoked as proof positive of pending doom. A food-conscious assessment seems to be overdue.

Climate and Famine Modeling

The subtitle of this book suggests rejecting "climate alarmism." The premise of my argument is that climate change is irrelevant to the urgent need to reform modern industrial agricultural practices. Conservatives must nurture local and organic/regenerative food resources regardless of whether they are convinced that the Earth is threatened by greenhouse gasses. This does not mean that I am a "climate science denier." On the contrary, I am quite willing to believe that human activity damages the planet: my whole point is that we are saturating it, and our children, with man-made chemicals.

However, the pitch for climate change urgency has devolved into a cultish alarmism that has sown political divisiveness because it has deviated from sound science. Moreover, it has been deployed in the frantic launch of the twin failures of top-down governmental response and renewable products that are themselves destructive and counterproductive—as opposed to the meaningful environmental improvements that can be achieved most quickly and effectively in agriculture.

Let us assume for the moment that humans are in fact warming the planet. What does the science actually say, and does it accord with the imminent doom constantly proclaimed by its proponents? These doom-sayers are everywhere, despite many past environmental predictions having failed to materialize. Why are these Chicken Littles still in ascendance and not dismissed like Millerites errantly proclaiming Christ's return?

Greta Thunberg's alarmist proclamations have been abundant and extreme. Alexandria Ocasio-Cortez, announcing her "Green New Deal," claimed in January of 2019 that "millennials and people, you know, Gen Z ... we're like: 'The world is gonna end in 12 years if we don't address climate change.'"[11] This was apparently based on an October 2018 UN proclamation that "humanity has 12 years left to avoid catastrophic climate change."[12] Yet the UN made a similar claim in 1989, leading some to logically question whether there are ulterior motives behind such unscientific (and demonstrably false) histrionics. George Mason University economist Walter E. Williams argues that there are so many apocalyptic predictions because "they have an agenda for more government control ... fear about the environment is a way to gain government control."[13]

The World Economic Forum claims that unprecedented global coordination is necessary to address the climate and pandemic crises. This raises questions about whether climate alarmism is in fact an Orwellian initiative to seed fear and consolidate power rather than a sincere effort to save the ecosystem. The WEF's top five long-term global risks are all environment-related.[14] The chief resource relied upon for climate change claims is the Intergovernmental Panel on Climate Change (IPCC). The predictions the IPCC makes are in turn founded on prediction models. But a cursory review of those models reveals that they do not offer clear predictions at all, but in fact seek to forecast a range of possible outcomes based on various presumptions, themselves based on variations not in climate but in human behavior.

A Climate Science Special Report, which purports to be "an authoritative assessment of climate change, with a focus on the United States," explains:

> Climate projections are typically presented for a range of plausible pathways, scenarios, or targets that capture the relationships between human choices, emissions, concentrations, and temperature change. Some scenarios are consistent with continued dependence on fossil fuels, while others can only be achieved by deliberate actions to reduce emissions. The resulting range reflects the uncertainty inherent in quantifying human activities (including technological change) and their influence on climate.[15]

As explained by the Massachusetts Institute of Technology:

> The Earth's climate is too complex for even the most powerful computers to fully simulate. Just as modern weather models cannot tell us with certainty whether it will rain next week, climate models can only predict a likely range of outcomes.[16]

Climate models presume causation (greenhouse gasses *will* cause temperatures to rise) and try to offer predictions of expected outcomes. This makes them doubly susceptible to inaccuracies. Dire proclamations about the urgent threat of climate change therefore deviate greatly from the underlying science:

> It's important to remember that these scenarios are not exact forecasts of the future. The scientists who created them are not making judgments about which ones are most likely to come to pass. "We do not consider the degree of realism of any one scenario," said Amanda Maycock, an associate professor of climate dynamics at the University of Leeds.[17]

The *science* argues that climate change forecasts are far from set in stone, and so conservatives are understandably cautious in ascribing ironclad certainty to predictions that are couched in cautions *against* employing their contents as prophetic. This is not extreme: what is extreme is concluding that the world is soon ending apocalyptically from greenhouse gasses and that the government should take over all human interactions to manufacture renewable products that will themselves accelerate the use of natural resources and release pollution (as well as greenhouse gasses) into the environment.

Models that seek to predict the weather are notoriously unreliable, even days (let alone decades) in advance. Scientists have been trying to read the tea leaves of an astoundingly complex atmosphere for centuries. It is folly to expect or presume that pinpoint accuracy will ever be possible. Steven E. Koonin observes: "Model projections of regional and local climates are currently nowhere near good enough to give guidance beyond vague statements like 'sea level will continue to rise.'"[18]

These limitations are commonly recognized in non-climate-change modeling. Those involved in drought forecasting acknowledge that it is extremely difficult to predict droughts even months into the future.[19] Famine prediction models are similarly limited. Scientists still tout the value of models because they "allow local governments to act and international funds to hit the ground before starvation does, preventing the worst possible outcome in already food-insecure regions."[20] Yet the WEF and Green New Deal seek to do the opposite in response to climate change— they preempt local governments from acting while extracting local funds to finance international globalists.

The irony is even more evident when organizations claim that climate change will impact or cause famines, when no model can accurately predict famines beyond a short period. The World Food Programme claims:

> The climate crisis is one of the leading causes of the steep rise in global hunger. Climate shocks destroy lives, crops and livelihoods, and undermine people's ability to feed themselves. Hunger will spiral out of control if the world fails to take immediate climate action.[21]

But this does not appear to be true. A Vox article about the World Bank and tech companies using AI to predict famines suggests that the unpredictability of people and politics is one of the biggest driving factors. "Overwhelmingly, famines in particular, but humanitarian emergencies in general, are politically caused. It's only a relatively small minority— and virtually none in modern history—that were caused exclusively, or even predominantly, by natural adversity," Alex DeWaal, author of *Mass Starvation: The History and Future of Famine*, told Vox.

As the world's future is increasingly determined by long-term, unreliable climate change models, there does not appear to be a chemical pollution model predicting where PFOAs, phthalates, or Ohio train wreck chemical plumes will reach–just CO_2. Such a model would necessarily include estimates of the heat and chemicals generated by EV and solar panel manufacturing. This analysis would make clear the true environmental costs of a massive shift to so-called renewables, against which people might rightly claim that

"We are about to sacrifice our civilization for the opportunity of a very small number of people to continue to make enormous amounts of money."[22]

Neither is there a famine prediction model that is reliable beyond at best a few months. Yet no prophets are required to predict that if a nation abandons its local food production and becomes dependent on factory food transported huge distances using a fragile and vulnerable infrastructure, that sooner or later there will be a profound famine. That is what this book is about—not alarmist predictions of death by carbon, predicated on an abuse of scientific models, but a common-sense alarm that becoming dependent on corporations and governments for food that can be grown locally is the ultimate human folly.

A food production prediction model would employ different data inputs than those for droughts, rainstorms, or climate change. It would weigh risks such as war, considering a scenario of a US conflict with China as well as Russia. The Ukraine conflict devastated that country's invaluable grain crops—a wider conflict would unleash exponentially greater havoc. Even a full-blown trade war with China could quickly spark hyper-inflation, if not panic, in the United States. Most of the world's microchips, upon which farm equipment in the United States now depends, are manufactured in Taiwan. Shortages of DEF (diesel exhaust fluid) during the pandemic nearly brought supply systems to a halt. DEF has been mandated for tractor trailer trucks since 2010 as a pollution control technology, but America depends on imports (mostly from China) to keep its truck fleets moving.[23]

Tensions with China have escalated well beyond spy balloons and the influences of TikTok: the menace of a Sino-Russian alliance looks very real. Reminiscent of the Cold War, the threat of nuclear Armageddon has also come to the fore. Indeed, there *is* modeling of what would happen to food supplies if a conflict arose that caused "nuclear war soot injection" into the earth's atmosphere:

> Atmospheric soot loadings from nuclear weapon detonation would cause disruptions to the Earth's climate, limiting terrestrial and aquatic food production. Here, we use climate, crop and fishery models to estimate the impacts arising from six scenarios of stratospheric soot injection, predicting the total

food calories available in each nation post-war after stored food is consumed. . . . So far, an integrated estimate of the impacts of the entire range of war scenarios on both land- and ocean-based food production is missing.[24]

Instead, Americans are plagued ad nauseam by fear-mongering over gun violence, domestic terrorism, and climatic destruction from greenhouse gasses. Where are the computer models with agricultural production scenarios in the event of a dramatic drop in synthetic fertilizer availability (China, Russia, and India have already cut back exports); an electromagnetic pulse that would halt tractors and tractor trailer trucks alike; civil unrest occasioned by economic or political turmoil; interruptions in fuel supplies; a dramatic decline or even failure of the currency or banking system; and—oh yeah—dramatic climate change?

Those embracing prescriptions to build unending supply lines of high-end EVs are ignoring their fields and soils—and grocery shelves—at great peril, ignoring also the economic collapse that their one-issue focus threatens. The conflicts between farmers in the Netherlands and Belgium foreshadow a widening conflict between grand globalist plans to save the world and the need for people to eke out a living and feed themselves and their families.

The voices of the Great Depression are faint in today's techno-exuberant culture, but the lessons of that time reveal that a more precipitous collapse of the economy, and the food distribution system upon which it is dependent, is more than merely theoretical. While most people shut out the very possibility of another such economic implosion with obstinate cognitive dissonance, a repeat is more than just likely—it is inevitable. Profligate spending at all levels of society now burdens the nation with so many tens of trillions of dollars of monetized debt that the currency's survival is increasingly in doubt.

Imagining a modern Great Depression exposes the unthinkable magnitude of threat such a disaster presents. America was a nation of a mere 100 million people in 1929, spread across the landscape and connected to hundreds of thousands of diverse, self-reliant farms. That America is now eclipsed by an industrial interloper of unprecedented power and control.[25]

An abrupt interruption of the industrial system that today's 320 million Americans are dependent on for their food would make the Great Depression look like a brief privation. The soil erosion, water drawdowns, loss of bio-diversity, vulnerable distribution systems, and long-distance transportation of vital foods that are now the lay of the American agricultural landscape threaten a cataclysmic decimation that is truly biblical in its proportions. Mark Bittman predicts: "That means famine for perhaps billions of people, maybe before 2050 and almost certainly by the end of the century."[26]

Increasingly, Americans will be forced to turn from cognitive dissonance toward the chorus of sensible, knowledgeable voices who know the land—the farmers. This will unite people across divisions of party, ideology, color, and economic status, as a shared plight will require a civilized, collective response.[27] America requires bold, truthful leadership to shift into full-gear mobilization to counter this rising menace, embrace regenerative agricultural practices rather than merely chattering about them, and increase local food production and processing.

The gradual desecration of the earth's productive soils and waters by industrial agriculture is akin to a steadily seeping, ever-growing Fukushima disaster. Conservatives have traditionally been advocates for strong national security. Today, our nation's food security is increasingly threatened by the expansion of global agricultural interdependency. Conservatives must lead America to strengthen resiliency against vulnerabilities that could cause food shortages or even widespread famine. In addition to the concentration of vegetable crops in the American West, an increasingly high proportion of fruits are now imported from overseas.[28]

There are numerous issues concerning food shipped from China relating to freshness (and chemical preservative or plant-hormone applications), chemical contamination in production, spread of disease to plants or humans, and nutritional value. Yet perhaps the most glaring threat is the potential disruption of global food shipping. As the pandemic revealed, those seemingly endless supplies of foreign goods can dry up overnight when the fragile system upon which they depend faces a hitch in any one link.[29]

The constant movement of Chinese barges stacked with stuffed containers has a limit of ability. The handful of US ports into which the barges crowd also have restrictions of scale, labor, and storage space. The ships and containers in turn depend on trucks to scurry away with the astronomical quantity of goods scuttled here from overseas. The trucks depend on underpaid (and overworked) human drivers, but also on freeways that are choked and diesel exhaust fluid (DEF) largely manufactured in China, along with the microchips and many replacement parts necessary to keep the fleet moving. DEF was scarce and costly during the Covid pandemic. Most of today's trucks will not function without it. America's modern miracle of commodity transport resembles a line of technological army ants, crawling over increasingly long distances and ever-greater obstacles. Just a single disruption of one link in this fragile chain can back up the entire colony disastrously.

That global, industrial, chemical- and techno-dependent food production and distribution system is deteriorating rapidly because the soils, nutrients, carbon (in soils), water, chemical inputs, and fossil fuels upon which it depends are all becoming more costly in both economic and environmental terms.[30] Many see the world's overproduction leading not to a gradual decline but a sharp implosion.[31]

There are two main drivers of imminent food price inflation and/ or scarcity: industrial dependency and fossil fuel inputs.[32] Even if fossil fuels were unlimited in supply, their prices will continue to rise due to increasing costs of extraction and continuing inflation pressures induced by profligate federal spending. Printing money will impact fossil fuel and other agriculture input costs, which are often layered. These inflationary impacts will strike at food and commodity prices viciously, while wages and real incomes inevitably lag.

The timely policy prescriptions of this book—to incentivize local and regenerative agricultural production—will aggressively fight pollution, reduce fossil fuel dependency and greenhouse gas emissions, and restore water and soils, while *increasing food availability and affordability*. Recent spikes in inflation are already notably steeper in food prices, quite independent of the war in Ukraine.[33] The real economic and environmental costs of food are most assuredly destined to rise steadily, and Americans are unprepared for this domestic threat.

Technology will not reverse the damage it has wrought to soils and water, nor will genetically modified crops improve productivity.[34] (Despite deceptive advertising by Monsanto that "Worrying about starving future generations won't feed them. Food biotechnology will."[35]) Although some genetic modifications seek to improve yields—particularly by designing crops that will grow in more arid climates than otherwise—the majority of genetic modification efforts are directed toward merely holding ground.[36]

Profit-driven corporations now "own" most seed genetics and possess near-total control over food supplies. But GMO technologies cannot overcome nature's own resilience in plant and animal pests, nor do they nurture the soils and water being decimated by the application of synthetic chemicals and fertilizers upon which they are *designed* to depend.[37] Most glaringly, all of these supposedly salvific technologies are utterly dependent on cheap fossil fuels. It is guaranteed that oil will not stay cheap, and there is no technology available to replace cheap energy.

Today's Americans, of all political perspectives, are accustomed to a level of affluence unprecedented in human experience. Although food prices are rising, they remain relatively low from a historical perspective, which has incentivized tremendous waste.[38] Worse, there has been a steady loss of gratitude and appreciation for healthy food and a concurrent deterioration of the appropriate respect society has historically reserved for its farmers. In a very short time span, farmers were all but removed from the food equation, displaced by impassive, massive corporate "entities." No society in human history has become so distanced from its food supply.

These cheap food supplies have created a false comfort (as well as alarming obesity rates). But like so many of modern human achievements, it is an illusion built on short-term profit and will lead to long-term disaster. Wendell Berry has raised this alarm, unheeded, for decades:

> Equally important is the question of the sustainability of the urban food supply. The supermarkets are, at present, crammed with food, and the productivity of American agriculture is, at present, enormous. But this is a productivity based on the ruin both of the producers and of the source of production. City people are unworried about this, apparently, only because they do not know anything about farming. People who know about farming, who know what the farmland requires to remain productive, *are* worried.[39]

The Green New Deal unashamedly advocates for massive public borrowing to finance polluting manufacturing industries of EVs, heat pumps, and solar panels as solution to an environmental crisis while ignoring the food crisis and looming famine entirely. This is a red alert of impending failure. Writer Kirkpatrick Sale warned of the dangers of the "economies of scale" problem that applies with particular accuracy to government power and bureaucratic sprawl: "Governments, whether meaning to or not, always seem to create more havoc as they grow larger, and the largest of them historically have tended to be the most disruptive and bellicose."[40] Today's Green New Deal government is *apocalyptically* disruptive and bellicose.

With oil prices rising, Democrats propose to inflate those prices further by leveraging massive manufacturing industries reliant on fossil fuel inputs for mining, energy, material, and transportation—compounding the economic and environmental emergencies that threaten the nation. That is the *opposite* direction from food security and the reversal of agricultural pollution.

California trucks massive quantities of goods nationally, plus America receives more and more food from overseas. This entire just-in-time distribution system could evaporate overnight, making recent supply-chain disruptions permanent. Military conflict, an electromagnetic pulse event, a large asteroid, earthquakes, volcanoes, a nuclear accident, war, another pandemic, flooding, and droughts are all potential disruptors of this fragile-if-miraculous network. Statistically speaking, it is only a matter of when one or more of these crises impacts food supplies, abruptly and perhaps permanently closing off the industrial-food spigot.

One hundred years ago the American food supply was resilient and immune to such catastrophes because it was locally based. Today, urban sociopolitical unrest could quickly disrupt more than just a few cities. An OPEC-style embargo of oil, broadening conflict in Ukraine or elsewhere, or other economic disruption could seed catastrophe. Perhaps the most obvious and immediate catastrophic event is the food inflation being amplified by massive federal spending via debt monetization (printing money).

Another long-term problem is the depletion of resources necessary for synthetic fertilizer production, particularly phosphate and nitrogen. The discovery and development of synthetic fertilizers enabled the continuation of improvements in world agricultural productivity, in turn bolstering an exploding human population. However, these modern marvels still require basic elements to make, a chief essential ingredient being phosphorus.

Phosphorus is present throughout our planet, but phosphate rock (of which there are hundreds of varieties with differing compositions) has been the natural resource from which most of the world's phosphate is commercially extracted. There are quadrillions of tons of phosphorus in the earth's crust, but the concentration there of 0.1 percent phosphorus is not commercially viable for application.

US production of rock phosphate peaked in 1980 at 54.4 million metric tons. In 2006, China surpassed America to become the world's largest producer of phosphate rock. There are finite supplies of phosphate rock on the planet, with Morocco possessing the bulk of the planet's reserves. Phosphate is an essential mineral for all life on Earth. Modern agriculture is completely dependent on this single resource, leading to debate over when the world will hit "peak phosphorus." Ensuring a sustainable supply without overburdening the ecosystem will remain a challenge.[41]

Rock phosphate prices have steadily increased in recent decades and spiked even more aggressively during COVID-19, rising from $70.75 per metric ton in April 2020 to $320 per ton in September 2022, a 450 percent increase in 30 months! The impact of high phosphate prices will continue to course through most industrially produced food products.

America is similarly dependent on foreign sources for vital potash and nitrogen. Along with fuel oil price spikes, the inflationary pressures related to these inputs will compound in the energy-layered systems that grow, process, and distribute food. Prices are going to rise, and phosphorus availability may one day single-handedly threaten the economic and human health of nations. All of these staple agricultural inputs require massive amounts of energy in their mining and transport. According to the USDA:

> In 2007, 58 million tons of fertilizers were shipped to U.S. agricultural producers by ocean freight, railroads, trucks, barges, and pipelines. Transportation is a significant component of total fertilizer costs. . . . In 2007, imports accounted for 49 per-

cent of the nitrogen fertilizer supply in the U.S. and 85 percent of the U.S. potash supply.[42]

Americans cannot flee these problems in spaceships bound for clean planets to destroy. We must clean up the soils we have neglected and return to self-reliance. Rather than trust the government or huge international corporations for our food, we must grow it ourselves or buy it from neighbors we trust.[43] This is not an argument for "prepping" (however sensible that may be) but for building local agricultural communities as bulwarks against the foregoing list of potential threats to food security. American food system vulnerability is a direct result of industrial food dependency, and reversing that dependency is the sole cure.[44]

As Dr. Robert Malone details in *Lies My Gov't Told Me*, backyard gardening became a vital patriotic American initiative during both world wars. Dr. Malone advocates resurrecting the practice today:

> With the advent of fertilizer, grain, petroleum, and energy shortages worldwide, it seems that the stage is set for the next wave of victory gardens. Growing a garden is a victory over the globalist agenda—a victory over those who wish to control every aspect of consumerism as well as every aspect of our lives.[45]

These are the tasks of current and future generations: to wean away from industrial agricultural methods; eliminate environmental toxins and toxic food products and their government subsidization; rediversify crops where possible and end monoculture dependency; rebuild damaged soils and their microbial denizens; preserve existing water supplies from drawdown and pollution; and rebuild local communities and local food production. This is not a grand proposal for expanded government takeover of citizens' lives or food supplies, but the very opposite—it's a call for the restoration of local autonomy and local food security. It views small farms and their farmer stewards—not popstars, astronauts, politicians, or tech wizards—as the *true* hope for America's future. It will also restore healthier diets for healthier humans, refill rural schools with smiling children, and resurrect lost agrarian communities and their vibrant contributions to human security and happiness.

There are some who believe that the best hope for our nation is in its collapse. They believe that people will not change their destructive, risky behaviors that despoil soil and ecosystem until a Great Depression–style emergency demands it.[46] Yet there are many farmers—and growing numbers of young farmer wannabes—who are eager to forge a civilization that is balanced and disavows self-destruction *before* and in knowing anticipation of that likely collapse. Thirty years ago, Wendell Berry summarized the solution presently required:

> Anybody interested in solving, rather than profiting from, the problems of food production and distribution will see that in the long run the safest food supply is a local food supply, not a supply that is dependent on a global economy. Nations and regions within nations must be left free—and should be encouraged—to develop the local food economies that best suit local needs and local conditions.[47]

Local food production is the foundation of national and local food security.

CHAPTER EIGHT

A Regenerative Economics

And this new economy would understand, first of all, that the ruin of farmers solves no problem and makes many.

—WENDELL BERRY, *Sex, Economy, Freedom & Community*

This book proposes a conservative, conservationist, environmental politics constructed on the bedrock of small-scale, local agriculture and implementing low-impact and regenerative techniques in existing large-scale agriculture. Such a shift is not only cost-saving but will stimulate economic growth on numerous levels. The perception that farming is unprofitable is built on the unfair economic advantages granted for decades to favored industrial producers. An even playing field in the midst of a food-inflation crisis will show very quickly just how profitable working the soil can be. Numerous young people wish to invest in a viable farm economics. The policies of this and other farming books are the blueprint for their success and will also boost and preserve existing small farms.

Like most starry-eyed technological discoveries, the initial results of industrial farming methods *looked* promising. Following World War II, large corporate actors ("stakeholders") influenced society toward ever-larger scales of agricultural production. However, the economic principle of "scale" suggests that any enterprise becomes less productive and/or less efficient when it becomes too large. This is especially true of industrial agriculture: food does not lend itself to mass production as easily as sterile widgets and techno-gadgets. A century ago Aldo Leopold predicted that this early illusion of industrial plenty would wane in time as reality prevailed:

> Man's invention of tools has enabled him to make changes of unprecedented violence, rapidity, and scope. . . . Agricultural

science is largely a race between the emergence of new pests
and the emergence of new technologies for their control.[1]

Leopold's prescience is proved in nearly every facet of modern man's
battle to subdue Creation. The unlocking of energy from fossil fuels
provided humanity with an unprecedented—an *unimagined*—power
to conquer its "environment." Combustion engines and a plethora of
technologies provided comforts and security previously unknown to the
species. In the area of food consumption, no innovation more dramatically
impacted the human world than refrigeration. All of these benefits have
been completely dependent on cheap fossil fuels.

Fossil fuels are referred to as stored energy. Their original source is
compressed plant material that derived its energy (and sequestered carbon)
from the sun through photosynthesis. Solar panels harvest current energy
directly from the sun, but are manufactured and transported using limited supplies of stored energy. Grass and plants also act as current energy
sources because they collect present-day sunlight. Cows and other farm
animals are thus solar-powered.

A return to local, regenerative agriculture requires several areas of
economic study, including assessing the profitability and productivity of
local agriculture versus industrial, economic viability for young people,
capitalist versus communist (or other) models of agricultural economics,
international economic factors, and policy initiatives (discussed in chapter
14) relative to these considerations. Unlike the Green New Deal, which
shamelessly estimates its taxpayer price tag in various trillions, policies that
restore farmers to fields and microbes to soils promise to stimulate long-
term, sustainable *economic* as well as agricultural stability, especially in
rural areas most in need of reclaiming that once-profitable sector.

The salutary benefits to hometown America of restoring agricultural
profitability are obvious, but they will be urgently evident as rising
(inflation-amplified) fossil-fuel prices gradually shift profitability away
from urban centers and toward rural operations. As stored energy becomes
pricier, current energy resources become more cost competitive. Thus,
for instance, locally grown Massachusetts lettuce could attract a higher
market price if the transportation costs of lettuce from the San Joaquin

Valley tripled due to a spike in the price of diesel fuel. Both lettuces were grown with current energy, but the cheap stored energy of fossil fuels that allowed long-distance trade in agriculture is becoming more costly. Its time of reckoning has come: industrial agriculture will inevitably become economically as well as environmentally bankrupt.

Capitalism versus Communism

As America evolves toward a sustainable agricultural system, it is necessary to understand the distinction between capitalist and communist economic models. The Green New Deal is overtly socialist; it essentially claims that food is a political issue and that wealth inequality, racism, and other social ills can be cured by reallocating money through a monstrous government bureaucracy. As has been considered in these pages, nothing could be further from the truth when it comes to agriculture and the environment. Neither problem can be addressed "globally" or "governmentally." Only local, individual responsibility and stewardship can save the world.

The vast majority of all wealth is ultimately derived from natural resources—from the land. Economic models differ in theory over what happens to food and other resources once they leave the land, but the essential dispute is not between sociopolitical theories; it is between big and small. At different times in its history, China has alternately eliminated and nurtured small farms, in both cases applying communist theory. And in the American (so-called "free market") capitalist system, the big has very effectively destroyed the small in agriculture—to the near extinction of true family farms. This has not been a free market by any honest measure. As Wendell Berry rightly concluded:

> Communists and capitalists are alike in their contempt for country people, country life, and country places. They have exploited the countryside with equal greed and disregard. They are alike even in their plea that it is right to damage the present in order to "make a better future."[2]

The moral dilemma of the Tragedy of the Commons, in which incremental, small extractions from a common resource destroy the whole, is constrained by neither communism nor capitalism. Social order—especially that most local of social orders, the family unit—is required for effective resource management. Just as global pollution is rooted in local (individual) consumption, the solution to wasteful industrial global overproduction is rooted in more frugal *local* production.

The terrifying economic threat presented by the Green New Deal is a climate change bureaucratic behemoth that will swallow up economic growth and any hope for environmental stewardship along with it.[3] A totalitarian federal bureaucracy benefitting narrow industrial manufacturing interests is not morally accountable, whether instituted by capitalists *or* communists. Proposed solutions requiring government domination eliminate any possibility of effective environmental remediation. China and the Soviet Union have both exhibited the consequences to ecosystems of expansive, centrally planned economies. As conservative scholar Rodger Scruton observed, "The environmental devastation that they caused remains as a permanent testimony to the folly of centralized government under monopoly control."[4]

The failure of the American food system to preserve small farms was caused not by an innate flaw of capitalism but an *immoral abuse*. Wealth disparity has been greatly exacerbated by technological advances and globalization, neither of which is unique to capitalism. But these are problems that will need to be ethically confronted by any economic system, including the socialists. The key, again, is size: small is equitable.

E. F. Schumacher is credited with popularizing awareness of the importance of reducing economic scale from industrial to human, emphasizing the fundamentals of regionalism and local efficiencies in economic productivity. Schumacher emphasized that an efficient agrarian economics is not accomplished by Buddhists over Christians, Democrats over Republicans, or socialists over capitalists. It is successfully achieved via the small over the big.[5]

The Case for Small-Scale Economics

Globalization is not a friend to the environment or to local or even national economies and cultures. If the principle of economies of scale holds relevance, a global economy is the largest available human economic scale, and its inefficiencies will ultimately be apocalyptic for humanity and life. In monetary analysis as well, this short-term boom leads to a global bust, increasing energy costs compound over time, along with increasing waste disposal costs.

A proper appreciation of the various energy and chemical inputs inherent in agricultural production, processing, and distribution is required to develop policies to reverse the destruction wrought on the world by industrial methods.

The key is to reverse policies that favor destructive industrial actors and practices (see chapter 14). This is not to abandon free-market capitalism, but to *restore* free agricultural markets. Reversing three chief areas of regulatory discrimination will transform the very foundations of America's industrial food system: (1) phase out federal subsidies for industrial monocultures such as corn and soy (and ethanol production); (2) provide improved regulatory, processing, and distribution structures for local, smaller farms; and (3) provide strong income, property, and/or capital gains tax credits or incentives for local food production, funded with savings from reduced federal subsidies to monocultures.

These policies support a free-market economics of local agrarianism. There are additional long-term economic benefits to this policy shift arising from consequent reductions in transportation expenses, health costs, and refuse generation, as well as ancillary income expansions in agritourism, satellite businesses, and improved efficiencies in schools and other public resources as more people return to rural communities.

This proposal for a new agrarian economics is simply a reversal of the things we moderns have inflicted upon ourselves.[6] Over decades, artificial fertilizers funded with destructive subsidies caused an artificialization of humanity as farmers and their families were pressed into urban servitude and spiritual and economic squalor. The grievous injustices caused by misguided government bureaucrats and academics who pressured farmers off their land in the name of "big" and "technological" are now laid bare, including the subsidies, burdensome regulations, and tax favoritism that stacked the deck against millions of farm families. Reversing those evils is *true* Farm Aid!

In *How to Think Seriously About the Planet: The Case for an Environmental Conservatism*, Roger Scruton proposes "free market" policy ideas to address the eternal moral challenge of "the Tragedy of the Commons." But as he explains, these are correctives for an industrial corruption in government and mega-agriculture that have denied small, local farms a level economic playing field:

> The replacement of local food economies by the global super-market is not the result of free and fair competition. It is the result of hidden subsidies and intrusive regulations—in particular regulations regarding "health and safety"—with which only centralized businesses can comply. It is the government, not civil society, that has destroyed the local economy; and if we see the local food economy as part of sustainability we must do what we can to counter the regulative machine, and to remove or redirect the regime of subsidies. . . . In general a conservative policy returns decisions and risks to the people who are most affected by them.[7]

Food prices are escalating rapidly, and the economic causes are tightly enmeshed in global interconnections and attendant risks caused by large-scale, short-term profiteering. Since the global food supply is largely dependent on industrially manufactured synthetic fertilizers for its productivity and economic viability, price spikes in fertilizer inputs ripple through the food system. In 2021, skyrocketing urea (the most common form of nitrogen fertilizer) prices contributed greatly to food inflation.[8] Increasing dependence on Chinese imports of fertilizers ensures the American food-price problem will escalate unless alternatives are found.

China is the world's largest exporter of urea and second largest exporter of phosphate.[9] China wisely protects its food production and so implemented fertilizer export limitations to ensure its own supplies. It similarly aggravated spiking fertilizer costs in 2007 and 2008 when phosphate prices soared.

Much like rebuilding flooded lowland homes in known hazard zones, industrial agriculture just shrugs its shoulders and awaits the great disaster that will compel action. The problem of natural gas price sensitivity is a recurring one. A 2022 USDA assessment reported:

Nitrogen fertilizers are a key component in the production of field crops. . . . Given the importance of applying fertilizer to meet yield goals for most field crops, a rapid escalation in fertilizer prices affects a wide variety of farming activities and decisions. . . . In late 2021, fertilizer prices began to spike alongside rising prices of natural gas—a primary input in nitrogen fertilizer production.[10]

Prices of natural gas declined from 2013 through 2017, then shot skyward as natural gas prices rose in late 2019, nearly doubling for the 2022 planting season. Natural gas increased in price more than 76 percent from March 2020 to March 2023.[11]

The third pillar upon which synthetic fertilizers are crafted is potash, which also is vulnerable to supply shortages that could create economic disruption, international conflicts, or food price inflation in the future. A significant disruption in the supply (or price hike) of any one of these three key industrial fertilizer inputs will induce either drastic loss of production, an alarming spike in food prices, or both. Eventually these costs will become prohibitively high. That alone makes industrial agriculture unsustainable. Industrial dependency (which also includes gigantic infusions of fossil fuels, herbicides, pesticides, and GMO seed) will become cost prohibitive, either before or after soils and water are depleted and fouled. In the meantime, food prices will inflate in sensitivity to these various inputs, in addition to inflationary pressures caused by irresponsible expansion of the nation's debt and money supply.

Within the range of potential downside scenarios that could threaten food security considered in chapter 7, economic disruption emerged as a significant one. Within that segment of agricultural vulnerability, there is an economic sub-range of potential food-delivery disruptors: trucker strikes, drought, flood, shipping port disruptions, currency fluctuations, inflation volatility, tariffs, or other unforeseen financial or economic turmoil.

Assessing the range of probabilities for various hypothetical future economic outcomes, there are two visible poles: fiat currency deterioration and eventual economic collapse versus solid, sustainable growth. The statistical probability of either of those two extremes might be low—perhaps

10 percent each—leaving America's economic future "likely" to fall within that broader 80 percent "middle." Shifting the economic needle from doomsday to secure is what small-scale economic growth—spurred positively by a self-funding local and regenerative agricultural revival—achieves.

Modern society is dangerously dependent on cheap oil and other fuels for all essential activities. Cheap energy has enabled urban growth that would otherwise have been unimaginable. Massive amounts of resources are transported to cities using cheap fuel, and the urban refuse flows back to the countryside. As more people have been economically displaced from the land, they have moved to the cities, where their migration inflates housing costs. In (economic) response, city workers buy houses in the suburbs, increasing their prices as well. The farther urbanites move into suburbia in search of lower housing costs, the more their transportation costs—both in dollars and in pollution—increase.

One response of the environmental movement (including the Transportation Climate Initiative) is to artificially increase fuel prices to discriminate against these commuters and squeeze them more tightly into the cities. The philosophy here is that this will reduce CO_2 emissions by reducing total miles driven. But it is unnatural and wasteful for everyone to commute to the cities; even more so to transport all the food and products needed in the cities from the country, rather than have the humans consuming them just live a rural life. As E. F. Schumacher observed:

> Economists, for all their purported objectivity, are the most narrowly ethnocentric of people. Since they are universally urban intellectuals who understand little of rural ways, they easily come to regard the land, and all that lives and grows upon it, as nothing more than another factor of production. Hence, it seems to them no loss, but indeed a gain, to turn all the world's farming into high-yield agri-industry, to depopulate the rural areas, and to crowd the cities to the point of chronic breakdown and crisis.[12]

This societal shift toward urbanization has itself been accomplished by virtue of cheap energy, and that period of energy excess is waning. Increasing extraction costs, depletion of supplies, and unstoppable inflation will now rapidly turn this short-term, artificial societal arrangement topsy-turvy. Spiking energy costs will make rural life increasingly more affordable relative to an energy-intensive urban lifestyles. This shift in energy efficiencies offers the opportunity to rebuild sustainable agricultural rural economies.

This is a bipartisan economic and environmental plan that will work. The Republican Party desperately requires environmental legitimacy, and the American people and the planet's ecosystem desperately require rescue from the Green New Deal. But economics and environmentalism are not severable: people do not want to pay to clean up the Amazon in preference to putting food on their tables, and that includes American people.

The policy initiatives proposed in this book will grow the economy while reversing ecological harms and increasing fresh food production for urban areas. Any shift back to the land is adversarial to big government and globalist control—that in itself is good cause to take notice and take action.

Why Small-Farm Economics Work

A persistent fallacy is that small-scale agriculture cannot compete economically with large industrial methods. The opposite is true for most crops: small-scale farming can and will be profitable, absent artificial regulatory and other hurdles that destroy profit margins. Vandana Shiva writes that productivity "in traditional farming practices has always been high if it is remembered that very few external inputs are required."[13]

Subsidization of monocultures and processed foods must cease. It is time to see how Monsanto, Cargill, and the rest operate without the economic training wheels of subsidies and regulatory favoritism. Consumer preference for better-quality local foods will continue to improve profitability for small, local operations. Rural farming income is mostly reinvested in the communities wherein it is earned, bolstering local businesses like hardware and feed suppliers, carpenters and lumber mills, restaurants and grocery stores. It is a trickle up—and down—economic boon to rural communities.[14]

Local farming is becoming increasingly profitable while nurturing culture, community, and environment. A 2020 *Forbes* magazine commentary acknowledged increasing profitability even after accounting for any declines in productivity:

> Many might point to decreases in yield, but under the right
> conditions, and by taking a holistic view of farmland opera-
> tions and the underlying asset value, the profitability of a farm
> can increase, all while reducing risk and crop loss. . . . Regen-
> erative agriculture can work and can increase farmland's prof-
> itability. Over time, this increased profitability can increase the
> value of an investor's farmland asset.[15]

Farmers understand the interconnectedness of soil and table, alongside
the values of common sense and humility with which corporate boardrooms have long been grossly deprived.[16] Local restaurants and diners
are also increasing their awareness—and willing to spend money—for
healthier, fresher, more trustworthy local foods.

As humans return to the land with rediscovered awareness of the
exciting possibilities in soil and agricultural husbandry, they will happily
learn that there is indeed hope in them hills. Improved soil management
employing regenerative agricultural practices does not require expensive
upgrades or equipment and can be implemented to some degree on every
scale. This is truly progress that has no downsides whatsoever for consumers, farmers, and the environment. It is an all-too-rare win, win, and then
win some more scenario.[17]

America's dependency on subsidized, environmentally destructive,
industrially produced foodstuffs is *economically* unhealthy. The return to
local and rural is a truly promising hope for Americans, built on wisdom,
experience, and science. Conservatives must seize this economic opportunity to avert starvation and societal collapse. Democrats must similarly
reject big-government solutions that reward large corporate interests and
join with conservatives who share these goals.

Distributism describes an economic structure in which those who raise
food control and retain the profits of their labor, rather than be exploited
by an ever-waiting contingent of large-scale corporate or government
interests. Distributism is deaf to ideological fallacies like socialism versus
capitalism. Either a farmer grows food productively on her land, or she
doesn't; either a healthy nutritious meal is ingested, or it is not.[18] Only by
a return to such simplicities will Americans revive the physical, cultural,

and economic health that have been sacrificed for the "quick and cheap" promises of our industrial destroyers.[19] It is time to search for better angels.

Wendell Berry's warnings against industrial destruction and dependency have consistently advanced a distributist view for decades. Mr. Berry often invoked Thomas Jefferson, who seemingly foretold of our current plight when he wrote, "If people let the government decide what foods they eat and what medicines they take, their bodies will soon be in as sorry a state as are the souls of those who live under tyranny." In Berry's words:

> I believe that land that is to be used should be divided in small parcels among a lot of small owners; I believe therefore in the right of private property. I believe that, given our history and tradition, a large population of small property holders offers the best available chance for local cultural adaptation and good stewardship of the land–provided that the property holders are secure, legally and economically, in their properties.[20]

This is a creed that Americans from all political parties, races, and economic strata can embrace *together*. Food price volatility will likely devolve into scarcity and then hunger. Phasing out subsidies for monocultures, implementing regenerative agricultural transition at every scale, and nurturing local farming in all its forms will benefit *all* human consumers of food *equally*. If famine is to be averted, the world does not have ten years to wait to procure secure, sustainable food supplies. Growing local food in rural America is increasingly profitable and promises to improve economic prospects for small farmers and rural small businesses.

CHAPTER NINE

Culture and Agriculture

> *To live, to survive on the earth, to care for the soil, and to worship, all are bound at the root to the idea of a cycle. It is only by understanding the cultural complexity and largeness of the concept of agriculture that we can see the threatening diminishments implied by the term "agribusiness."*
>
> —WENDELL BERRY, *The Art of the Commonplace*

There is a dangerous urban-rural division within today's culture wars. To hate rural culture is to hate humanity and the source of its food and natural resources; to hate urban life is to scorn art and society and to dehumanize millions. The growing cultural divide between rural and urban threatens both rural and urban people—with discrimination, economic decline, mass starvation, and cultural nihilism.

For decades, natural resources and human capital have been extracted from the countryside for the economic growth of cities, sapping the vibrant rural culture in the bargain. This is indeed the most revolutionary of accomplishments of the Industrial Revolution, and it is not at all beneficial.[1] Rural America has endured this assault with dignity, but the inequities of this prolonged cultural denigration have created understandable resentments in the countryside of which urban America remains ignorant, or perhaps merely ambivalent.

Economics, liberties, and societal tranquility all enter into this cultural conflict. At root is an industrial techno-mysticism that has been blindly embraced by rural and urban Americans alike to the detriment of both. Americans have inexorably shifted from an *agri*culture to an *industri*culture or *techno*culture, from connection to the land to a separation caused by consumption addictions that leave corporate profiteers in unsupervised control of the land once stewarded by humans. Humanity now confronts the consequences of its thoughtless embrace of technological ease, what Wendell Berry called a "creation in reverse" and "man-made cosmic terror."[2] The *only* solution is an agrarian reformation; a small-farm revival. To neglect rural culture is to reject all culture: "it must be asked if we can remove cultural value from one part of our lives without destroying it also in the other parts."[3] Raw-milk artisanal cheeses and Doritos are both *cultural* food products, yet they reflect completely different, even alien and oppositional, "cultures." "Agriculture is in so complex a sense a cultural endeavor ... that food is therefore a cultural product."[4]

America is waking to its deadly dependence on what Joel Salatin satirically derides as "our Greco-Roman western linear reductionist system-atized fragmented disconnected parts-oriented individualized culture."[5] The gradual destruction of rural culture is a consequence of the industrial "development" that has destroyed agricultural communities. Uniformity of big-box stores and chain restaurants displace homestyle meals at local diners, fresh-baked breads at hometown bakeries, and the intimate com-munity news shared by neighbors waiting in line at traditional general stores. Cheap and tasty is a quick path to cultural decay as well as bad human health. Americans must unite in a food *culture* movement, the foundation for which is local, diversified farms.

Culture and agriculture are inextricably woven together, and techno-logical "advances" cannot displace one without killing the other. America has errantly embraced a "community-killing agriculture" that cheapens culture and community along with food.[6] Rural farmers need city buyers of their goods, as they always have. Plus, they need a place to visit the opera or buy specialty manufactured goods not viably produced in rural areas. But the *rural* knowledge and skill sets to deliver nutritious food to the city are *cultural.*[7]

In *Beyond the Hundredth Meridian*, Wallace Stegner ominously revealed the centrality of food and self-reliance in the culture wars that destroyed Native American tribes:

> However sympathetically or even sentimentally a white
> American viewed the Indian, the industrial culture was certain

to eat away at the tribal cultures.... One's attitude might vary, but the fact went on regardless. What destroyed the Indian was not primarily political greed, land hunger, or military power, nor the white man's germs or the white man's rum. What destroyed him was the manufactured products of culture, iron and steel, guns, needles, woolen cloth, *things that once possessed could not be done without.*[8]

The fate of the Native Americans and their demolished cultures is the same fate unfolding before us, by familiar exploitative actors. Once the knowledge of local cultures is lost, it cannot be recovered. The cultures of Native American peoples were decimated in much the same fashion as is being repeated today against rural farming communities and their invaluable collective knowledge. Wes Jackson cautions that this loss may destroy America even if the ecological crises faced are resolved:

Species extinction and genetic narrowing of the major crops aside, the loss of cultural information due to the depopulation of our rural areas is far greater than all the information accumulated by science and technology in the same period.... The information that has left the countryside [is] the kind of information that is a necessary basis for a sustainable or sunshine agriculture.[9]

Instead of replacing grass-fed meats with vat-bred synthetic alternatives composed of polluting industrial soy, Americans should eat *more* grass-fed meats for their health and to reduce pollution. This will restore rural economies *and cultures* instead of increasing dependency on urban processing. Preparing for an age in which fossil fuel energy is no longer "cheap" requires Americans to migrate *out* of cities and back onto a food-rich, nurturing agri-rural landscape. Rotationally grazed livestock and well-tended soils and gardens offer the best course for that transition.[10]

It is not just politicians who have lost the wisdom of the land, but consumers culturally conditioned to quick, fast, "tasty" food spewed from factories. More and more Americans are growing in awareness of the enslaving food distribution and retailing industry that grinds American workers with subsistence wages while beguiling "customers" to feed at their dubious operations.[11]

Modern commercial globalization tears through cultures internationally and if unchecked will eventually blend all cultures into something like T. S. Eliot's apocalyptic poem "The Waste Land," in which no traditions or histories hold meaning because none remain distinctly intact. Eliot's title was not directed at industrially decimated soils and water, but today's ecological destruction mirrors the cultural one he described. Industrialization has pushed farmers into sterile servitude in cities, suburbs, and factories, where they learned to "commute." For most of the farms that remain, these same forces have created an industrial factory-farm servitude for animal and farmer alike, wherein crushing contracts exploit farmers and restrict their ability to creatively run their own businesses. This has contributed to a homogenization of culture toward the banal and the dependent.

It is imperative that our nation confronts the costs of its cultural disintegration, including drug addiction; escalating anxiety, depression, and suicide rates; alarming wealth disparity; unraveling dystopian cities; and increasing rates of homelessness and hunger. All of society benefits when families tend the Earth with care, thereby connecting urban and rural citizens to a shared, humble dependency on soil and animal.[12]

As Americans become more informed of the infirmities of their industrialized food system, they culturally revert to appreciating their local food, local region, and the trust that can only be certain there. That local culture is a diverse agricultural one, varying from state to state, between regions within states, and between varieties of farming scattered in variegated topographies. What is "local" varies, adapts, and is flexible. It is more resilient against national and international threats and natural disasters.

In their dawning environmental awareness, Americans were first moved to protect and preserve awe-inspiring national treasures in a National Parks system. Later, Rachel Carson and others alerted Americans to the harms of chemicals like DDT that killed bald eagles. The 1980s brought attention to swollen, leaking landfills and contaminated groundwater. In all of these cases, action was initiated in response to public sentiments. If America can preserve its wilderness, protect its endangered species, and contain its stinking landfills, why can it not preserve and protect the lifeblood of its culture and sustenance—its rural farmers?

Much of that traditional agricultural knowledge still remains. Many young and retiring Americans are taking interest in agricultural ventures for profit and/or sanity and/or food security. In contrast to Europe, some American regions still shelter a remnant of rugged local farmers to draw from. Chris Smaje encouragingly claims:

> Few local autonomies remain anywhere in the world today, perhaps least of all in the wealthy countries. And of those wealthy countries, my home country of Britain is among the sorriest of the lot, lacking the historical continuity of small-scale agrarianism that clings on in pockets in the Americas, and lacking the local food cultures and peasant traditions that cling on in parts of Europe.[13]

The agricultural stewardship and independence that dominated the American landscape in colonial times has been eroded by industrial pressures, but still rural patches of America persist. Much valuable local farmland can yet be reclaimed with the aid of the farmers who still possess the cultural and practical knowledge of how to renew the land. More people wish to move back to the land to seek and carry on that knowledge.

The promising agricultural marvels of the postwar industrial boom proved to be mirages. It is vitally important to local culture and the very identity of America to preserve and nurture vanishing *cultural* knowledge for local food supplies and local culture to be sustained. The Great Depression exposed the vulnerabilities of dependence on a national government and industrialized system. Since that time, America has amplified that dependency exponentially and must roll up its farming sleeves with gusto to rebuild what has been neglected.

In this time of supposed reckoning with prejudices and social injustices, perhaps Americans will reflect on the abysmal record of their nation in its debasement of farms and farming. Wes Jackson writes: "Part of that War against rural culture can be seen in the negative attitude of our larger culture toward rural places and rural people. They run as deep as the worst forms of racism."[14] No reparations have been proposed for the economic damages and social distress this forced impoverishment has inflicted. Indiscriminate of skin color, gender, or religious affiliation, small farmers have borne the brunt of modern neglect and discrimination.

Popular culture has come to sneer at "dirty" farmers and farming. The national opinion has been shaped by industrial propaganda to view farming as unprofitable and unrewarding. The powerful wealth of large commercial interests hijacked government policy to undermine profitability for small family farms by securing massive subsidies that benefited large producers; dominated university research; and promulgated regulations that unduly and fatally burdened small producers who could not afford to comply. This assault chipped away at rural farms and communities for decades, until the lack of profitability ensured an accompanying dismay.

This "culture war" against rural agriculture has been chronicled and lamented for decades by Wendell Berry, who observed:

> This loss of local knowledge and local memory—that is, of local culture—has been ignored, or written off as one of the cheaper "process of progress," or made the business of folklorists. Nevertheless, local culture has a value, and part of its value is economic. . . . Lacking an authentic culture, a place is open to exploitation, and ultimately destruction, from the center.[15]

Berry explains that this destruction is reciprocal in that all society suffers when local culture is destroyed, because local culture mediates between competing interests, as the glue of nurturing community:

> The indispensable form that can intervene between public and private interests is that of community. The concerns of public and private, republic and citizen, necessary as they are, are not adequate for the shaping of human life. Community alone, as a principle and as fact, can raise the standards of local health (ecological, economic, social, and spiritual) without which the other two interests will destroy one another.[16]

The culture war in today's America is divisive and multifaceted. But identity is only built on skin color, gender orientation, or other tribal reductions by an alienated society deprived of healthy traditional community associations historically and almost universally bound together by agri*culture* and a shared battle against famine and mortality. That culture must be earnestly resurrected. Identity politics can only destroy both republic and citizen. It pits different cultures into endless conflict along with racial, socioeconomic, and even ecological divisions. The chaos of tribal politics thrives in the void created by the gradual diminution of authentic local culture.

The cultural value of small farms, local farmers markets, CSAs, roadside farm stands, and other social interrelations that extend from local food and agriculture are priceless in their contribution to America's identity, vital for its economic and agricultural survival, and popular with many Americans despite the larger culture's regrettable ignorance of its own root dependence on soil for health and food security. Only by revitalizing local farms and communities with a determined effort can a restoration of these deteriorating foundations be accomplished. Restorative agriculture regenerates much, much more than just soil.

CHAPTER TEN

A Cry for Food Freedom

We still (sometimes) remember that we cannot be free if our minds and voices are controlled by someone else. But we have neglected to understand that we cannot be free if our food and its sources are controlled by someone else. The condition of the passive consumer of food is not a democratic condition.

—WENDELL BERRY, *The Art of the Commonplace*

My personal path from tax attorney to animal farmer entailed a conversion from consumer to producer, in which I learned not only how to make hay, raise animals, and harvest milk and meat, I also learned about the quality, freshness, and healthfulness of this food and way of life. That journey also became an education about the market and government forces that have conspired over the decades to inhibit and control this way of life for profit and power.

In 2016, we were renting a former dairy farm in Irasburg, Vermont, a town with no zoning, and rural even by Vermont standards. I advertised to sell halves of beef on Craigslist. One day shortly thereafter, a car pulled unannounced into the dirt driveway on our dead-end back road. I went out to greet a Vermont Agency of Agriculture Food and Markets (VAAFM) meat inspector and was soon lectured on how selling this meat was illegal.

This was news to me and seemed senseless—I had been doing this for almost twenty years, and many of my Vermont family and community had raised or sold their own meats for as long as Vermont has been a state. I challenged the VAAFM rep, who told me I could only sell *whole* animals, not halves, and that I could only sell by live weight, not hanging weight. Since I had a legal and commodity-market familiarity, this was immediately ludicrous to me. I was bemused, and so I pressed this poor guy for over an hour.

It went like this: the federal government, instigated by industrial meat producers who don't like farmers like me "stealing" their commercial market share with grass-fed local meats, awards grant money to local state agriculture agencies to hire more people to prohibit on-farm slaughter practices in the name of "public safety." Ironically, those massive meat recalls are always from the gargantuan meat facilities that grind thousands of tons of dubious animal parts together for McDonald's and Jack in the Box. The meat from my small herd of cows is much safer on all levels, which is why my customers will pay more. My customers also wish to ensure humane treatment of the animals and avoid antibiotics and hormones in their meat.

The new meat inspector waltzed onto my little farm to inform me of all these new rules. I asked him a few basic questions, such as why was the VAAFM restricting the sale of halves of beef slaughtered on-farm but not whole animal purchases? Why was it requiring on-farm slaughtered animals be weighed live rather than after slaughter? And what about the impact of these rule changes on the itinerant slaughterers and custom processors whose livelihoods depended on on-farm slaughter traditions?

As to the difference between selling whole animals versus a half, the market distinction is huge. I have never had a customer buy an entire cow. That would require about $5,000 and two large freezers (and a very big family!). What, I asked the meat inspector, is the health and safety purpose behind requiring the sale of only whole animals? That is, what is the difference in food *safety* when both halves are still slaughtered and processed identically? His answer was built on the agency's determination that selling parts of animals violated federal law: "Well, you can only sell a whole animal." I explained that I was an attorney, and that's not how the Constitution works. I told him that the government has the burden of demonstrating a substantial state interest when it puts people out of business with over-regulation, whether that government is federal, state, or municipal.

I then pressed him about the new requirement that animals be weighed alive before slaughter, which he justified using the agency's determination that only live animals could be legally sold for on-farm slaughter. "Is it better for health and safety to compel me to truck my animal to a local facility to be weighed before sale?" I asked. I explained that the animal is stressed gratuitously by trucking, which hurts meat quality (stress causes the excretion of cortisol), risks injury, and also exposes it to whatever pathogens are in the commercial truck and/or the weighing facility (in this case a local commission sale, where hundreds of sick and compromised cows were sold every week). Also, my cows were born on the grass we slaughter them on and never got trucked anywhere, let alone pushed through gates for scaling. So much for humane animal treatment. The inspector told me, "Well, if you are hanging it before weighing it you are not selling a live animal." "Well, that's absurd," I explained. " *Of course* contract law allows me to sell a live animal, the price of which is determined post-slaughter using a scale—at the state-inspected processing facility where the clean carcass is hung, instead of the nasty, uninspected commission sales barn where the living animal would be needlessly agitated." I protested that futures prices were routinely determined for commodities including meats on the Chicago Mercantile Exchange based on such systems. There was not one conceivable health and safety benefit to these new mandates, but there *was* plenty of financial benefit to large corporations, whose meats are less safe and healthy than local, grass-fed ones.

My uninvited guest left somewhat challenged. I promptly sat at my computer and researched the new "safety" laws and learned that *all* on-farm slaughter was legislatively destined for elimination in Vermont in a few more years. The so-called "health and safety" statute incorporated a "sunset" provision that was slated to ban all on-farm slaughter entirely in 2019. Yet my research revealed that New York and some other states were quite liberal in their on-farm slaughter laws. New York and other states allowed much more leeway in not only on-farm slaughter but also animal processing regulations. This was vital to serve cultural minorities such as Jews and Muslims who will not under religious tradition consume mistreated industrial animals.

I then read David Gumpert's important book, *Life, Liberty, and the Pursuit of Food Rights*, which traces the story of how federal and state authorities have quietly tightened the regulatory noose on local foods, especially raw milk and related products. It was evident to me that Vermont's statutory scheme to prohibit on-farm slaughter traditions was a corporate scam dressed up as "protecting the people." In actuality it was doing the *opposite*, compelling people to eat *less* safe and healthy meats to benefit large corporations at the *expense* of local businesses like mine. I joined the Farm-to-Consumer Legal Defense Fund and learned more about Amish farmer Amos Miller and various raw milk battles. I wrote to Wendell Berry and Joel Salatin, appealing for support. Both of them encouraged me to rally my allies and fight for small farms.

I was still struggling with fibromyalgia daily, and our finances were very modest. But this attack on small-scale, rural farmers was just intolerable, and as an attorney and farmer, I smelled a mega-rat. I said to Jackie: "Farmers can't afford $300-per-hour attorneys to fight this, and even if they did, the lawyers wouldn't really understand farming the way we do. I think I must fight this." Blessed as I am with a supportive wife who shares my passion for human and animal health and vibrant local farming communities, she agreed. Jackie encouraged me to stand up against them.

I called a press conference with my cows in their pasture and announced I was going to ignore the VAAFM, continue to sell halves of beef, and that the proposed health and safety laws were an unconstitutional farce. I challenged the State of Vermont to charge and arrest me, so that I could prove in court that their laws were unconstitutional. I also wrote a strong letter to the hapless meat inspector, challenging these new policies as well as VAAFM's power to regulate me.

I galvanized area farmers, slaughterers, and custom processors, and we traveled to a Vermont State Senate Committee on Agriculture hearing to testify against the pending legislation and demand on-farm slaughter liberties. The full story need not be recounted here, but after another year or two of wrangling, we farmers secured a repeal of the proposed on-farm-slaughter restrictions and now sell halves *and quarters* of animals legally in Vermont!

This experience was eye-opening for me. I became aware of the ongoing commercial and government pressures to shut down small-scale food processors under the guise of protecting public health. I became not just a passionate farmer but a patriotic one. Large industrial interests view small farms and their human farmers as impediments to greater market share and profitability. Similarly, the federal government has long viewed this rural demographic as the greatest threat to its complete totalitarian control of America. If there was ever an area that should be shielded with guns from "enemies domestic," it is local food production.

The premise that food liberty is a necessary requisite for any liberty at all is largely lost on the modern consumer. Whether or not Americans trust their government, they mostly trust their nation's food supply—it has been reliable, plentiful, and diverse for eighty unprecedented years of productivity. But this passivity opens the door to the domination of citizens through food control, which is the dispute that gave rise to the American revolution against the British. This food liberty history has faded from popular memory, but it was the effort to tax and control food supplies that most rankled American colonists.[1] Thomas Jefferson was a consistent supporter of the liberty to farm.[2] He was essentially a proponent of distributism who believed that the more *local* farming was, the more secure would be both food supplies and fundamental liberties.

In his 2007 book, *A Revolution in Eating: How the Quest for Food Shaped America*, historian James McWilliams recounts that the ways Americans cultivated and prepared food inspired their resistance and eventual defiance of the British Crown, whose intrusions were "a violation that transgressed the very item that shaped the social and economic life of the colonists: food."[3] The stifling domination of food production and distribution that has unfolded in recent decades is more threatening to American liberties than the colonial British Crown could have ever fashioned or even imagined.

Here in America's early history are strong warnings that something is greatly amiss in 2022. Americans have long taken it for granted that they are free to grow food, even as those freedoms have been chiseled away in the name of progress, aesthetics, health and safety, and modernity. This slow-drip erosion of rights has accompanied the destructive industrial erosion of soils, air, and water. It is evident that certain powerful interests, including particularly the federal government, have long endeavored to control all aspects of food production.

A significant clue to this insidious violation of the nation's founding contract was revealed in the telling 1942 US Supreme Court case of *Wickard v. Filburn*.[4] If ever there was a case in which the exception swallowed the rule, it is *Wickard*. The "rule" at issue was the clear constitutional provision that the federal government would have authority over interstate, but not *intra*state, commerce. *Wickard* essentially eliminated that local, states-rights protection.

The case addressed the 1938 Agricultural Adjustment Act, which sought to control wheat prices. Roscoe Filburn was an Ohio farmer who raised wheat for his own home consumption, exceeding the permitted sowing acreage under the federal act. In response to regulatory action to penalize him, Filburn alleged that the excess wheat produced was never intended for the market but only for personal consumption by his family on its farm.

In a decision that sweepingly eviscerated Commerce Clause protections, the *Wickard* court ruled against the small farmer, finding (and thus establishing as law) that a home farmer's activity is governed by federal commerce power even if it has no direct effect on interstate commerce, as long as the effect is "substantial and economic." Roscoe's wheat was not exempt, the court ruled, because "his contribution, taken with that of many others similarly situated, is far from trivial." The result is that small farmers growing for *subsistence only* are deemed to be involved in national, interstate commerce because they "may forestall resort to the market by producing for [their] own needs."[5] That is, farmers are subject to the market they exclude themselves from and may be compelled to buy industrial products shipped interstate because not doing so hurts commerce!

Here's what the court had to say:

> A factor of such volume and variability as wheat grown for home consumption would have a substantial influence on price conditions on the wheat market, both because such wheat, with rising prices, may flow into the market and check price increases and, because, though never marketed, it supplies the need of the grower which would otherwise be satisfied by his purchases in the open market.[6]

This novel "aggregation" standard erased restraints of the federal government intended under the restrictions of the Commerce Clause and has been affirmed since. Most recently, the court held that the commerce provision of the Controlled Substances Act gave the federal government power to regulate local marijuana use because it affected supply and demand in the national marijuana market.[7]

Since America's founding, the federal government has expanded into a behemoth not favored by the founders. Indeed, this type of federal domination is exactly what the Constitution and Bill of Rights foresaw as the greatest threat to personal liberty and what they were enacted to forestall. In addition to expansions particularly of congressional and executive powers, the shift has become more partisan, allowing one political ideology to seize greater national control of laws. Both of these developments are precisely what the United States Constitution was crafted to *prevent*. Americans must advocate for a "primal constitutional right" to grow and sell food from neighbor to neighbor.

On November 2, 2021, Maine became the first state in America to correct this federal domination of food rights by amending its state constitution. Those voting for the measure victoriously added the following language in Article 1:

> Section 25. Right to food. All individuals have a natural, inherent and unalienable right to food, including the right to save and exchange seeds and the right to grow, raise, harvest, produce and consume the food of their own choosing for their own nourishment, sustenance, bodily health and well-being, as long as an individual does not commit trespassing, theft, poaching or other abuses of private property rights, public lands or natural resources in the harvesting, production or acquisition of food.[8]

Wendell Berry has vividly described the modern American condition as a three-sided battle in which both conservationists and farmers have lost out over time to the "third side . . . that of the land-exploiting corporations."[9] Maine proves that the other two sides are mounting a forceful challenge to the modern land-destroying corporate barons. A rising national effort is next.

Those early voices of distributism bear a rehearing: they were essentially advocates for a strong agrarianism. This goes a long way to an argument for a constitutional liberty in 2023 America to raise and choose one's own foods. In a time when the government seeks to coercively and unconstitutionally inject experimental toxins into unwilling citizens, the assertion of food rights becomes more urgent than ever. As Americans fall deeper into poverty, the omnipresent neoliberal, increasingly socialist, "state" stands at the ready to expand its power to "solve" the problem it seeded—just like industrial agriculture and technology, that third side of the triangle. Informed Americans from all sides must align their two sides against this tyrannical domination.

The Constitution is silent about food rights in the same way that it is silent about the right to breathe oxygen. It was unfathomable to colonial Americans that the government would dare seek to control food or that citizens would abdicate their self-determination in allowing themselves to be so enslaved. It is axiomatic in any culture that people should be permitted to subsist—any and all "laws" or regulations that purport to restrict that universal right are direct attacks against the people's liberties.[10]

There is big money in food—growing it, shipping it, processing it, selling it. It is a multi-trillion-dollar business, as well as the most basic necessity of all human consumption. Controlling it conveys unlimited power, making it the greatest of all political weapons. The Obama administration staunchly supported Monsanto in its dispute with farmers to patent and own genetically modified seed supplies. *Bowman v. Monsanto Co.* held that a farmer could not grow and keep soybean seeds for replanting when he had purchased the original seeds from Monsanto.[11] This means that corporations designing new seed strains own *all progeny* of that seed, in perpetuity. The Obama administration again failed American farmers and consumers when it preempted state efforts to clearly label GMO foods by enacting weak and unreliable federal labeling requirements that confuse and mislead consumers. This benefited industrial food producers at the expense of human and ecological health.

Wise voices are rising to challenge the tightening noose around Americans' food supplies. Inner-city vegetable gardeners have faced legal action for violating zoning laws that restrict gardening; other disputes involve chicken or animal rearing where those activities conflict with zoning laws designed to maximize property values for rich people! Many states and municipalities have enacted laws designed to prevent citizens from living off-grid, most notably by mandating connection to the electric grid, regulating rainwater collection, or banning composting toilets. A number of informed academic voices have now joined the fray to combat this forced dependency, and many citizens are standing up against such draconian oppression.

In *Life, Liberty, and the Pursuit of Food Rights,* David Gumpert alerted America to the use of stifling "health and safety" regulations to inhibit home slaughtering of animals, raw milk products, and other locally produced food products. Gumpert establishes that the motives are usually not really to protect public health and safety but to preserve corporate profit margins and market share. Slaughter rules have sprung up across the country that suddenly seek to ban on-farm slaughter traditions that have existed for centuries—not for human health, but because citizens raising grass-fed beef began to draw market share from Cargill and other mega-producers of inhumanely raised, unhealthy, grain-dependent CAFO beef. The pretense of protection disguises the true motives for these stifling initiatives.

These abuses of regulatory power have been inflicted to the detriment of local economies and landscapes as well as human health. Joel Salatin relates an experience with Virginia authorities who seized his calves for supposed noncompliance with health and safety laws.[12] Wendell Berry recounted the same intrusion into Kentucky that *destroyed* local meat production back in 1978.[13]

The Farm-to-Consumer Legal Defense Fund exists to help farmers fight legal battles across the nation, as this power-grab by the feds and their industrial masters heats up with time. It is obvious that the increased stranglehold on food by corporate America is very jealously guarded. The more citizens resort to producing their own alternatives, the more the tyrannical backroom actors pull the strings of their elected marionettes to subdue any threat that could undermine profits and monopoly in food sales.[14] And what is the real purpose of the USDA acquiring inventories of semiautomatic weapons with Tritium night sights?[15]

Attorney Baylen Linnekin documents the magnitude and broadness of these regulatory attacks by bureaucrats against farmers and their customers in *Biting the Hand That Feeds Us: How Fewer, Smarter Laws Would Make Our Food System More Sustainable*:

> Many food-safety rules ... bar people from using sustainable methods to grow, raise, produce, prepare, sell, and buy a variety of foods. ... Many government rules favor—and even promote—large scale food producers.[16]

Joel Salatin notes that a "culture that will not allow its citizenry autonomy in matters of personal food intake will certainly destroy other freedoms very quickly."[17] The pandemic revealed a society prepared to surrender freedom of movement and commerce to lockdowns; medical choices to Big Pharma and Herr Fauci; freedom of speech to Twitter, Facebook, and mainstream media. As the push to seize guns gains steam, and all aspects of government are saturated with a "woke" social justice ideology that connects food access to race, will Americans stand idly by as the Department of Homeland Security determines who will eat and what? Historian John Lukacs warned of this coming devolution of the American experiment into totalitarianism: "A puerile presidency may be but one symptom of the devolution of this republic into a military superstate."[18]

Americans can readily see that the voices calling for food security and a return to local agriculture are being conscientiously ignored by proponents of the Green New Deal. Could it be that an agenda to dominate food and energy is unfolding before voters' eyes? The greatest vulnerability of the citizenry is the destruction, deliberately or negligently, of the food system and soils upon which all human life depends.

Wendell Berry advocates for a local, sustainable agriculture because "the orientation of agriculture to local needs, local possibilities, and local limits is indispensable to the health of democratic liberties as well."[19] This is not a contemplation of a 1970s-style hippie-commune return to the land; this is an ancient power struggle that has never faded. The two poles of future human society are rural, agrarian interdependence versus a global domination of every aspect of human experience.[20] America's small and midsize farmers have always presented a defensive bulwark against totalitarian domination, but their numbers have dwindled—by corporate-government design. Those claiming they oppose multinational corporations and corrupt government systems strive to impose a new world order dominated by precisely those interests. Vandana Shiva has raised the alarm about this domination by multinational corporations:

> What we are seeing is the emergence of food totalitarianism, in which a handful of corporations control the entire food chain and destroy alternatives so that people do not have access to diverse, safe foods produced ecologically. Local markets are being deliberately destroyed to establish monopolies over seed and food systems. . . . This food totalitarianism can only be stopped through major citizen mobilization for democratization of the food system.[21]

A proper course to democratize the food system would institute two policy areas to advance regenerative, environmentally sensitive agricultural methods: (1) phase out subsidies for destructive monocultures, particularly corn and soy; and (2) provide short-term tax credits and long-term regulatory relief for small-scale farms to improve profitability and encourage entrepreneurial investment. This is a radical transformation that challenges *both* corporate cronyism *and* limitless government regulatory oversight.

For decades, the federal government has tightened its regulatory domination of every nook and cranny of the nation's food supply. Any time there is an actual health issue related to food, the government is at hand with regulations to "protect consumers." Ironically, it is often contamination of food by large production facilities that results in regulations being enacted that are disproportionately burdensome on smaller operations. This has been the case in meat slaughter and processing in particular.[22]

Whole fields of regulatory domination are mapped out at the federal level, then introduced as "consumer safety" initiatives in state legislatures in exchange for federal grants to hire more state inspectors and rule-implementing bureaucrats. Bureaucracy grows; farms close. It is the nature of government to feed itself at the expense of soil, human, and food health.

The Orwellian pretense is always that the government is "protecting" people, yet experience proves it more often protects big business and its own food fiefdom. Joel Salatin puts it bluntly:

> Look, folks, if we want to talk about elitists, I think the real elitists are the people in this country who want to deny you and me the freedom to buy the food of our choice. . . . The government's track record on deciding what to promote as safe food is abysmal. The government told us to feed dead cows to cows and gave us mad cow disease. The government told us to subsidize corn growers and cheapened unhealthy high-fructose corn syrup.[23]

Tom Philpott explains this further in *Perilous Bounty*:

> What drives this creeping disaster is the rise of a virtual oligarchy of companies that capture most of the profit generated by the trillion-dollar-a-year food economy. Three massive, globe-spanning companies—Bayer-Monsanto, Corteva, and Syngenta—sell the great bulk of the seeds and pesticides available to farmers. A handful of others—Tyson Foods, JBS, and Smithfield Foods—slaughter and pack the majority of meat we eat. The market for trading corn and soybeans largely belongs to Cargill and Archer Daniels Midland. In California, a single firm—the privately held Wonderful Company— dominates the water-sucking almond, pistachio, pomegranate, and mandarin-orange markets.[24]

A silent chokehold of utter domination has been creeping into American kitchens, targeting, abusing, and profiting from our frail human dependence on food. Industrialism seeks not only to addict its consumers but to control their very access to the substances upon which they are made dependent. A further maturation of this process is in progress in the synthetic meat industry, which would have humanity shift from the flesh of animals raised on sun-fed grass to a complex, patented factory "product" reminiscent of pink slime. As Diana Rodgers and Robb Wolf lament, "Where once there was independence, there is now serfdom."[25]

The alternative to global techno-domination is the reduced scale of local production, distribution, consumption, and decision-making. Kirkpatrick Sale founds humanity's future prognosis on its ability to downsize from the current "oligarchy of the elite" to resist this liberty-throttling domination:

> It is on breaking the terrible dependence on imports and exports, and the economic vassalage that results, that self-sufficiency must depend.... We have sacrificed our citizenship to bigness, slowly over the decades—more rapidly in the last half century.[26]

Sale suggests that a true measure of affluence would not be fiat currency notes, but self-sufficiency. By this gauge, he reckons, Paleolithic humans were perhaps the most affluent in history due to their self-reliance. Wendell Berry similarly argued that "Free men are not set free by their government. Free men have set the government free of themselves; they have made it unnecessary."[27]

Self-reliant agriculture has always been central to securing liberties, including by early Black activists who pioneered civil rights efforts in the South through the Freedom Farmers movement.[28] Americans share *equally* the need for healthy local food, and people of all colors and orientations must unite against Big Ag. During the trauma of the COVID-19 pandemic, citizens of all political persuasions witnessed their extreme dependence on a precarious industrial food supply when grocery store shelves stood empty. Homesteaders are the antidote to a growing effort to transfer responsibility to the government and mega-corporations for that which we once did ourselves—grow healthy food, store it, and then eat it. Covid has revealed the folly of industrial food and has armed many more Americans with the desire and awareness to respond *locally* and *regeneratively*.

With increasing dependency on Chinese and other foreign food producers that are often subjected to lax food safety regulations, it is dubious to further curtail local farmers and consumers from their centuries-long traditions of commerce in the name of "protecting public health." As growing awareness of the importance of healthy local food motivates more people to try their hands at home gardening, chicken-rearing, or milking a family goat, the political frictions with a corporation-influenced, oversized government will increase. It is imperative that the right to grow one's own food be granted its proper priority for the pursuit of human health and happiness.

Socialist endeavors of the past have always eyed land and food control. Joseph Stalin and Vladimir Lenin targeted peasant farmers, known as "kulaks," resulting in class genocide that seized productive, fertile farmland that was transferred to agriculturally inexperienced political beneficiaries. Lenin created "Committees of the Poor" to implement the "dekulakization" of the land and the subsequent execution, starvation, and imprisonment of millions of family farmers. In China, the Great Leap Forward employed a similar strategy.[29]

The failed effort to craft a utopia in Cambodia by Pol Pot sought to control all agricultural production by compelling large populations of inexperienced urban Cambodians into the countryside, while rice was exported to China. Millions died as starvation ravaged the country. Zimbabwe's race-driven populist effort under Robert Mugabe to create racial "equity" involved seizing land from white farmers. This was distributed to Black partisans lacking farming know-how. Agricultural production plummeted, and hyperinflation ravaged the country's economy. The nation continues to struggle to recover.

Now the American government proposes to "rescue" citizens from the plight it has created, subsidizing yet more consolidation and mechanization in food production. In the stated interests of feeding the world, improving food safety, and the recently added argument of ameliorating climate change, governments worldwide and domestic are enacting vague legal mandates to reduce carbon dioxide emissions by such-and-such an amount by such-and-such a date. Wendell Berry points out the biggest threat from such intense government control:

> A government that could do enough, assuming it had the
> will, would almost certainly be a government radically and

unpleasantly different from the one prescribed by our Constitution. A government undertaking to protect all of nature that is now abused or threatened would have to take total control of the country.[30]

Weaponizing food and land in America for political purposes is nothing new. As related throughout this book, the oppression of and prejudices against small family farmers of all races have persisted in America for most of the last century. Wendell Berry has chronicled the government-industrial pressures that pushed America's farmers into cities for factory jobs and has condemned elitist prejudices against rural dwellers:

> As a rural American I was of course fully aware of the prejudice, equally conservative and liberal, against rural America and rural Americans. I knew that "rural" and "country" and "farmer" were still current as terms of insult. But I was not quite prepared for the venom, the contempt, and the stereotyping rhetoric that some liberal intellectuals (so proud of their solicitude for "the other") brought down upon their fellow humans.[31]

A cultural division in the United States will become evident in the coming years between those who can produce food self-sufficiently and those who are helpless to realistically contemplate the task. In his argument that modern civilization will enter a long but steady decline, John Michael Greer writes approvingly that small, rural communities still cling to "the freedom and power most Americans long ago surrendered to the cultural machinery of a mass society."[32] A local, regenerative shift in agricultural production, processing, and distribution will unite rather than divide Americans in seeking a reliable, sustainable food system for all that reinvigorates rather than undermines those freedoms.

Green New Deal fans appear unfazed. Typical of the wave-of-the-hand nonchalance with which the New Socialists of the Green New Deal gush faithfully about its societal reconstruction is Stan Cox in *The Green New Deal and Beyond: Ending the Climate Emergency While We Still Can*:

As the struggle for the Green New Deal and other legislation proceeds, there will be much wrangling over the question of what is politically acceptable. That's inevitable, but we must keep at the center of the public debate the most urgent question of all: What actions must be undertaken to eliminate greenhouse emissions in time?[33]

Urgency is thrust out as priority over "political acceptability" of what used to be called constitutional rights.[34] In *Green Fraud: Why the Green New Deal Is Even Worse Than You Think*, Mark Morano accurately sums up what is proposed:

> The alleged "climate emergency" is merely a premise for achieving the political goals that the Left has sought for decades. The Green New Deal will mean a complete takeover of a massive swath of the U.S. economy, disrupting and destroying lives as formerly free decisions are turned over to the bureaucratic state ... taking choices out of the hands of individual consumers and businesses and putting them into the hands of those who are allegedly more enlightened.[35]

Morano documents that the Green New Deal is in fact a "massive government intervention" that was originally drafted to guarantee incomes for those "unwilling to work." His book *Green Fraud* argues that the Green New Deal is an insidious, deliberate attempt to eviscerate American constitutional liberties. He writes, "The morphing of the public health bureaucracy and the climate establishment is at hand, and a technocracy or rule by unelected government 'experts' is now upon us."[36]

Small farms and direct connections between consumers and those who grow their food have been the foundation of successful, thriving societies since man first grew a pea plant. These traditions and the food security, economic stability, and vibrant communities they support are only established by means of the small farms that American industry and American government have conspired to gradually destroy. It is time for We the People to stand up and firmly reverse this slide into enslavement and reclaim the agrarian heritage that gave rise to this nation.

Joel Salatin accurately dubs our current corporate-government collaboration to control Americans' food supply as the "food police state."[37] American consumers must stand with their farmers and get informed about where their food comes from. They shirk this duty at their peril and at the peril of liberties that must no longer be taken for granted.

Americans are rousing from their food stupor and becoming aware of both the dangers in their food supply and the monopolistic creep of corporate-government domination of its production, processing, and distribution. Controlling the entire food supply is the end game. Dr. Joseph Mercola and Ronnie Cummins offer the prescription to counter this totalitarian effort:

> If we want to stop the Great Reset that is being furthered by power-intoxicated globalists. . . . We need a new family-farm-based agricultural system that can provide "food as medicine," organic and healthy food for all, while regenerating the environment and biodiversity.[38]

In that battle, the great state of Maine is leading the way. Interestingly, this effort to secure a constitutional right to grow food has been going on for some time, despite efforts by corporate actors to quash it. It should not have been necessary to codify a right so fundamental and basic, but the furious effort to prevent the passage of the "food liberty" amendment (now codified as Article 1, Section 25) speaks volumes. It is time that a federal recognition of these basic human rights was assured, whether via a constitutional amendment or by other means. As with the right to teach one's own children rather than have them indoctrinated by government institutions, it should be axiomatic that Americans possess these simple food and farming rights. The current "food climate" demands reaffirmation of these truths.

Re-localizing food production favoring traditional and regenerative agricultural practices is a rescue package for food sovereignty, economic growth, healthier food, and preservation of constitutional liberties. Americans must wake up to the food tyranny in their midst and get informed so that they can alert others.[39] National security is compromised by the gradual elimination of the local food-production network that fed the American revolutionaries.[40]

America's political future will be increasingly fueled by food policies that are important to Americans and their families, in the midst of what will likely be unrelenting food price inflation within a deteriorating economy. Citizens must embrace the political *liberation* power of this fast-growing movement.[41]

Americans face a looming food Armageddon. If it is to be averted, individual rights and personal choice must be *defended at all cost*, not abandoned in foolish terror. These problems have been swelling for decades, as corporate profiteers have tried to tamp them down or steer them aside. Spiking food prices will spark the next American revolution—against corporate-government domination. Wendell Berry has issued the challenge: "How can he be free who can do nothing for himself? ... Men are free precisely to the extent that they are equal to their own needs. The most able are the most free."[42]

The political force that comes to the rescue of that land and people is what is desperately required for this pivotal time. Regardless of whether it is Right or Left, it must be food- and soil-centered.

CHAPTER ELEVEN

The Illusion of "Renewables"

To accurately evaluate the environmental impacts of any particular human activity, total costs must be assessed. For instance, in monetary-based economics, the costs of a particular agricultural activity are the cash inputs—real estate taxes, fertilizer and feed, diesel fuel, electric and insurance bills, equipment purchase and parts, seed, and so on. Profitability is calculated after receipts for sales of goods, measured in dollars and cents.

But this profit measure excludes costs that were involved in production that are not evident in dollars—for instance contamination of air and water, chemical pollution, soil erosion, water depletion, and other environmental damages that are passed on to the ecosystem without being "paid for" by the farmer. These are what are referred to as externalized costs.

Measuring externalized costs exposes the complexity of weighing and balancing various competing inputs and resultant consequences. And this extends to all human activities. There are externalized pollution costs for every TV, cellphone, laptop, or other gadget purchased; for every lawn being mowed and fertilized for aesthetics; for ski trips and flights to Aruba; for ATVs, snowmobiles, motorboats, and jet skis; for sheetrock, plywood, PVC pipes, concrete, and asphalt shingles. Additional unconscionable nonmonetary consequences of agricultural goods may include inhumane treatment of animals, child or slave labor, or sexual or racial discrimination. Every aspect of human consumption incorporates externalized pollution or other potentially adverse moral costs.

The most rudimentary awareness of these costs, and of how to reduce their environmental impact, can only exist on an individual level. Unless government is to ban all snowmobiles or regulate who gets to use them and when, such decisions will be voluntary and individual, whether for good or ill. This is why scale matters greatly in environmental policy; consumption is *individual* and "local."

Extending this perspective from agricultural and household goods to proposals for manufactured renewable energy, it is clear that there are externalized costs inherent also in the production of solar panels, electric vehicles (EVs), windmills, heat pumps, and hydroelectric facilities, and so on. In most analyses of renewable energy technologies and throughout the pro-renewables propaganda push, these externalized costs are generally just ignored. This is either grossly ignorant or grossly unethical: none of the supposedly "renewable" manufactured technologies survive even a cursory analysis of this sort.[1]

When we consider the environmental impact of manufacturing EVs and solar panels, the chemical inputs and outputs far outweigh any energy gains from their use. Furthermore, the *energy* required as an input in the manufacturing and transportation of those same EVs and solar panels increases rather than decreases fossil fuel usage. Manufacturing solar panels requires monumental inputs of diesel fuel to mine raw materials and transport them to factories that then consume even larger amounts of energy (from natural gas or coal) to fabricate solar cells to generate energy from the sun. The net impact is not energy-saving, but energy-depleting![2]

None of the alternative energy technologies presently known can even remotely replace current human fossil fuel consumption—they all *increase* and *accelerate* overall pollution and energy consumption. Equally harmful, they defer effective action that could in their stead make a difference, due to the false sense of accomplishment the illusory promises of renewables provide.

Renewable energy is most certainly *not* efficient, and it does not reduce levels of consumption. It just offers people new ways to keep on consuming. This is unsustainable. Even if renewables were not counterproductive (as most are), shifting human consumption to replacement technologies will do little to avert continued environmental decline. As Aldo Leopold said of government land conservation projects, "In the long run it is exactly as effective as buying half an umbrella."[3]

Renewable energy efforts do not seek to reverse unsustainable consumption, but to enable it with new technological (profit-making) manufacturing that is as damaging to the ecosystem as ever. The Green New Deal is a deal for corporate America to receive massive subsidies to destroy the planet at an even more accelerated rate than in the past, driven by profits but painted up as salvific. The environmental chicken coop doors are being flung wide, inviting industrial foxes to dine as never before. And the cultish devotion of many converts to this magnificent boondoggle leads to a stultifying cognitive dissonance that must be countered with cold, hard facts. The truth is undeniable: these products simply do not save the planet.

Not all pollution is the same. When resources are limited, logic dictates that energy resources should be allocated in priority to those efforts that are most vital. Food, housing, and heat are the priority uses of energy; golf carts, fireworks displays, and flights to Hawaii for martinis are secondary. It is absurd to treat all energy usage and pollution generation as identical, and this includes cars and trucks people need to earn a living versus yacht trips for the wealthy and electricity that elderly and poor people use to run their oil burners or see at night versus the electricity used for flatscreen TVs and Jacuzzis.

This analysis savages renewable energy policies. For one, both EV and solar panel projects are regressive and disproportionately impact the poor. Rural blue-collar workers still need to drive to work and may not have access to public transit; retirees on fixed incomes still need light and heat in their homes. Residential arrays are especially inefficient and inequitable. Low-income residents are less likely to be able to afford residential installations and are thus left paying higher electricity rates to subsidize those who can under most net metering programs, and rooftop installations cost approximately twice as much as commercial applications.[4] Rooftop arrays are much more inefficient (more costly per unit of energy) than large-scale solar installations, and their benefits accrue only to the individual homeowners.

Leftist proponents of the Green New Deal are aware of these inequities—and justify them with perverse, paternalistic rationalizations. One climate change resource guidebook touts the following flippant justification for these glaring inequities:

> Low-income people around the world are particularly affected [by harms from climate change] because they do not have the

resources to easily adapt to climate shifts. These impacts on vulnerable people dwarf any regressive economic effects of the emission abatement policies themselves. Accordingly, even an emission abatement policy that has a regressive economic effect is, on the whole, probably beneficial to lower-income people and justified.[5]

"Probably." That is a moral and policy judgment impacting millions of people, and it merits better evaluation—especially by voters expected to pay the tab.

But not all energy has the same usages. How can a society equate energy used to produce food with energy used to watch a movie? There has been a rush to stop farmers from polluting, even if it puts them out of business and drives up food costs or results in shortages. The same disconnected urban idiocy that enacts zoning laws that ban chickens is hellbent on taxing food production while giving a pass to recreational pollution like snow-making machines at ski resorts, water and amusement parks, and the international tourism industry. So much is being done to curtail dairy farms, yet there is zero attention to the 600 million gallons of gas burned annually in American lawnmowers lacking pollution-control technologies, routinely mowing an area that now exceeds the state of Texas. Farms are ever more regulated, while parking lots and asphalt are constructed with little pause.

The Green New Deal and the environmental movement are, in their current form, just a modern fad with no policy meat. The hype and emotionally charged celebrity displays are built on absurd mistruths and oversimplifications. Cows are suddenly targeted as eco-culprits, the world is ending any day, all other issues pale in comparison, and the poor people in the Amazon must be saved by American virtue-signaling consumers with no clue.[6]

This is not only counterproductive, it is a dangerous thrust toward domination.[7] That the Green New Deal is a scam is plain from the failures of its proposed policies to do much more than dream. The truth is that these technologies cannot begin to replace existing fossil fuel energy sources and so are just a delay.[8] The failures of the Green New Deal and these "sustainable" product frauds must be juxtaposed against the positive benefits of transforming America's industrial-agricultural dependency. A local and more regenerative agricultural infrastructure will actually reduce the threats of food inflation and food insecurity, preventively rather than reactively.

The ethanol debacle is a perfect example of the co-opting of environmental policy by corporate and government crooks who try to divert such movements to their own profit. Let us not forget the Obama administration's quick move to do the same with GMO-labeling requirements, quickly pivoting to make national labeling as fuzzy and useless as possible—a result that did *worse* than nothing to inform consumers. Instead, the ability of corporations to deceive the public was enhanced.

Ethanol, too, has done worse than nothing to improve the environment. It subsidized an expansion of soil-eroding and water-polluting fossil-fuel-dependent corn production to provide profits to manufacturers who could compel the guaranteed purchase of their new commodity while it destroyed small engines and cars and reduced their useful lives, increasing overall pollution (and, yet again, corporate profits). Additionally, this policy shift drove up corn prices and contributed to global hunger and poverty.[9]

As with renewable energy manufacturing, ethanol didn't simply displace gasoline without a cost. Massive amounts of gas and diesel were absorbed in plowing fields, trucking natural gas–derived fertilizers to field and corn to factory, pumping water for irrigation, and processing the corn into a refined product, which is then transported yet again. This is an environmental gag that keeps on going without interruption because the corporate profiteers are not answerable to voters. As John Michael Greer calculated:

> If every square inch of American farmland were put to work filling our gas tanks—with none left over to grow food or anything else—the total yield of ethanol would only be a little over 110 billion gallons, which is just a bit more than half of our current gasoline consumption.[10]

This is hardly the first time the environment has been sold out using dysfunctional policy prescriptions. "Cash for Clunkers" was an Obama-era initiative. Officially released with the acronym CARS in 2009, the Car

Allowance Rebate System purported to be environmentally motivated. It provided financial incentives to car owners to trade in used vehicles for newer, allegedly more fuel-efficient ones. But the primary purpose of the program was as a short-term economic stimulus to pump up auto sales, which it succeeded in doing. But examining the externalized environmental costs of this scheme reveals that it benefitted large manufacturers (regressively, because only more affluent buyers of brand-new cars received the benefits) while increasing both pollution and greenhouse-gas emissions. Moreover, the economic "stimulus" was short-lived: CARS ignored the total life cycle of the scrapped vehicles, which had required massive amounts of energy and raw materials in their manufacture. It also blindly avoided recognition of the environmental costs in energy and pollution generated in new-car production. And once the program expired (supporting the sales of about 690,000 new vehicles), new-car sales again plummeted.

Like true bureaucrats, the Department of Transportation reported that Cash for Clunkers was an environmental success. But CARS mandated that the trade-ins not be recycled for parts, and many were in good running order. These are lost miles on the road by functioning vehicles. However inefficient older vehicles may be in terms of gas mileage, each one represents tremendous inputs of energy and resources in their initial manufacture and mining and transport of constituent materials. Replacing them before their useful life is over wastes those resources, while *prematurely accelerating their replacement* with brand new vehicles that require similar or even greater energy and other inputs. Thousands of tons of landfill wastes were generated from the prematurely retired vehicles.

CARS was shamelessly regressive and thus inequitable. Low-income Americans cannot generally afford new vehicles, especially the more expensive fuel-efficient models that qualified for government subsidy under the program. Such subsidies also encourage ill-advised financial decisions by low-income drivers to incur loans on vehicles beyond their means to own. The government conspired with car dealers to prey on consumers through CARS, dressed up as an environmental benefit when it accomplished the opposite.

Burning biochar or wood for energy is another demonstrable scam that has gone way too far without critical reflection or correction. The push to burn wood or refuse has long been tried, but like the legendary mystical perpetual motion machine, success remains elusive. There is surely a place for such technologies in the human future, but harvesting trees or other natural resources for energy production is a net polluter and creates no new energy.[11]

Efforts to "sequester carbon" by subsidizing the growing of trees reveal the breakdown of critical thinking in environmental policymakers and academics. It is a farce that these incentives are monetized as so-called "carbon credits"—they allow the worst of corporate actors to "buy" the *right to continue polluting*, measured solely in CO_2 and thus ignoring particulate and chemical pollution that continues. Further, this disincentivizes preservation of precious and diverse agricultural lands for food production, which are already growing back to forests due to an artificial loss of farming productivity created by prohibitive residential property taxes and federal subsidies for large industrial producers. Subsidizing reforestation undercuts family farms.

Supporters of renewable technologies often concede these problems.[12] Certainly there is no long-term or large-scale solution to human energy consumption in burning trees for energy or storing substantial quantities of greenhouse gasses in forests. It persists solely as a profit-driven scam that wastes time and resources while environmental problems *increase*. Sadly, this is true of *all* of the Green New Deal's proposals.

Consider anaerobic digesters. Touted as an amazing breakthrough technology and installed widely, they don't actually accomplish much aside from enriching corporate coffers and appeasing an easily sated need to feel a solution has been discovered. Many of these technologies are more like magic displays to enthrall the public. Anaerobic digesters are fundamentally questionable, as they merely convert methane to CO_2 while also releasing into the atmosphere nitrogen oxides, sulfur dioxide, and other dangerous air pollutants. It is also a very expensive process that requires substantial investment in large tanks and other equipment as well as the incineration technology, all of which also consume energy and create pollution in their manufacture and delivery. Notice that those externalized costs are, per usual, simply ignored as if they didn't exist.

To sit at the knee of enlightened climate pollution solvers, these wonderful tools to save humanity (including from cow farts!) are the best thing since sliced (bleached, sterilized, nutrition-less) bread. One supposed climate policy guide gushes:

> The primary method of reducing these emissions is to process manure in anaerobic digesters, which convert the produced methane into electricity. This benefits the environment and provides power for farm or dairy operations. Anaerobic digesters are a commercialized technology, making them a promising method for achieving emission reductions from livestock.[13]

This is the direct opposite of reality on every level. But the acolytes of environmental deliverance via corporate-industrial rescuers are divorced from reality. These authors also opine that a better solution would be for people to stop eating meat.[14]

There's an idea—let's just make people stop eating healthy, grass-fed meat and let them eat toxic, factory-manufactured cakes made from soy. If ever there were a proposal made in hell to address humanity's current plight, it is the elimination of cows from the food chain. The very suggestion is proof of a stellar disconnect between the environmental problems presented and their solutions.

Proponents of a sickly, meatless diet exclude from consideration the numerous environmental *benefits* of grass-fed, rotationally grazed meats versus confinement-raised, grain-fed animals. Typically, after mangling the agricultural facts to malign poor, sweet cows, they then propose vat meat synthetically derived from industrial soy or other monocultures as substitute, excluding entirely their externalized costs.[15]

As with EVs, solar panel installations both residential and commercial, heat pumps, industrial windmills, and almost all of the technological "solutions" to energy pollution, the motives of vat-meat proponents may be something less than beneficent. In *Sacred Cow: Why Well Raised Meat Is Good for You and Good for the Planet*, Diana Rodgers and Robb Wolf explain:

> There's not a lot of profit to be made in industrial agriculture, but there's gobs of money to be made in processing foods into

something new. If they can control the whole supply chain and make a product that few others can make, which they'll convince the public is better for the environment and causes less harm to animals, the profit margins on a product like this are enormous.[16]

Similarly, solar panels have always dazzled the techno-imagination, but the technology will never suffice to rescue humanity to any meaningful degree. The environmental harms from the extraction of mined materials and fossil fuels (including coal) in the manufacturing of solar panels and components are immense. Additional environmental impacts of transporting and eventually disposing of these products are also significant and counter any claims of "renewability" in the larger picture.

Those who seek to compel all humanity to dependence on an ever-larger scale of production and distribution seem always to do so by focusing on the narrowly defined, insignificant, and usually false "benefits" of their gigantic eco-delusions. Thus climate warriors point to Cash for Clunkers, ethanol production, solar panels, EVs, and other failures as "successful" by narrowing critical thought to a set of sub-data. Thus, the CARS program has been labeled successful based solely on comparative MPG figures for the replaced cars and ignoring the massive waste and increased overall manufacturing production it caused. The ethanol program is hailed as "clean" while ignoring damage to soils and water. Solar panels are measured economically against grid power while excluding destructive manufacturing and fossil-fuel inputs as well as future disposal costs. EVs are praised while avoiding their myriad practical problems and the enormous resource inputs and chemical and CO_2 pollution required in their manufacture and transport.

In recent years, the truth about solar panels has started to emerge. There is growing awareness of horrendous manufacturing and labor conditions in the solar panel industry in China, particularly in the Xinjiang region. The US State Department has determined that genocide is being perpetrated there against Uyghur and other mostly Muslim minorities.[17]

It is not unreasonable to expect that environmental policies directed at prevention and redress of anthropogenic environmental harm would be concerned about the extremely cancerous chemicals being generated, along with fantastic amounts of CO_2 released, in the *manufacturing* of "renewables." It is hopeful that at least forced Uyghur labor has caused eyebrows to rise. If human rights abuses matter, and the avowed purpose of averting pollution is to protect human health, then solar panels and EVs are both false solutions—regardless of whose labor constructs them.

Neither concern (pollution or forced labor) arises in a truly regenerative push to nurture small, local agriculture, which if widely implemented will do more in one year to curtail both pollution *and* CO_2 than all the solar panels and EVs on the planet. And every year after. Without enslaving anyone.

The inconvenient truth is that the various renewable energy proposals on display are all technologically unfeasible, depend on predictions premised on impossibilities, and consistently aggravate rather than remediate the environmental problems they purport to solve. They all share the additional attributes of strong support from industry "stakeholders" and their bevy of lobbyists; endorsement by self-serving politicians; NGO support, indirectly funded by industry special interests; coerced taxpayer support via government subsidies, tax credits, and regulatory favoritism; and increased power over individual choices in the name of saving the planet.

Many of these ventures are being launched—and funded—without anything other than a fantastical wish and a secular prayer.[18] Ah, what faith—techno-mysticism puts all of humanity's eggs in the same putrid basket that this idiotic industrial religion has crafted. For decades, government and university research policy and investments have been directed away from regenerative agriculture and toward the imperative of more machines to clean up the machine mess. It is a cycle of modern madness.

The Green New Deal and existing policies propel Americans off a cliff of travesty and risk. Mark Morano observes as much in *Green Fraud: Why the Green New Deal Is Even Worse Than You Think*: "Banning energy that is powering America while mandating energy that is not ready to take over is not the moral or rational option."[19] Ill-considered initiatives are undermining grid security and shuttering existing energy plants in hopes of technologies not yet existent.[20]

The more closely the boondoggle frauds of "renewables" are scrutinized, the more obvious the pattern becomes. In their book *Bright Green Lies: How the Environmental Movement Lost Its Way and What We Can Do about It*, Derrick Jensen, Lierre Keith, and Max Wilbert warn, "We are fighting for the living planet. The bright greens are fighting to continue this culture—the culture that is killing the planet."[21] This includes false hopes in hydrogen as "fuel," which does not exist in pure form in nature as an energy source (except in the flaming ball of the sun). Creating pure hydrogen requires more inputs of energy than are stored in those chemical bonds. Hydrogen is thus at best an energy-*storage* vehicle, still reliant on some external source of energy to create it.

It is impossible to charge electric cars at gas stations using current technologies—the two-hour charging times would back up every gas station permanently. There is insufficient battery technology to accomplish needed goals; batteries are largely controlled by China; and batteries generate massive amounts of externalized pollution in manufacture and disposal. No matter: "Build it and the technology will come!" And when the technology fails to arrive, the short-term profiteers will be long gone—their disaster left for the citizens to clean up.

The Green New Deal and its supporters seek to redesign the entire world and transfer wealth as they deem equitably fit to further their grand designs. Vocal Green New Deal proponent Stan Cox proclaims that the "national economy will need to reorient toward ensuring sufficiency for all rather than feeding the accumulation of wealth by the few."[22] Does blaming pollution on the wealthy distract voters from the wealthy profiting from regressive, government-mandated, "renewable" manufacturing initiatives?

In contrast with these various snake-oil deceptions, a revitalized local food economy coupled with widespread adoption of regenerative agricultural practices will significantly decrease chemical applications of fertilizers, herbicides, and pesticides; reduce fossil fuel consumption in plowing and other machinery usage, as well as in transportation; restore instead of deplete soils (none of the renewable technologies address this); decrease water loss from irrigation from aquifers and rivers while reducing water pollution; increase water retention by soils to conserve water and prevent drought; create real, long-term, local economic growth instead of short-term work for renewable manufacturing laborers and solar panel installers; create a healthier, more secure and sustainable food supply for urban and rural Americans alike; and sequester exponentially more carbon than all the renewable energy technologies combined.

E. F. Schumacher was wary of the potential for large-scale industry to destroy and ensnare and advised developing nations not to follow the United States into industrial folly and its inevitable destruction and enslavement.[23] The Green New Deal relies upon a hyped "crisis" for which it proposes foolish responses dependent on a nonexistent "progress" of technology, to unleash a radical totalitarianism upon the economy and nation. If environmental policy is to be designed to save the world and prevent carbon dioxide and chemical pollution, why is economic transformation and wealth redistribution the primary focus of the Green New Deal? If CO_2 reduction is an actual desire, effective policies will always begin and end with soil health, because healthy soils sequester carbon while improving crop yields and food quality. Soil experts Grace Gershuny and Joseph Smillie claim "carbon is the ultimate fuel for all soil biological activity, and therefore of humus formation and productivity."[24]

Buried within the renewable laundry list of the Green New Deal is a bare-bones declaration that it will support regenerative practices:

> Working collaboratively with farmers and ranchers in the United States to eliminate pollution and greenhouse gas emissions from the agricultural sector as much as is technologically feasible, including—
> (i) by supporting family farming;
> (ii) by investing in sustainable farming and land use practices that increase soil health; and
> (iii) by building a more sustainable food system that ensures universal access to healthy food.[25]

That's a nice, if brief, wish list, but there is no meat on those bureaucratic bones. Quixotic ruminations will not save family farms any more than renewable energy technologies will save the planet. There is essentially no benefit to soils from any renewable energy technologies.[26]

Regenerative and local agricultural transition contrasts sharply against the Green New Deal alternative. It does not ask for yet more debt at the worst of times and will achieve far, far more environmentally while *reducing* government expenditures and boosting economic growth. Survivors of the Great Depression may be few as we approach the centennial of that disaster, but many of their descendants still appreciate frugality over profligacy and can readily spot the difference.

There are very substantial crises facing America's food supply and ecosystem, regardless of whether carbon dioxide or other gasses are contributing to climate change. The relatively rapid depletion of soil, water, and natural resources has been accomplished through the truly marvelous achievements of human ingenuity and technological advances, themselves made possible by the abundant source of stored energy unlocked by fossil fuels. However, these priceless resources are finite and must be stewarded carefully.

Renewable energy illusions of a simple conversion from oil ignore the scientific truth that all solar panels, EVs, industrial windmills, anaerobic generators, heat pumps, and other technological gadgets depend for their production on complex and consumptive processes that are themselves wholly dependent upon, and thus rapidly drawing down, those finite fossil fuel reserves. Machines don't last forever, and a planetary network of "renewable" solar power grids and electric cars would literally *destroy* the planet in the making. Even if these technologies *were* efficient, they would still be unsustainable.[27]

A cursory examination of the true externalized costs of the manufacture of renewable power and transportation technologies reveal they fail the basic common-sense test—they delay real action while amplifying existing damage and dependency. This may be good business for Big Government, Big Ag, and Big Food, but it will be a *nasty* business when food inflation spikes on and on, and food scarcity and hoarding become the new normal.

America will soon hit the environmental iceberg that has not melted but grown, while humanity dithered over the existence, or degree, of global warming. Food scarcity and hyperinflation are upon us. As this catastrophic ship of industrial dependency lurches unfalteringly toward that iceberg that brings famine and collapse, the proposal of the Green New Deal is to assist the industrial monsters who created it to leap comfortably into the lifeboats, while the passengers are handed "renewable" oars of granite to cling hold of in leaden hope.

The Green New Deal careens America toward greater economic and environmental deterioration than any human society in history, which together could create a self-defeating vicious cycle. When the government needs funds to feed millions of starving Americans, it can only print so much of that inedible dough. Rapidly increasing local and sustainable and regenerative food production will blunt the threat of this growing, unthinkable menace rather than accelerate the consumption of those limited fossil fuels that must be stewarded responsibly for use by future generations.

CHAPTER TWELVE

Regenerating Human Health

Sir Albert Howard saw accurately that the issue of human health is inseparable from the health of the soil, and he saw too that we humans must responsibly occupy our place in the cycle of birth, maturity, death, and decay, which is the health of the world. Aside from our mortal involvement, food is our fundamental connection to that cycle.

—WENDELL BERRY, *Another Turn of the Crank*

Americans are becoming aware of *where* their food comes from— geographically, but also the process by which it is seeded, sprayed, harvested, preserved, and distributed. As they rouse from their junk food–induced lethargy, the cause of their declining physical health, lower life expectancies, increasing cancer rates, and decreasing fertility is becoming increasingly evident: the industrial food supply. Crafted monolithically with the eager cooperation of an incompetent if not corrupt government, subsidized toxic food production and processing is sickening Americans. COVID-19 has exposed these truths more widely, both because being physically healthy provides improved immunity to the disease and because the pandemic has exposed the extreme food vulnerability in a system people took for granted and believed to be sound.

If human health is the criterion for evaluation, America's food production and processing system is extremely *un*sound. The need for a solution to this issue transcends partisan lines, yet *both* major political parties have been complicit in the subsidies and regulations that have contributed to our plight. Much like confined, silage-fed cows that suddenly see a gate open to fresh green pastures, American diners have begun to tire of the same dubiously produced diet and are flying the CAFO-coop for far healthier fare. It is time for farmers, rather than politicians and chemical-pushing mega-corporations, to be heard regarding the best practices to ensure healthy, sustainable food supplies for all Americans.

This chapter cannot begin to recount the sheer magnitude, in degree and breadth, of the health problems being caused by poor diet and toxic pollution in America and the world. Instead I offer a sampling of excellent resources for further examination. It is imperative for human health that "consumers" become informed about what it is they are consuming rather than trust the proven liars in the food industry, aided and abetted by corrupt or foolish bureaucrats. As Dr. Sina McCullough warns: "Our food is more dangerous than it has ever been in the history of our nation, and it's largely because of our veil of unearned trust."[1]

It is becoming increasingly difficult to either trust the food supply or discern the truth about its ills. This sad and deteriorating condition is the inevitable result of a century-old push to enslave nature's agriculture to mankind's profit-motivated industrial technology. That push has sent human health over a deadly cliff, while destroying soils, water, and ecosystem. By enslaving nature, we have enslaved ourselves instead.[2]

The great threat to humanity is not anthropogenic climate change, but chemicals and other pollution destructive of human, animal, and soil alike. While Americans wrangle over CO_2 and other greenhouse gasses, the chemical spigot has been spewing overtime. Republicans in particular must get up to speed on toxic chemicals, which quickly make CO_2 irrelevant, and leave that issue appropriately in the rearview mirror. In restoring a healthier agriculture and food supply, consumers will also restore soil, water, and animal health while sequestering enormous amounts of carbon back into the soils from whence much of it has been released.

Both political parties have been asleep at this regulatory/policy wheel—that's why our family farms are nearly extinct and our food system damaged nearly beyond repair. But nature has abilities to heal that technology will never achieve. The question now is, will *both* of the parties that united to help corporate America destroy our soils and agriculture now unite to *reverse* that profound betrayal?

The Democrats are well on their way to address carbon dioxide sequestration in agriculture. Will the Republicans meet them in the public debate and champion food and soil health, *regardless* of the climate question? That is the question of this book, and the question for which millions of Americans will increasingly await an answer.

This win-win improvement of ecosystem and human health is the agricultural/environmental breach into which conservatives must fervently leap. Food prices are already soaring, and they will continue to rise. Inflation pressures will compound rather than abate: fertilizer supplies are scarce, vulnerable to disruption, and spiking in price; increasingly expensive fossil fuels affect plowing, spraying, harvesting, processing, and transportation costs; farming and transportation equipment often cost more than median homes. And today, China controls more of the US food supply than is healthy for any nation's sovereign independence. If that is not a concern for conservatives, they have already taken up residence in coffins and are just waiting for someone to throw in the dirt.

The gradual elimination of small-farm families and local agriculture has long been excused with talks of "the market" and "progress," but the market was defrauded with corruption and greed, and the result is a "progress" toward self-annihilation. The cheap fuels that made this extermination possible (and suburbia popular) are reversing permanently in cost, and so, too, will the forces that destroyed local agriculture. Rather than blame either political side for the condition into which Americans are now gradually awakening, it is the task of conservatives to take up this vital cause earnestly and invite all Democrats with a shared concern and desire for real solutions to stand in unity for these goals. Healthy soil is not the property of a sole political party, however much the Democrats seek to secure a proprietary ideological monopoly on environmental issues via their CO_2 obsession.

The chief Achilles heel of farmers that the urban regulators and food fearmongers invoke for their domination is "health and safety." Tragically, this pretense has been employed to make Americans' food supplies consistently *less* healthy and *less* safe. This excuse for bureaucratic regulatory oppression of small operators has increased in recent years. In Vermont, the newly added farm-killing mantra is that the state must "protect the Vermont brand," a rationalization employed to erase the Vermont small producer. But the justification to create rules that destroy good farms based on anecdotal misdoings of the minority of unethical or poorly qualified operators has been "the exception used to create the rules" for many decades.

This false pretense of "protecting" the food supply has instead sterilized it and largely eliminated small-scale diversity. Along with the spectacular array of personalities, local foods, and plant and animal varieties that blanketed America a century ago in the form of its small family farms, there was a diverse supply of foods essential to human health. The devil's bargain of cheap food is before us: industrial technology has supplanted nature's processes at the expense of human and environmental health.

Want to cure cancer? Stop giving it to yourself by ingesting cancer-causing chemicals at drive-through, factory-dining outlets. Don't like the blunt truth of that assessment? Then get cancer. It is free choice, personal responsibility, cause and effect, and the government won't save you—it *did this to you.*

Dr. Sina McCullough, who personally suffered devastating diet-related illness before investigating these truths, warns Americans with scientific evidence:

> Half of all Americans currently suffer from one chronic illness such as heart disease, cancer, or diabetes. In addition, one in three adults are obese.... Of all the chronic diseases, the leading killer in the United States is heart disease, which is responsible for one in every four deaths. ... Chronic disease is currently increasing at a steady rate across all age groups.... Even children are sicker.[3]

There is *no question* chemical "additives" to processed food are sickening Americans. The health question becomes: To what degree will nutritious whole foods prevent cancer, diabetes, obesity, autism, birth defects, high blood pressure, migraine headaches, fibromyalgia, chronic fatigue syndrome, Covid, and other ailments that have increased exponentially since the advent of cheap industrial food-fare? In their book *The Truth About COVID-19*, Joseph Mercola and Ronnie Cummins write:

> Junk food and sodas are manufactured to be tasty and addictive, cheap and plentiful, but they are ultimately poisonous.

They certainly can quickly and conveniently fill your belly, especially if you're operating on a limited budget, but they can make you fat, clog your arteries, and lead to cancer, heart disease, and dementia. Junk foods destroy your health and damage your gut biome and immune system, setting you up for chronic disease and viral triggers such as COVID-19 that can aggravate and magnify existing disease.[4]

If sickness alerts the public of "product risk," the government and industry are always there to placate these consumer shifts: awareness that cigarettes cause cancer gave Americans "light" cigarettes; fattening sodas were joined by *more*-fattening "diet" sodas; the push for organics gave us overnight industrial "organics" that *aren't*. If there is an identifiable consumer concern about food, it will be marketed and rebranded for profit at every turn—with zero regard for human health. And the beginning of unhealthy food production begins at the crop-rearing agricultural level, then extends to industrial animal-rearing facilities that toxify meats.

It is not so easy to shift back from this cheap-food disaster. Huge swaths of once-fertile farmlands have been "developed" for human habitation in the suburban age. One's home is located where one neither works nor grows food, totally dependent on cheap fossil fuels to connect with either. Those former backyard, local sources of food called "home gardens" and "family farms" are mostly cookie-cut into fenced "lots" with ample investment in ornamental, nonedible shrubberies and pachysandra, and soils have often been drenched with lawn fertilizers and weed killers. This is why America cannot realistically revert all agriculture to pastoral dreamland. But it is also why the nation must economically encourage the preservation and restoration of remaining farmlands. Existing large-scale, industrial-sized operations can still implement beneficial practices such as reduced tilling or no-till practices, reduced fertilizer applications, increased sowing of cover crops, and so on. The problem cannot be remedied overnight.[5]

America's soils and waters are being contaminated with massive amounts of sickening chemicals. So, too, are the humans who consume the foods grown in those soils, sprayed with desiccants and pesticides, processed with additives and preservatives, packaged in plastic. Like viruses and bacteria, chemicals are invisible, and some are harmless while others are highly toxic, carcinogenic, sterilizing, or otherwise health-compromising. For the vast majority of chemicals, their impacts on human health are unknown—let alone their impact when *combined*. And they are indeed combined, in a myriad of mixtures and processes, in the production of "processed" foods. Mercola and Cummins explain:

> These junk foods and beverages, which make up 60 percent or more of the calories in the typical American diet, are highly processed, sugar- and carb-laden, and laced with pesticide, antibiotic, and chemical residues. In toxic combinations with the typical American's overconsumption of factory-farmed meat and animal products, US junk food diets are a virtual prescription for chronic disease and premature death. . . . Typically, junk food sells at one-quarter of the price per calorie of real whole foods (vegetables, fruits, grains), with the true costs of production and consumption, including damage to public health, the environment, and the climate, concealed from the public.[6]

Food manufacturers invest billions of dollars luring customers to purchase products for which specialized researchers seek ever-new technological means of addiction. Compulsive eating disorders are just one of a myriad of modern dysfunctions aggravated by profit-driven food tampering.[7] There are now more than 85,000 manmade chemicals that have been added to Creation, with little or no regulatory oversight on their impacts on life.[8] Americans of any political view should be alarmed at just how terrifyingly foolish this is.

In the intense passion of her sincere concern for the planet, Rachel Carson warned in 1962 of the dangerous, poorly labeled chemicals in residential products like floor polish and lawn pesticides. She raised specific scientific concerns about the sensitivity of the human liver and endocrine system (which controls vital hormones) to the effects of even miniscule exposures to some "endocrine disruptors." She warned, with good common sense, of the risks of multiple, or continuous, exposures that are cumulative.[9]

Modern research confirms that Rachel Carson was exactly correct. Likely the most damaging chemicals to humans in the world are the endocrine disrupters. This category of nasties has been linked to obesity, male and female reproductive dysfunction, cardiovascular disease, some forms of cancer, birth defects, growth failure, and neurological and learning disabilities.[10] This damage can be not only cumulative, but epigenetic—it can be passed on to children.[11]

There is some evidentiary suggestion that hormonal imbalances caused by toxins in food and the environment may be contributing to transgenderism in humans. But there is little doubt that environmental contamination is compromising the *fertility* of American youth. Since there is such a plethora of toxins, it will be quite a scientific challenge to isolate which ones—or which of the virtually limitless combinations of "ones"—is chiefly triggering hormonal and fertility damage.[12] The most immediate way to prevent illness from pesticides and other chemicals is to avoid ingesting them by eating organic, fresh food whenever possible. The title of Dr. Leonardo Trasande's book *Sicker Fatter Poorer: The Urgent Threat of Hormone-Disrupting Chemicals to Our Health and Future . . . and What We Can Do About It* tells much about his prescription for better health: "Aside from banning chemicals, what can we do to prevent our exposure to them? Eating organic has been documented to reduce levels of organophosphate breakdown products in the urine."[13]

Conservatives surely grasp that these chemical exposures are potentially harmful and that it costs a lot more money to extricate these chemicals from the environment (and human bodies) than the profits gained by their release. How much would it cost to remove the dioxins from the bodies of wildlife like deer, and how many universities and government programs are researching and funding that initiative? The more the causes of this chemical pollution are investigated, the more it is evident that regenerative agricultural practices reduce chemical applications and thus exposure to both ecosystem and humans.

The human health impacts of the currently toxified food system are serious, diverse, and still not fully understood. The microbiome (which is impacted by foreign chemicals that inhibit or kill the growth of beneficial gut bacteria) is a recent awareness for laboratory and diner alike. These toxic foodstuffs are killing more people than COVID-19, every year, with little public concern.[14]

The food additives that are causing human illness are directly connected to the industrial food supply and the unsustainable agricultural system upon which they depend. The substances most sickening Americans are easy enough to identify. The obvious culprits are artificial preservatives; artificial colors and flavors; artificial sweeteners; bleached flour; trans fats; hormones and antibiotics; and high-fructose corn syrup, often summarily called "the harmful seven." The American addiction to sugar (which literally stimulates dopamine and brain activity, even more than many addictive drugs) has also had horrible health consequences.[15]

Another example of the illnesses caused by the industrialization of natural whole foods is the dismissal of the importance of human breast milk. Human breast milk is essential and irreplaceable by human technological "industry." Yet an entire market, assisted by the federal government, encouraged women to raise their children on an industrially produced and processed "replacement." Baby formula allowed companies to profit by squeezing their unnatural products in between a mother and her child, replacing a fundamental connection that should never have been interfered with.[16]

It should horrify the public that these practices—enabled by a modern "faith" in all things technological—were inflicted upon anxious young mothers and their infants. Beginning in the 1920s, women *scheduled* childbirth for hospital induction, were sedated completely, and their babies were routinely extracted with forceps. Had the "scientific industry" procured a pill for child delivery, many mothers would have taken it.[17]

This harvesting of American citizens for profit via corporate-government collusion has been underway for a long time in America. People around the world rose up to warn women about "the benefits and superiority of breastfeeding," and created the International Code of Marketing of Breast-Milk Substitutes, yet the United States refused to adopt the code.[18]

Moderns may consider themselves immune from such folly, were it not for the pushing of prescription opioids by doctors for conditions that did not require a narcotic. Legal settlements have held drug manufacturers but also distributors—including Walmart, CVS, and Walgreens—accountable. The restriction on these pharmaceuticals led to a street heroin epidemic, ironically followed by a massive provision at public expense of synthetic opioids manufactured by pharmaceutical companies.

Nor is there comfort in the vaccine debacle when one examines the propaganda used to spread fear about COVID-19, lies about the disease's gain-of-function origin, bunk science used to push vaccine efficacy and safety, and horrifying infliction of an experimental vaccine on young children who face little risk from Covid. Vaccine manufacturer Pfizer paid the largest criminal fraud settlement in US history for misrepresenting the safety of its drugs. Are food supplies safer? Walmart and Walgreens were implicated in improper distribution of regulated drugs. How much can such retailers be trusted when selling less-regulated foodstuffs?

This pattern of government-industry collusion meets one definition of fascism. Food fascism should concern antifascists of all political inclinations. A profoundly disturbing disinformation "system" surrounds this human generation, and America has consistently been the world leader in inflicting new profit-making experiments on its citizenry. In the name of national security, the US government exposed military personnel to radiation, chemicals, drugs, and psychological experiments. Experiments on US civilians range from the well-publicized Tuskegee syphilis debacle to deliberate exposures to plutonium and to pathogens used in "germ warfare testing programs" in places as diverse as San Francisco, New York City, and Florida. And there is little question the government has also spied on Americans in direct contravention of federal law.

This inculcation into industrial codependency and resultant toxification begins in the womb and is then "nurtured" from baby formula to baby food to children's sugar-soaked cereals. Children are thus "primed for a lifelong sugar-rich diet," as Mark Bittman puts it.[19] And now pop culture and mainstream and social media condition youth with the unhealthy notion that obesity is "healthy." Shockingly, the American Academy of Pediatrics is now recommending surgery and novel weight-loss drugs for young obese children, even as obesity rates continue to increase. Since the 1980s, obesity rates have tripled in children and quadrupled in adolescents, a trend that accelerated during the pandemic.

Into this mix of unhealthy ingredients and perverted dining advice are added a host of man-made chemicals, often created for purposes quite distant from food production: aspartame was originally developed as an ant poison; glyphosate began its chemical career as a "descaling and chelating agent" used to "clean out calcium and other mineral deposits in pipes and boilers of residential and commercial hot water systems."[20]

Echoing Rachel Carson's foresight in *Silent Spring*, it appears the most immediate threat to human health from these insidious contaminations of intricate bodily functions may not be cancer but sterility. According to Shanna H. Swan and Stacey Colino, an unknown plethora of chemicals that interfere with natural human hormone production called endocrine-disrupting chemicals (EDCs) are "playing havoc with the building blocks of sexual and reproductive development."[21] America's young people are becoming sterile, and the scientists scratch their heads at what could be the matter.

Plastics are a tremendous problem unto themselves, and they are not easily replaced. They are doubly harmful because they are manufactured from fossil fuels that damage the environment and then wreak havoc on human health while dispersing in fragments from mountaintops to ocean depths, saturating the planet in irretrievable, endocrine-disrupting, nano-time bombs. But as with soils, water, and wide-scale chemical contamination, the Green New Deal leaves the problem unaddressed.[22]

Reestablishing the centrality of localized and regenerative agriculture practices reduces both plastic production *and* exposure to humans by increasing local agricultural production and distribution networks of fresh foods through farmers markets, CSAs, hospitals, prisons, schools, and so on. When food is grown, purchased, and distributed locally, plastic packaging can often be avoided altogether, along with chemical preservatives and growth-inhibiting hormones used to extend shelf life of many fruits and vegetables.

High-fructose corn syrup profits corporations at the expense of human health. This processed concoction was in few foods, but now comprises about 8 percent of Americans' daily calories (versus 1 percent from vegetables).[23] This is not healthy living! Soybeans now comprise about 10 percent of total calories; about half of all farmland is planted with genetically engineered, government-subsidized crops[24]; and lab-created "flavorings" are used to restore flavors lost in processing. Just one artificial flavoring may employ more than 100 chemicals!

The myriad of toxins, inhumane practices toward animals in rearing and slaughter, wasteful inefficiencies, threats of parasites, human labor abuses, dubious ethics, unsafe regulations, and other negative impacts of industrialism on food production, processing, storage, and distribution, is surveyed thoroughly in Joel Salatin and Dr. Sina McCullough's outstanding resource, *Beyond Labels: A Doctor and a Farmer Conquer Food Confusion One Bite at a Time*.[25] Another informative book is *Nourishing Traditions: The Cookbook That Challenges Politically Correct Nutrition and the Diet Dictocrats*, by Sally Fallon and Mary G. Enig.[26]

One area of industrial agriculture technology that has particularly concerned many people is genetically modified crops. The chief problem with these crops is their dependence for success on *chemical inputs*. Some are genetically designed so that they will not thrive without the addition of a particular chemical ("traitor" technology); others have chemicals woven right into their DNA to fight off pests with toxins. And massive amounts of these crops are dependent on their genetically modified resistance to glyphosate, which then kills everything else around them.

But the weeds have quickly developed resistance to glyphosate, requiring heavier and heavier applications of the stuff (and thus heavier ecological, microbial, and human damage), or even additional herbicides such as atrazine.[27] Stephanie Seneff provides a frightening tally: "Since 1974, about 8.6 billion kilograms—some 19 billion pounds—of glyphosate have been applied worldwide."[28] Glyphosate is often used just prior to harvest as a desiccant, including on non-GMO crops such as potatoes and wheat, but also oats, legumes, barley, rye, canola, safflower, sunflowers, linseed, and flax. Use as a desiccant increases overall applications, is not restricted to GMO crops, and greatly increases concentrations in harvests.

In *Toxic Legacy: How the Weedkiller Glyphosate Is Destroying Our Health and the Environment*, Dr. Stephanie Seneff concludes that "a growing body of scientific literature strongly suggests that *no amount* of glyphosate is safe" and that it "is becoming increasingly clear that overexposure to toxicants is playing a role in the autoimmune epidemic."[29] She also warns that the entire planet has been saturated with this factory-favorite, including organic crops, and that an FDA analysis of *honey* in

2017 revealed glyphosate in all twenty-eight samples tested.[30] Bees don't discriminate when gathering pollen.

Perhaps this chemical, so beloved in the agricultural industry, is simply harmless. But political history teaches that if it *is* harmful, influential corporate interests will invest billions to perpetuate profits at the expense of human health. The chief purpose of GMO crops is to take advantage of these chemicals—if the chemicals go, so do most GMOs. There is big money, and thus big incentive to lie, in glyphosate. Most glyphosate crops also end up fed into factory-farmed industrial animal production.[31]

A fitting adage might be "when in doubt, leave it out," but instead America is *soaking* its soils—and foods—in Roundup (the popular product containing glyphosate, as part of a chemical cocktail). This is an irrevocable decision as far as any hope of extracting these substances from soils. It is also a strong argument why protecting *some* fertile agricultural lands from steady applications of these dubious concoctions might be wise policy—just in case. Regenerative farming practices do that while increasing productivity on those smaller-scaled parcels, securing local healthy food in the bargain. They also increase nutritional content in fruits and vegetables, which have been declining for decades.[32]

Straining soils by extracting crops without replacing minerals and by dousing fields with chemical fertilizers, glyphosate, herbicides, and pesticides that kill soil microbes depletes trace minerals from crops vital for human health.[33] Other compromises to food nutrition arise from long-distance shipping: preservatives to prevent decay, hormones to inhibit plant growth or ripening in transit, fungicides to protect from mold, additives to preserve color.[34] Unnatural augmentations are more necessary as distances increase. And foods picked early for long-distance shipping are less nutritious.

This raises the prospect of internationally shipped food products—foreign-produced, processed, and inspected—on American grocery shelves, including increasing inventories from China. Today, most so-called "grass-fed" meats in American grocery stores are not grass fed at all and are labeled as "Product of USA" when in fact they are foreign. Perhaps America's conservatives trust Chinese-origin foods more than the Chinese people themselves do.[35]

The industrialization of animal products ushered in another new range of human illnesses from pathogens that thrive in the immuno-compromised, stressed bodies of creatures compelled into unnatural eating habits and housing systems to maximize profitability. Far more antibiotics are now used in farm animals than in humans, to protect them from illness caused by these profit-driven conditions.[36] This results in a bizarre vicious cycle, as bacteria dangerous to humans (and potentially made resistant to antibiotics) are bred in factory-farmed animals, negatively impacting consumer health so that sickened people have to ... *take antibiotics!*[37]

This has increased the risk of foodborne diseases in America's meat supply, and outbreaks of food poisoning from industrial meats have consequently become more common. The increased dangers have been used to justify tighter regulations, which are applied equally to small operations that cannot economically bear them. Large producers thus benefit economically from the new harms they manufacture, which are then used to eliminate smaller, safer competitors. This is a moral hazard, and the true costs to human and animal health are becoming more evident.

These unnatural processes also increase the likelihood of pandemics. Some two-thirds of bacteria and viruses that can cause human disease are zoonotic, which means that they originate in animals. Intensive factory farming consolidation increases the breeding grounds and means of transmission of diseases like swine flu and bird flu.

Instead of nurturing the local farms that protect human beings from these various threats, the new technology initiative—backed fully by the cow discriminators and the Green New Deal—is to coerce people to eat synthetic vat meats derived from proprietary industrial processes that convert polluting, polluted (with chemicals and glyphosate) soybeans and other industrially grown plants into "meat." This is yet another example of how corporations seek to cheat nature and its processes—in soils, animals, and humans—for short-term profits, and how government actors and political interests are quickly compromised to serve this sleight of hand. Grass-fed beef is *much* healthier than chemically tainted soy burgers, and beef cows and other ruminants restore soils damaged by monocultures and their chemical companions.

Old-school, regenerative agriculture methods improve soils and human health. The Green New Deal seeks to compel Americans to shift to a product fabricated from toxically produced soybeans. However, using current models of GMO soybean production to meet this need would be catastrophic to our health and our planet, compounding chemical contamination of humans, plants, and soils; increasing water and soil depletion; creating total techno-dependency; and eliminating the food security arising from diversified local operations using diversified biological species of both plants and animals.

The tiresome argument for vat meat is that cows are destructive, and synthetic meat is "the only hope" to feed the world. One author compares synthetic meats that accelerate environmental degradation with the miracle of mRNA vaccines:

> As unnatural as applying the new tools of synthetic biology to animal agriculture may seem to many people, this approach has the potential, over time, to help ensure that people everywhere have access to high-quality, safe, affordable and tasty animal products—while decreasing the environmental footprint, cruelty and adverse human health effects of industrial animal agriculture. The COVID-19 mRNA vaccines have helped people internalize, quite literally, that our increasing ability to hack the code of life has real benefits, but few of us fully appreciate how broadly these new capabilities will apply well beyond healthcare.[38]

The industrial Siren is calling, extolling the miracle of growing meat in a creepily named "bioreactor" rather than animals' bodies, the author proposes to create a new, massive bureaucratic arm of the very agencies that have for decades conspired with Big Ag to monopolize Americans' food supply![39] Big Brother Ag aspires to become much bigger!

Another threat to human and environmental health caused by technological advances is water extraction and contamination in the fracking industry. Because the nation's aquifers so desperately need the water being withdrawn for hydraulic fracking processes, it is being returned to aquifers after use in a patented process that employs undisclosed chemical additives. The water is "reinjected" into groundwater systems using some 50,000 "disposal wells" in California alone that redeposit over 20 billion gallons of water annually under lax regulatory standards. This water is then pumped out to irrigate crops for human consumption.[40]

Industrial agriculture continues to generate not just excess toxic manure, toxic synthetic fertilizer runoff, and other pollutants, but also herbicides and pesticides that can be particularly insidious. One such chemical, named 2,4-D, is one of the most widely used herbicides in the world. Much like the pharmaceutical push for synthetic opioids that were deceptively advertised as nonaddictive, this chemical (found in more than 100 brands of herbicide) contaminates most US drinking water. It is an endocrine-disrupting pollutant that transfers directly to breast milk and is linked to reduced sperm count, damage to testes, and genetic damage. The Centers for Disease Control estimates that some 25 percent of Americans now carry 2,4-D in their bodies, and it is accumulating.[41]

This partial list of the damaging human health impacts caused by agricultural "marvels" that are anything but marvelous recalls the ominous prediction of Aldous Huxley that "medical science has made such tremendous progress that there is hardly a healthy human left." Industrial agricultural and a miscellany of industrial processes that thoughtlessly spew contaminants into the ecosystem have been a sort of quasi-religious faith in science that are ensuring that there will indeed be no healthy humans left if this trend is not reversed. As America launches headlong into transhumanist agendas to unleash mRNA technologies into organ fabrication research and gender hormone "improvements," it is obvious that humanity must instead reverse course. And the number one area in which humanity can effectively and quickly reverse-transition is industrial agriculture and local food production.

The closer food is to home, the healthier it is likely to be for human, animal, and soil alike. Roger Scruton presented this as a conservative environmental policy:

> Localization is not merely the best hope for a sustainable agriculture and food economy. It also creates a strong disincentive

to the externalization of costs. . . . At this local level a conservative environmental policy is not one in which the government strives to secure environmental benefits; it is the one in which the government enables people to secure those benefits for themselves.[42]

The healthiest food will always be the "localist." And the only viable path toward environmental stewardship and the restoration of an embattled ecosystem is individual responsibility, community connection, and localized production where possible of all products—without chemical inputs or outputs! This is why the locavore movement has grown steadily despite corporate America's constant battle against small farmers. When it comes to human health, locally sourced foods raised in dynamic, life-nurturing soils are priceless.

CHAPTER THIRTEEN

America's Youth Are Our Small-Farm Future

If we want the land to be cared for, then we must have people living on and from the land who are able and willing to care for it.

—WENDELL BERRY, *Another Turn of the Crank*

Today's average farmer is an old farmer. The cultural heritage and hard-won agricultural information that are fading with the older generations who still understand them cannot be regained by textbooks or institutional instruction but must be taught in the field. In order to steward land regeneratively, ensure local food security, and reduce pollution, it is imperative to attract younger generations who are willing and able to care for the land. Currently there are financial and cultural disincentives for this path. Both must be reversed.

With growing consumer awareness of food origins and safety issues, local and organic food sales have improved small-farm profitability. Removing the artificial subsidies for Big Ag and regulatory impediments that have greatly hurt small farms will make farming substantially more profitable for the small-scale operation. Sharply rising food prices, food scarcity, and increasing consumer demand for trustworthy, environmentally friendly, nutrient-rich local foods will carve a path right to the gates of local farming operations. More and more, intelligent young people will be able to make a living off the land.

Many young people are already searching for stability and meaning in an increasingly nihilistic and narcissistic America. Especially if they wish to raise children, young people seek a secure, unpolluted, community-oriented locale in which to nest. Tens of thousands are already moving to rural Americana, a trend that accelerated under Covid and will grow with increasing urban disorder. Many of these people wish to farm, commercially or for home subsistence; others wish to live in a pristine escape from urban population density and are able to work remotely from a laptop.

The proposed tax and policy supports outlined in chapter 14 are progressively ("equitably") structured and will help young people disadvantaged by intergenerational wealth disparities. For those of greater means, these same policies will encourage young people to invest their trust funds or inheritances into a regenerative agriculture business plan that is viable and a lifestyle that is attractive. We must preserve our small farms as foundations of community, economy, health, and culture.

Today's young people face an especially dystopian future. Rural life can be difficult, but that may be exactly what is sought by increasing numbers of youth disenchanted by materialism and hedonism. Many young people want to not only consume less but be part of the solution. And the sole solution, in any real sense, remains regenerative agriculture. Many of those who do not seek to participate directly in agriculture still desire to consume more eco-aware and healthy products, especially foods, and will pay a premium to support their production.

Chris Smaje advocates for a return of humans to rural land stewardship and local food production. He observes in his book *A Small Farm Future*:

> This modernist phenomenon of well-paid and materially comfortable but meaningless and alienating work is increasingly apparent.... The problem is a whole-world one for two reasons. First, it creates large numbers of people with a lot of money in their pockets to draw down on global resources but no capacity to restore the resource stocks they're depleting through their work, as—for example—farmers can. Second, it fosters a kind of morbid cultural psychology that invests feelings of alienation and incompetence or, worse, a narcissistic embrace of modernism's capacity to deliver endless personal service.[1]

High rates of anxiety and depression, sociocultural anarchy roiling the nation, and a wobbling faith in "progress" and government to provide for the future make the appeal of country living more than just nostalgic. Young people seeking stability, especially to raise children, are attracted to the type of agrarianism described by Wes Jackson as being typical in 1935:

> Because the fabric of community was more intact, ordinary human problems were dealt with more directly, inside the community rather than outside it. Under the watchful eye of adults, rural teenagers experienced rites of passage, such as putting up hay or canning tomatoes. With those rites of passage largely gone, it's little wonder that teenage drug and alcohol abuse and teenage suicide are so high.[2]

The agrarian rites of passage that helped young people develop emotional stability and character have deteriorated with the shift to urban, consumptive lifestyles. By abandoning small farms, Americans lost the best child-rearing system it ever possessed. Small-farm childhoods are not only joyful, educational, and purposeful, they are healthier. These benefits increasingly appeal to broad swaths of young people waking up to this modern condition.

As chapter 12 chronicled, America's children are being horribly sickened by the industrial food system. Dr. Sina McCullough correctly warns that "for the first time in the history of the United States, children may live shorter lives than their parents."[3] Most Americans suspect what science proves: living on a farm is good for children's physical health. This has long been popularly known, paradoxical to the general consensus that farming is a dirty, impoverished life.

Interaction with healthy ruminant bacteria bolsters the immune system, as do fresh, organic, whole foods. The "hygiene hypothesis" holds that children's immune systems need exposure to dirt and pathogens to develop and function normally.[4] Regardless, avoiding toxic chemical exposures in early life is good child-rearing policy.

A proper understanding of nutrition and agriculture reveals that it isn't just that farm life is good, but that industrial consumption and dependency are very bad. School lunches created under the policies of the Farm Bill sicken children. Not only are the chemical applications to soils subsidized through support of monocultures, the highly processed concoctions industrially created with those crops are again subsidized for school lunch programs. Americans and their children are essentially double-taxed and double-toxified.[5]

Supporting small farms, and returning young families and their developing children to the land, is the antidote to dependency—for Democrats and Republicans alike. Americans must reverse the false, foolish contempt for farms and farming, beginning in America's schools. This generation is being groomed for dependency and deprived of basic common sense.

Children in today's schools are being taught about Native American agriculture and even racialized agriculture—but they are not being taught that being a farmer is "good" regardless of skin color or that becoming a farmer is a wise career choice. If the false notion that farming is dirty, unprofitable, and for the unintelligent is perpetuated, there will be no inculcation of the proper values of stewardship into our young. Agricultural programs that connect young people with experienced farmers are essential both culturally and educationally. Americans must encourage and equip the next generation to take the Earth-tending heritage that still remains into hand and return to the land—regeneratively and locally.[6]

America's youth require economic incentives and training in regenerative agriculture to solve the grave ecological problems that modern industrial agricultural production has created. This will seed economic growth and revitalization across rural America, supporting rural economies to reclaim what has been wrongfully stolen. This will still take a generation or more to accomplish, but in as little as a decade, these young innovators could begin to reclaim leadership of a more eco-sensitive, sustainable, and profitable agriculture.[7]

Instead of preparing children for a life of challenging conflicts requiring strong ethics and solid character, Americans have for several well-intentioned decades tried to "make life better for them" in ways that deprived them of important lessons. The people who lived through the Great Depression were grateful, humble people. Those raised in convenience and ease incline toward the opposite. Children are not benefited by coddling: farms and other healthy work environments are where the young are socialized in positive values and communication skills, self-direction, and decision-making. Video games, social media, and textbooks do not nurture, but often undermine, these important developmental processes.

Agricultural knowledge is inherently humbling and compels gratitude. This benefits people of any age group but is a powerful foundation with which to enable the young. The environmental angst America's youth often direct at older generations benefits no one. These young people pollute and consume with vigor (using more energy and tech gadgets than their forebears) and should be taught to examine the proverbial logs in their own environmental eyes.

Americans who seek to imbue conservation of rural agricultural knowledge and of lands must encourage young people to learn trades, including agriculture, and the important values that will improve their lives. The young must be weaned from the industrial, materialistic value system that has compromised the environment and threatens their health and food supplies. They must be taught to eat wisely and healthfully and that farming is a noble if arduous pursuit that is returning to economic profitability.

The young have a lot of work to do, as do the old. But for those parents (whether liberal or conservative) who routinely drive their children through a fast-food "dining experience," their children are being conditioned to poor health by addictive, polluted, industrial food. As childhood illnesses have increased, more would-be parents seek a healthier lifestyle and ecosystem in which to rear their children, as well as healthier, more trustworthy and nutritious foods. If farming were more economically viable and destigmatized, more young parents would make the leap to commit to localized, rural agricultural ventures.

The policies proposed by this book are to reduce government subsidies and regulatory favoritism for industrial agriculture and provide tax credits and regulatory relief for small-scale, local agricultural businesses while greatly improving soil, water, food quality, local culture, and the environment. This is an attractive package for growing numbers of American youth, especially during the Covid chaos of many larger cities and especially for those who wish to raise families in health and security.

Young people must shirk off the destructive industrialism that threatens their health and the health of the world. There is no path forward without small-scale farming as a vital component. Conservatives must attract young Americans back to the land, where they can heal the damage inflicted upon our landscapes, heal soils, and heal themselves. That is a *True Green Deal* for future small farms and farm families!

CHAPTER FOURTEEN

Policies That Let
Small Farms Breathe

As it stands now, it is not the farmer who is being subsidized so much as the lords of corporate agribusiness. Why shouldn't the profits be plowed back into the rural community instead?

—WES JACKSON, *Nature as Measure*

The policies I propose as a regenerative politics will quickly and cost-efficiently advance environmental benefits while preserving and nurturing liberties, food security, human health, and rural economies and cultures. These policies are tailored to focus resources on regenerative practices by reversing historic regulatory, tax, and subsidization policies that have favored large agricultural interests. It also seeks to implement flexible supports for local food production, processing, and distribution that are market-based and economically beneficial.

One of the primary focuses of an effective shift in agricultural policy will be to relieve unfair income and property tax burdens that discourage small-scale farming in favor of both larger, industrial-sized interests and suburban/residential development that compete inequitably for farmable land. Both property and income tax relief are necessary, not as subsidization of otherwise unprofitable ventures, but as respite from those unwise and inequitable tax burdens that have *crushed* rural agriculture for decades.

If Americans are to farm the land for the benefit of all, then it is to the benefit of all to immediately end or phase out policies that destroy market competitiveness for the agricultural methods that will most benefit the environment *and* society. Not only does more localized agriculture help improve community and food security, but regenerative practices yield the greatest return at the lowest cost in environmental terms. Soil-building practices can be encouraged with appropriate policies, simultaneously encouraging young people to farm by making these methods more profitable.[1]

There is no dispute that shifting human reliance from industrial to regenerative agricultural practices offers the most effective, least costly area within which to most rapidly implement these dramatic improvements. Effective public policy initiatives must focus on shifting away from industrial agricultural production. In addition to the issues of water and soil loss, human health, and food security discussed throughout this book, implementing common-sense regenerative farming supports will do more to reduce fossil fuel consumption and sequester carbon than all the other options on the table combined *while* bolstering rural economic growth.

This is both good agricultural policy and sound political strategy. It has nothing but positives to offer voters. It unites people of disparate partisan, socioeconomic, and cultural backgrounds and disappoints only entrenched quasi-criminal corporate profiteers. It is thus a political, economic, and environmental win-win-win.

Policies that encourage renewed investment in small, local farming are not an effort to exact retribution or secure rural agricultural "reparations" through government meddling. To correct regulatory, subsidization, and tax loophole imbalances is simply to reset the landscape *fairly*; prices will adjust, and large producers and industrial corporations will adapt. Government policy should prefer and encourage improved agricultural management practices.

However much a complete shift away from industrial agricultural production might be desirable or beneficial, it is impossible. Bayer's board of directors is not going to disband into yeoman homesteaders on idyllic plots, nor would that be desirable due to the precipitous collapse in food production that would follow. Corporations are often responsive to public sentiment; many food producing and processing companies are already implementing regenerative practices. Thus large-scale operations, being necessary, must be positively encouraged to adopt regenerative practices where feasible and be rewarded economically for doing so. Corporations must be encouraged to be partners, not adversaries, in this transition.[2]

The inherent negatives of industrial agriculture chronicled in these pages should not be interpreted as a call to abolish all conventional large-scale agricultural production, any more than repeated support for organic production should be seen as a purist vision. The reasons for this tension are that a complete transition to organics is not feasible, and the conflict between these two alternatives causes both sides to dig in as adversaries rather than work together complementarily. Indeed, some uses of chemicals will likely always be necessary, as with organic dairy and cow wormers—some modern tools are just irreplaceable. This is particularly true with regard to certain pesticides, without which some crop yields would be decimated. Until effective alternatives are developed, a middle road is the best course. However, longstanding subsidies for industrial agriculture *should* be phased out and local and regenerative farming methods subsidized.

The bulk of the policy proposals considered here are intended to nurture small agricultural ventures, including start-ups and backyard toe-dipping. Yet, large landowners and operators must be brought into this discussion as well because their impact is enormous, and their needs and concerns are distinct from those of small operators. This is particularly true of commodity price volatility.

For standard crop staples that are international commodities—such as corn, soy, and wheat—price controls (or the absence of price protections) can cause devastation to farmers and agricultural producers, and developing markets for local goods does not protect large-scale producers of those grain crops that will still be required. It was, after all, a deliberate policy push by the federal government to compel farmers to migrate into urban areas by depressing agricultural commodity prices.[3] That same government must reverse the damage this foolish transition has inflicted.

At a national level, a system of government-assisted price and production coordination could be implemented using modern technological marvels to reduce bureaucratic error. Bigger is not always better. These monoculture crops face unique market vulnerabilities that countervail their vaunted benefits.[4] International tariffs, regulations, and other potential disruptions of markets are also unavoidable when staple crops are traded on today's global scale. Government has a continuing, important role to play in responding to those challenges. Sensible food policy must incorporate and improve current industrial practices. Support for medium-sized agricultural businesses is also important.

The current system degrades human health and processes the earth's bounty into addictive, sickening, unhealthy products that are peddled with glittering labels and slogans to children and to a vulnerable, stressed-out generation of Americans. Both the food production and food processing industries—Big Ag and Big Food—are joined by the oxymoronic "Big Healthcare" to profit increasingly from this process while *all three* pollute the environment furiously. A profitable regenerative, localized agricultural resurgence circumvents this warped, profit-driven desecration by returning land stewardship to a diffuse community of human entrepreneurs. America must restore nutrients, carbon, and bacterial life to soils.[5] It must restore water to aquifers. To do so, it must restore humans to the land.

No matter the size of their farms, farmers aren't the bad guys. They are victims of a relentless economic effort to maximize profits at the expense of family farms and local communities.[6] Agricultural policies must be advanced that will embrace and support the entire agriculture system, not pit one group of farmers against another or inflict economic harm on one group of farmers. This means America must pause and heed the voices of the farmers instead of the politicians who ineptly present themselves as authorities on agriculture.[7]

Monsanto Corporation boasts gross annual revenues of some $15 billion and pays its estimated 21,900 employees an average of more than $83,000 annually. That massive wealth has been siphoned in part off the taxpayer dime via a prolonged infliction of environmental destruction that would make the Lorax load his AR15. An appropriate policy response would seek to eliminate the public policies that have exacerbated and accelerated this almost genocidal assault on America's family farms for the past century.

In partnership with its diversified, diffused regenerative farmers, humanity needs animals. Cows are not co-destroyers of the ecosystem but the regenerative bridge to soil health and carbon sequestration. The ungodly horror of slaughtering North America's bison herds was intended as genocide of Native peoples but inflicted a legacy of soil deterioration. Bison built the rich soils of the continent from the solar power of rich grasses and the churning, creaturely cultivation of the land—from sun through plant through rumen to microbial bloom. The federal government extinguished that in a flash.

Policies that promote a return of ruminants like cows, goats, sheep, and pigs to the land will improve soil, human, and animal health while decreasing chemical and antibiotic pollution, water loss, and fossil fuel consumption. As MIT senior research scientist Stephanie Seneff explains:

> Factory farming is not beneficial to our health or our planet's ecosystem. It's also not humane.... Pasture-raised animals are a different story. Cows that free range over a large area make manure that naturally fertilizes the grass, and their grazing stimulates its growth.[8]

Farm animals can also improve soils in topographies and areas unsuitable for crops.[9] Breaking their historic connection to the land using industrial methods has exponentially compounded the damage done to our lands and environment.[10]

Industry "stakeholders" have tried to hamper this urgent return of animals to the land, some alleging that the longer life required to raise a cow on grass alone emits more methane—ignoring the much higher environmental costs inherent in the grain production required to raise CAFO animals more speedily. The numerous win-win-win benefits of releasing animals from confinement operations are manifest. Grazing improves soil quality, tilth, and water retention, which in turn allows more efficient grazing with more animals fed per acre of recovered land.[11]

Three areas of policy must change: grain subsidies must be phased out, burdensome regulations must be pared back, and tax relief (both income and real estate) must be offered to small farmers and food producers. If current subsidies of corn and other large crops were phased out over a five-year period, farmers of those products would have time to transition to more profitable crops, and reduced production would boost crop prices. Less industrial fertilizer and chemicals would be spread, and less-productive fields at high risk of erosion would be reverted out of tillage. Over the same five years, small start-ups and family farms could be offered favorable income or investment tax incentives, or perhaps favorable grants or financing, that could then be phased out over time.

The industrial takeover of agriculture by the so-called Green Revolution was driven by a techno-mystical fervor of government and academia that pumped money into an ultimately failed business model.[12] These industries must be weaned off those destructive subsidies *without* capsizing existing large-scale production.

For those deceived into believing farming is unprofitable, consider the magnitude of money devoted to the industry. Subsidies of many billions of dollars ultimately accumulate not in farmers' pockets but in the coffers of grain dealers and other corporate conglomerates.[13] A particularly inefficient and harmful policy area is the boondoggle of highly subsidized ethanol production, which absorbs some 30 percent of US corn production.[14] Corn subsidies hurt rather than help farmers of all sizes.[15] Dr. Sina McCullough has documented the extent of this dangerous economic and environmental chokehold:

> In the United States, roughly 300 million acres of land are planted with food. Half are dedicated to corn and soy, while 50 million are for wheat. . . . Through the Farm Bill, government incentivizes U.S. farmers to grow corn, and it works. America is the world's largest corn producer, growing 90 million acres of corn each year. . . . Government-subsidized soy takes a close second to corn, with over 77 million acres planted every year. . . . The Farm Bill costs taxpayers between $15 and $35 billion each year.[16]

The US government subsidizes corn and other unhealthy monocultures, then subsidizes the consumption (by children in school lunch programs) of the unhealthy, processed foods into which these are manufactured, and *then* subsidizes the healthcare system swollen with food-caused illnesses.[17]

This corn-centric focus has pushed unhealthy sweeteners into the American diet, increasing consumption of high-fructose corn syrup by more than 25 percent.[18] Corn is the single most destructive offender to the environment according to the USDA,[19] and all that corn competes for finite amounts of farmland. Nearly 40 percent of corn acreage in the United States is used for producing fuel ethanol.[20] *And* that fuel ethanol is a fraud: it destroys healthy farmland, but it likely requires more energy to produce ethanol than is yielded by the fuel, a net energy loss.[21]

Nevertheless, astronomical sums are continuously poured into corn production through government subsidies, and GMOs and industrial crops are systematically favored over healthier, less chemical-dependent options. This includes warped insurance rate structures that are prejudiced against organic crops and favor GMOs.[22]

The rate of transition to regenerative practices for both existing and new operations must be accelerated. Current subsidies to Big Ag must not be withdrawn abruptly because of the potential for market disruptions, but these subsidies will in the interim continue to compromise small-farm profitability. Relief for regenerative and small-scale producers must be fashioned and implemented immediately. Though farmers needn't be paid specifically to sequester CO_2, subsidizing production to offset unfair real estate taxes will result in practices that will do so.[23] Capital grant funding for start-ups, as well as to assist transition by existing operators large and small, is another important tool to ensure a speedy and nondisruptive changeover.

Wise agricultural policy will improve soil fertility and phase out government subsidies, while bringing much-needed economic growth to rural America and improving diet and food security. These are all policies that should and must galvanize Americans to join together at a time when the nation is horribly fractious. Conservatives can lead the nation positively and confidently with the policy proposals being advanced. Because carbon dioxide emissions become relatively unimportant in the discussion, conservatives can positively and sincerely engage with people of all walks of life and political positions to find *that common ground that is fertile soil*—not industrial-corporate domination.

Many of the hurdles to successful small-scale agriculture, which for decades have undermined family farms, arise from regulations that create unfair or disproportionate burdens for small-scale enterprises.[24] Regulations that unfairly inhibit small farming enterprises must be eliminated and replaced with separate regulatory structures or appropriate exemptions for qualifying local or regenerative businesses.[25]

One area of regulatory obfuscation is food-origin labeling. For most of the last century, Americans have been promised that they will know where their food comes from pursuant to "Country of Origin" labeling laws (COOL) originally guaranteed by the Tariff Act of 1930, which provided: "Unless excepted, every article of foreign origin (or its container) imported into the U.S. shall be marked with its country of origin." In 2008, Mexico and Canada sued to overturn COOL, alleging discrimination, leading the World Trade Organization to determine that its requirements violated international law.

In a 2015 $1.4 trillion omnibus spending bill signed by President Barack Obama, beef and pork were exempted from foreign-source labeling requirements. Essentially, foreign beef can be ground into burgers in the United States and then labeled a US product because it "undergoes substantial transformation." This has benefitted large international meat corporations at the expense of consumers, but also of domestic small farms and ranches, most especially grass-fed (grass-finished) regenerative farming ventures.[26] This results in local American farmers being subjected not just to unfair economic competition, but *more* stringent regulations than multinational corporations selling deceptively labeled foreign meats because domestic producers must comply with labeling requirements from which foreign producers are exempted.[27]

A sensible policy shift toward regenerative and local production will not splinter farmers into factions, especially not based on an arbitrary organic certification. It supports local conventional farming as much as distant organic, weighing the complex balance of externalized energy and environmental costs attendant on diverse products. Joel Salatin explains it well:

> If all the money and time spent regulating the word organic had been spent freeing up local food entrepreneurs, we'd be spinning circles around industrial food by now.... If you want good food, focus on farmers. If you want good land stewardship, focus on good farmers. Farms control more of the landscape than anyone else. Doesn't it make sense to populate the landscape with good farmers?[28]

This is particularly sound advice when one considers the dubious track record of industrial food producers and processors. The closer the consumer is to their farmer, the greater confidence they can have in what they put in their bodies. The trustworthiness of organic food labels is little better for Americans than the origin labeling of their beef and pork. As conservative Roger Scruton has written:

> Once marketers realized the possibilities of "organic" in junk food, health food, off-season grapes from Chile, milk from tortured cows, and much more—shampoo and clothing, for example—the industrial vision of organic boomed. . . . Traditional organic farmers suffered. The approval process for organic labeling requires extensive record-keeping and expensive applications.[29]

In addition to labeling flaws, sanitation regulations must be dramatically revised.[30] These have long been used to make small and midsize processing businesses unprofitable, particularly slaughterhouses and meat processors.[31] To improve regulatory policies, government rules should be eliminated that promote unsustainable or destructive food production or that prevent sustainable or more healthful agricultural or processing practices.[32]

To effectively implement food production and regenerative agriculture policy, a thoughtful long-term plan would:

1. Implement a five-year (or other intermediate period) of tax credits supporting local food production, in concert with the gradual phasing out of current federal subsidies for industrially produced monoculture crops.
2. Offer favorable credit terms and/or grants and tax benefits including accelerated depreciation for water and soil preserving technologies and equipment.
3. Prohibit zoning regulations that interfere with basic American rights to grow food.
4. Enhance public marketing and distribution networks for locally produced food.

5. Implement immediate favorable regulatory revisions to protect and encourage investment in small-scale, widely dispersed slaughtering and processing facilities, milk houses, cheese houses, and other value-added food production facilities, including maple syrup.
6. Invest in research and development of programs to reduce waste (especially food waste) and to compost more biomass (especially food waste).
7. Inform the citizenry about the benefits of regenerative agriculture and local farming. Public relations is pivotal to reversing misinformation about food and correcting disastrous stigma against the farmers who are needed now more than ever.
8. Dramatically shift university investment away from industry-controlled research that undermines farmers and the environment and saps talent for industrial hegemony and instead fund research into regenerative techniques that reduce fossil fuel and fertilizer dependency, secure nutrients in soils, and protect plants and animals from pests and disease using natural organic (chemical-free) methods.

Additional areas for creative policy discussions include:

- Local real estate tax credits for small- and medium-sized farms, or federal income tax credits designed to offset those property taxes. This would particularly benefit farmers in states (such as Vermont) with exceptionally high property taxes (often attributable to regressive funding of education using real estate).
- Tax credits or grants for additional employment hires at small farms.
- Tax credits or grants linked to diversifying products or expanding processing or value-added products.
- Link tax benefits to increased productivity per acre.
- Tax credits for reduced erosion.

The important factor is to avoid or eliminate policies that can be exploited by large industrial producers at the expense of small or midsize farming operations. This includes agricultural carbon markets, which suffer from numerous weaknesses including: failure to measure microbial improvements rather than simply carbon; unreliability and inconsistency of carbon measurements; ability of large producers to benefit at the expense of small and family farms; the encouragement of ongoing pollution by credit purchasers (who essentially buy "pollution indulgences"); insecure payment guarantees; rewarding chemical-based operations at the expense of organic. An insightful discussion of the many problems with agricultural carbon markets is "Agricultural Carbon Markets, Payments, and Data: Big Ag's Latest Power Grab," a March 2023 policy brief prepared jointly by Open Markets Institute and Friends of the Earth.[33]

Tax Credits for Small Farmers

America must reverse its decades-long tax preference for large industrial agriculture.[34] Currently, US federal tax law supports agriculture marginally through tools that recognize the economic realities of the farm venture: current deductions for certain capital expenditures, favorable capital gains tax treatment for farm asset sales, cash accounting, and farm income averaging. Existing federal subsidies for soil, water, or environmental protection, or for care for conservation areas or wildlife are sometimes tax-free, a consideration for small-farm subsidies that boost food production. Additionally, all fifty states have adopted some form of property tax assessment designed to reduce local and state property tax burdens on farmland.

To encourage a quick conversion from industrial to regenerative agricultural practices, the government must offer tax credit subsidies based on food production, but to small farms. For instance, if a 20 percent gross tax credit system were implemented, all those who grow and sell food would receive a (preferably nontaxable) tax credit equal to 20 percent of gross (not net) sales. This would encourage newcomers to investigate the profitability of small-scale food production, support them as they got their feet wet (muddy), and help offset significant initial capital outlays.

Of additional consideration would be a property tax credit or deduction provision to help offset farm-crushing real estate costs. Farmers need much more acreage than small businesses that work from an office, factory, or warehouse, and steady real estate inflation fueled by urban development and suburban sprawl has made farmland ever more scarce, and it is not easily brought back into productive use once chopped up or converted. Land is generally valued at its highest development (residential) price, whereas agricultural lands cannot sustain a profit when capital investment is pressed so high. As Joel Salatin explains:

> Business and agriculture subsidizes residential on a prorated income-exempt basis. . . . If a community really wants to pre- serve green space, then change the tax ratios so green space is not subsidizing residential housing. This inequity is growing each year; it's not decreasing.[35]

Land-use and other state programs seek to support small farms to vari- ous degrees, but these often favor non-farm holding of lands as investments by wealthy investors, taking *yet more* existing farmland out of productive agricultural use. An additional federal income tax credit or deduction for real estate taxes incurred on *working* agricultural lands would reduce the unfair property tax burden on existing and new farmers and encourage new market entrants both to grow food and to buy land on which to grow it.

Tax Credits for Regenerative Technologies

Tax credits, or favorable accelerated depreciation provisions, for regenerative farming technology investments and equipment would encourage faster transition to regenerative practices at all levels of business size and should be implemented in addition to other credits or tax benefits. Additional sup- ports should be offered using favorable credit terms and/or grants for invest- ments that yield positive environmental results, including no-till cropping equipment, composting systems, and improved irrigation equipment.[36]

Rather than attempt to pay farmers direct subsidies for sequestered carbon, retained soils, or preserved waters (all very difficult to monitor or regulate), subsidizing favorable methods that are also economically profit- able will more than accomplish those add-on environmental benefits. Subsidizing food production will make farming more profitable, and farmers will fashion ways to improve the land beyond what government regulations could ever do.

Protecting the Rights of Individuals to Grow Food

Attacks on food production have not been limited to commercial growers. Much like the federal government's bullying drive to regulate wheat that a farmer grows and eats on his own table as "interstate commerce," Big Agriculture seeks to compel consumers to dine from its factory trough, lest they "endanger" themselves by eating something less adulterated and chemical-free.

Increasingly, state and municipal governments in America seek to restrict the liberty of citizens to grow food on their own property, usually through zoning laws that value food-sterile, synthetically fertilized lawns over squawking chickens and the smell of manure. "Right to Farm" laws in many states seek to shield farmers, but these are often used instead to protect larger commercial operations and are of little benefit to homesteaders. Some state and local regulations have made it essentially illegal to live off-grid or to milk a cow in one's own garage for personal consumption.

Hospitals are not full of people getting sick from raw milk or home-slaughtered meats: they are dying of obesity, diabetes, and heart disease worsened by decades of profit-driven government policies that subsidize unhealthy-but-profitable ingestible "products." Taxing these sugary and unhealthy foods is the government's response—*increasing* power and taxation to *punish* those it has victimized.[37] The government has lost credibility in food and agricultural policy. If trust is to be regained, laws must protect human health, not compel servitude to a deadly industrial slave diet. Americans will revolt against laws that force-feed them toxins and make them sterile—as well they should!

In England as in America, "the countryside acts as a dormitory for wealthy urban workers." As more urbanites buy rural homes, they seek to curb the countryside to their idyllic vacation tastes rather than embrace and nurture a culture that is alien, even unknown, to them. "Current zoning regulations, allied to the symbolic economy of capitalism, make a reinvigorated countryside of smallholdings a virtual impossibility in England at present," Chris Smaje writes.[38]

America has not gone as far down this road as the United Kingdom and still boasts many pockets of countryside eager for proper agricultural reinvigoration. To follow England and Europe into government-dominated, suburban folly is the path of the Green New Deal, not sensible Americans who remember the Great Depression. American conservatives especially know better than to surrender complete authority to *any* government.

Enhance Distribution Networks for Locally Produced Food

No matter how much food is produced, it must be efficiently and fairly distributed.[39] Distribution is crucial for a multitude of reasons: food security, freshness, and local sourcing (and thus local economic growth) are all improved the closer food is to home. But also, the greater distance food is transported, the greater the amount of fossil fuels, and thus pollution, are attached. Some 10 percent of agriculture's greenhouse gas emissions are attributable to trucking and shipping, often in climate-controlled vehicles.[40]

As small, local farms have been closed (due to industrial-government policies *designed* to close them[41]), so, too, have the small shops, roadside stands, and other local outlets for their produce disappeared. Restoring these vital hubs is the "chicken-and-egg" challenge of expanding access to local products and reconnecting consumers directly with their farm-neighbor producers.[42]

It is imperative that farmers markets and community supported agriculture (CSA) models are supported and expanded. Recent years have indeed seen growth. Tom Philpott notes, "The number of U.S. farmers markets rose from less than 1,800 in 1994 to more than 8,000 by 2013."[43] This initial growth showed consumer enthusiasm for trustworthy, fresh, local food, but also the limits of access due to income and geography. Subsidies of cheap, unhealthy processed foods have made better-quality food unaffordable for many if not most Americans. Policies must be implemented that incentivize farmers markets and CSAs, as well as reduce costs and provide subsidies to local farmers, making those local foods more affordable to a broader range of consumers.

Many states have developed programs that prioritize the purchase of fresh, local produce and foods over industrial products for incorporation into local school, hospital, and prison meal programs. The federal government should rethink the food stamp program and limit (or favor) support to purchases of healthy food—easily done in today's high-tech, bar-coding world. This would be eminently more sensible than "sin taxes" or other secondary behavioral pressures. It also seems morally necessary, given the additional healthcare costs to the nation resulting from unhealthy eating by those on food stamp assistance with paltry nutritional or dietary guidance—that is not doing either taxpayer or benefit recipient justice.

The federal government owes America's children a balanced, nutritionally informed, *local* school lunch. Decades of dominance of the school lunch market by food Goliaths must be unwound in favor of active purchasing by informed buyers of fresh, nutritious, preferably organic, local produce, baked goods, dairy, meat, and locally made value-added foods such as preserves, lacto-fermented or canned specialties, and other healthy, artisanal foods. Children will be healthier while learning better eating habits and a proper food pyramid; local businesses will benefit from feeding local mouths; and chemical and fossil fuel inputs used in the production, processing, and transport of this massive amount of food will be dramatically reduced. This might be called "trickle-down environmentalism": stop consuming products that contain toxins or hurt the Earth, and the industrial chemicals that saturate food production will stop trickling down and collecting in our children's bodies and in their soil, air, and water.

Federal incentives and support structures should fashion an immediate implementation of comparable cafeteria buying programs for all public food provision in prisons, hospitals, rehabilitation centers, women's shelters, mental health facilities, and all other feasible areas of government food influence. An area of special focus should be the nation's armed forces, who merit the healthiest foods Americans can procure; provision for the "first fruits" of the freshest, most nutritious foods should be ensured wherever possible for our soldiers and government cafeterias, including statehouses nationwide. Healthier soldiers (and legislators) will sharpen mind and body, reduce both short- and long-term healthcare and disability costs, and support local regenerative agriculture and thus the environment. And while MREs (Meals Ready to Eat) may still endure on battlefields and in US training exercises, those, too, could incorporate foods sourced from small, regenerative farming businesses—once there are enough of them to meet that demand.

This is the empowerment of local agriculture to restore those various benefits that have been lost to rural farming communities. The markets for these healthier, tastier foods will thrive, and then more people will farm. Declining rural school enrollments will reverse healthily. With more profits and economic stability, more ancillary entrepreneurs will open coffee shops and art galleries near popular agrarian gathering places, and those satellite businesses that support farms with expertise, organic grains, hardware or farming supplies, labor, craftsmanship, and other skills will have new fertile ground in which to seed their small-scale businesses.[44]

Create Regulatory Structures That Support Farms

Much like improving distribution systems for small-scale, local agricultural products, regulatory systems must be restructured to support and encourage investment in small-scale, widely dispersed slaughtering and processing facilities, milk houses, cheese houses, and other value-added food production facilities. These businesses are essential for farmers to get their goods to consumers, but excessive regulations and attendant costs have (deliberately?) made them cost prohibitive, and so many have vanished. The small-farm infrastructure has gone the way of the small farms—and both must be restored in tandem.

Federal and state "health and safety" regulations have been used to swell bureaucratic enforcement at the expense of human health and food security. It is imperative that this imbalance is quickly reversed. During the Covid pandemic, many new farmers attempted to raise animals for meat, only to discover there was such a dearth of processing facilities that they could not get their animals to slaughter. (This includes both larger, federally inspected slaughter and processing facilities but also, where legal, custom processors for on-farm slaughter.) Without improved infrastructure, small farms will continue to flounder. Further, this problem exposes the vulnerabilities to the food supply created by overconsolidation: local processing facilities, along with protections for basic traditions such as on-farm slaughter, are essential to food autonomy and security. Expanding these supports using sensible, less burdensome regulations, combined with appropriate grants and tax incentives, is crucial to restoring the infrastructure necessary to support the economic viability of small- and medium-size animal farming businesses.

One important legislative initiative that has been bogged down for years is the PRIME Act. The title acronym well summarizes the bill: "Processing

Revival and Intrastate Meat Exemption." The PRIME Act would provide individual states with greater freedom to permit intrastate distribution of custom-slaughtered meat such as beef, pork, or lamb to consumers, restaurants, hotels, boardinghouses, and grocery stores. The importance of this legislation was exposed during COVID-19 when several federally inspected slaughterhouses were closed, requiring farmers to drive long distances to find slaughter facilities, or even to euthanize animals for a lack of ability to process them for market. The PRIME Act amends existing law under the Federal Meat Inspection Act to expand exemptions for custom slaughtering of animals for personal or household consumption to include meat sold within individual states to restaurants, hotels, grocery stores and other establishments, as well as directly to consumers. It is a telling travesty that for years now efforts to enact PRIME Act legislation to support local food production have been blocked. That existing effort must be streamlined for implementation!

Invest in Regenerative Research

Fancy gadgets and techno-gimmicks have proved that scientific shortcuts are not always the rosy paths they seem. More and more, science is finding ways to unlock the power of existing natural processes rather than monkeywrenching them with perverse industrial profiteering. Microbes in soil, compost, and human and animal microbiomes all interact in ways that scientists are still seeking to comprehend. One recent study in Austria found that microbes in cow stomachs can break down plastics! Imagine what additional natural gifts await discovery if resources are shifted to studying the miraculous processes at play in the regenerative, sustainable agricultural cycle built on photosynthesis, plant and animal life, and then death, decay, and regeneration.

Two related areas of particular promise to reduce adverse anthropogenic environmental impact are reduction of food waste and biomass recycling. An estimated 40 percent of food produced in the United States ends up in landfills, along with the energy inputs and water resources that went into producing, processing, and transporting it. Even greater environmental damage occurs in trucking that wasted food to landfills, where it takes up scarce dump space and generates methane and other gasses.[45]

People do not value food when it is cheap. Much of this low pricing is artificially created by hefty federal and global subsidization. As these subsidies are pared back, some food prices may increase modestly. However, eliminating corn subsidies in ethanol production would free up a great deal of maize for humans, and returning more and more animals to working the landscape via intensive rotational grazing will reduce corn and other grain consumption by animals dramatically, freeing up more grains for the human market. As farms shift away from destructive monocultures, more land will be made available for growing fruits, vegetables, and grass-fed meats, increasing supplies and competition and reducing relative prices while improving human, soil, animal, and environmental health.

The United States is likely entering a period of sustained inflation in which food and energy prices will increase steadily, continuously outpacing wages. Food prices are particularly vulnerable to layered inflationary impacts from fuel, transportation, fertilizer, and other fixed-price agricultural inputs. All of these input costs are reduced for the regenerative farmer, allowing the prices they charge to be more inflation resistant. But given that the vast amount of US food is industrially produced, each year's food prices will soar past the previous, as this year's higher diesel, fertilizer, natural gas, and wage costs impact next year's grain and beef prices, and so on.

Higher food prices mean consumers should waste less food. Highly nutritious foods like native, grass-fed meats and artisanal cheeses cost more, are worth more, and will be wasted less, regardless of food inflation. Additional food waste can be averted by government programs to redistribute aging food inventory at dramatically reduced prices to avert landfilling. Currently, huge amounts of edible food are simply disposed of as garbage once its sell-by date has passed. Market forces often wastefully disincentivize businesses from freely distributing perishable foods such as bread, dairy, and meat products to those in need rather than throw them in the Dumpster. These foods—whether or not derived from regenerative agricultural sources—can be diverted for distribution to homeless shelters or used in prisons or other government facilities and eventual composting rather than landfilling. Businesses can convert a liability (Dumpster and trucking expenses) into an asset, without undercutting their own sales.

There are three general stages of waste production by humans: generation, recycling, and disposal. Reducing food waste will greatly reduce pollution, but the next stage is still not to rot in a landfill—it is to rot in a compost pile and be recycled into "soil complements"—natural fertilizers to feed soil microbes that in turn build thriving communities that provide plants with all they need. Lawn rakings or clippings, as well as neighborhood compost collections, can join food wastes in this process of diverting soil-building assets away from landfills.[46]

The most effective and immediate regenerative improvement in agriculture would convert current industrial animal confinement facilities into grazing operations so that mountains and lagoons of manure currently threatening the ecosystem can instead be used to nurture it in place of chemicals. It is estimated that a mere third of the manure generated by American livestock could replace the phosphorus applications that feed the nation's entire corn crop.[47]

Small farms built on manure are more productive, build soils, and sequester carbon, whether or not CO_2 warms the planet. These are win-win-win benefits of an environmental policy constructed on the solid ground of regenerative agriculture.

Launch Pro-Farming Public Relations Initiatives

The government has an important, low-cost role to play in fostering an improved public awareness of the promising environmental, health, and economic benefits of regenerative and local farming. Government has been used for decades to inculcate false ideas: about nutrition, advocating for high-carbohydrate diets and discouraging healthy meat, eggs, and dairy products; about food safety, implementing costly regulations that hurt small farmers while increasing market dominance for CAFOs and manufacturers of highly processed foods; and also about the profitability and numerous nonmonetary benefits of farming, as the USDA and other agencies pushed farmers to consolidate. It is now evident that this has harmed small farms and consumers alike, requiring *informational* rectification to both farming culture and society.

The costs to government of abusing public trust to consume unhealthy, environmentally damaging foods are a growing loss of credibility and decay of trust of government to do anything that is not similarly corrupted. The cost to consumers is sickness and death. Americans are sicker than the populations of most developed nations in the world. The vast majority of this illness is caused by poor diet and lack of exercise. Americans generally, and conservatives in particular, must counter decades of industrial advertising of industrial foods as equivalent in nutritional value to wholesome, natural foods. As Dr. Joseph Mercola and Ronnie Cummins explain in their book about combatting the Great Reset and preventing extreme illness from COVID-19:

> You can combat insulin resistance and obesity, as well as prevent most chronic diseases, with a healthy diet. Of course, what you don't eat is just as important. This is why eliminating as many processed foods and fast foods as possible is your first priority. We need a new family-farm-based agricultural system that can provide "food as medicine," organic and healthy food for all, while regenerating the environment and biodiversity.[48]

Instead of dismissing farmers and farming as quixotic, anachronistic, or uncivilized, Americans must see them—accurately—as intelligent, innovative, frugal, and resourceful. The disgraceful, elitist condemnation of farmers that has increased with their destruction must be reversed. Farmers are needed now more than ever—especially young farmers.

A century ago, Aldo Leopold wisely called for a public relations campaign of this kind "for positive and substantial public encouragement, economic and moral, for the landowner who conserves the public values—economic or esthetic—of which he is the custodian."[49] Public relations is pivotal to reversing misinformation about food and to affirm the farmers on whom all human health ultimately depends, now and in the future. Instead of publicly funded derision, "public encouragement" is well overdue.

Just as with warnings about the risks of cigarette smoking and the importance of wearing seat belts, it is time government started alerting children to the dangers of processed food. Children can be taught about soils and microbiomes rather than "dirt" and reductionist perversions of the natural life cycle. Children can be taught to eat local foods, whole foods, and organic foods and to recognize what the differences are. The government that increasingly takes over the moral rearing of America's children regarding sexuality, abortion, gender identity, and "social justice" has yet to teach children how to eat healthfully or turn the lights and TV off when not in use. That should increasingly constitute food for parental thought.

Public service announcements on radio and television need not warn children of the dangers of illegal drugs or drunk driving. Exponentially more lives will be spared a slow, costly, painful death from toxic food intake by informed nutritional knowledge than by stopping all drunk drivers and drug use combined. Maybe rare school shootings by insane individual actors should be considered less important in the national conscience than the daily shootings of chemical toxins, unhealthy fats, and obesity-causing sugars into the diets of millions of young children by their government!

Agricultural classes in schools and colleges would never have disappeared in an intelligent society that properly prioritized food above leisure, recreation, and sterile, decorative lawns. As detailed in this book, the looming food inflation that threatens America compounds existing contamination of the food supply from unhealthy production and processing methods. Inflation will aggravate efforts to supply *any* food to Americans, let alone healthy sources. Inflation will similarly inflate housing and transportation costs, as well as the escalating healthcare costs of treating the conditions caused by poor diet. These combined inflationary pressures will leave less room in the household budget for any food, let alone healthy options that are often more costly.

Children need to be taught where food comes from and how it is grown. They may understand the processes of photosynthesis but do not attach that miracle properly with the microflora in their guts and the sparking neurons in their brains. Once they do, many of them will wisely chart a course for a rewarding career in farming rather than a corporate enslavement in an office or warehouse. America's children are being conditioned to be factory slaves, not self-reliant patriots. Sadly, most of their parents—including conservative Christians—have been unwittingly or lazily complicit in the conditioning of their own offspring for ill health, dependency, and thus modern serfdom.

It is time to teach the truth: small farmers are the hope for both present and future. Their hard work and extensive knowledge are increasingly more valuable than all the engineers in NASA. In time, all Americans will come to this realization. America's conservatives must wake up and become part of that rousing conversation *urgently*.

Mobilize Universities to Research Regenerative Practices

Unknown to most Americans, almost all university research in agriculture is devoted to newfangled efforts to conquer nature yet further and to cheat the natural processes of soil and food growth with methods or machines that can be commercialized for profit. Additionally, corporate recruiters have long siphoned off the best talent from our universities to become immoral coconspirators in their own destruction.[50] This has been the case for decades, and the number of farmers has been whittled down while NGOs and administrative bloat have come to dominate the economy and government policymaking. Monsanto and other companies desire to eliminate farmers as potential competitors and enlist them as serfs, and the government has been happily assisting. Wes Jackson foreshadowed synthetic meat and taste-enhancing technology when he observed that much of the research underway "may even lead to food production without either farmers or farms."[51]

The technology-worshiping delusion that science will conquer nature through bioengineering ignores the limits of biology imposed by finite energy resources. A healthy dose of human humility must infuse the funding for agricultural research that presently focuses investment almost entirely on nonorganic methods that center around continuing abuses by chemical- and energy-intensive monoculture. Some estimate that $49 billion is spent annually on global food and farming research, with less than 1 percent devoted to organic or regenerative methods.[52]

America's blind rush to eat "convenient," low-cost, industrial "snacks" has infected the nation with the escalating externalized costs of depleted soils and water coupled with often irreversible health problems including cancer, congestive heart failure, diabetes, hypertension, and other chronic conditions. Most of the world does not trust this corporate system for its nutrition, and most other societies have so far resisted this suicidal, self-destructive path. Small-scale "peasant" farming currently supplies food efficiently to 70 percent of the world's population using just 25 percent of its agricultural resources. The argument that "only industrial agriculture can feed the world" is more than just farcical—it is the exact opposite of the demonstrable reality of agricultural production.[53]

Imagine if the universities hijacked by industrial powerbrokers devoted their future studies to regenerative agricultural practices, composting plastics with cow bacteria, reducing agricultural applications of fertilizers or other chemical or fossil fuel inputs, securing more nutrients or carbon in soils, eliminating antibiotics and hormones from animal husbandry, and protecting plants and animals from pests through nontoxic means. Indeed, in 1962 Rachel Carson championed what she called "biotic controls" of insects: "A truly extraordinary variety of alternatives to the chemical control of insects is available."[54] Instead, profit motives have triumphed over proper agricultural stewardship.

Society is becoming aware of the human microbiome and is concurrently growing in collective understanding of the primacy of the soil biome. This key area of focus impacts every aspect of our ecological disaster in agriculture, including not just the threats of pollutants but also of soil and water depletion. America must shift research and development to reward solutions to these soil-killing threats rather than perpetuating this folly.[55]

America must bolster the research and development resources available to support knowing regenerative farmers, large and small, to fashion methods to counter the destructive profiteering that has dominated food production, and the deteriorating American rural landscape, for over a hundred increasingly destructive years.

Oppose the Green New Deal

The grotesque inadequacies, even counterproductive harms, proposed by the Green New Deal are apparent. Conservatives must lead the charge to defend Americans from this government-expanding, polluting, exploitative *fraud*. The Left seeks to explode corporate domination through faux environmental urgency to control every aspect of the global economy. Climate activists universally proclaim that "a climate drive needs to be international."[56] Yet, the converse is true. Just as only local food production can cure industrial consolidation, only local action can prevent an indus-trial Armageddon guaranteed by frenzied large-scale mass manufacturing of "climate technologies" that are not in any real way renewable.

A climate-saving drive must first be *sane*—paying wealthy investors and polluting corporate actors to battle "climate change" by letting trees grow in exchange for license to pollute is pretty much the definition of insanely idiotic. In contrast, turning CAFO animals out to a healthy life on grasslands sequesters far more carbon than forests or "renewable" boondoggles while diverting destructive food-rearing practices from soil-eroding industrialism. The Green New Deal would reward rich people with money to foster *more* carbon dioxide generation and a reduction in available farmland. That is simply ridiculous.

To the extent that government does have a role to play in remediat-ing the billions of daily individual decisions that cause pollution, Aldo Leopold emphasized that "government ownership and rehabilitation is a remedial, rather than a preventive, expedient."[57] This founding father of sus-tainable land stewardship grasped that which eludes today's government-worshiping policy wonks: government can neither replace nor compel individual (small-scale) stewardship.[58]

Modern man has displaced human husbandry with an abusive tech-nological imposter. At the root is not just an abandonment of land, but of responsibility for the Earth, and even for one's own health in relation to that Earth. What has changed is not just what moderns eat, but how sterile and alienated is their eating. It is not just nutrition, but reverence, humility, and gratitude that have been sacrificed for cheap gluttony. Government cannot provide or impose these vital fading values, even by global Green New Deal proclamation—even *if* the Green New Deal embraced these values. It does not.

At the root of this tragedy is not just an abandonment of human con-nection to the land, but what it is to be human—self-governance, free will, personal responsibility. How does a population separated and divorced from the land ever expect it—or themselves—to be cared for? The very concept of liberty is bound to agriculture.

The proposals in this book call for protections for the small man and the small farm family, by cutting the government apron strings of corn and other subsidies that have permitted the pillaging of America's farmers and land, sapping rural economic vitality and children's health, unchecked for a century. This is a "land back" movement that pits humans against government tyrants, not Black people against white or rich against poor or Democrats against Republicans. These policies will unite Americans along all of these lines!

A proper, nonpoliticized appraisal of the appropriate balance between government and individuals is warranted. The battle is not between socialism versus capitalism, or even the state and the "free" market, which as we see has not been free for small farms. Environmental challenges will never be solved by delegating them to someone else—especially not by handing that responsibility to an Orwellian, omnipotent state. Not only will government be unaccountable, it will be tempted and even incentivized to profit at the expense of success—exactly as has been done in agriculture.

One cannot sensibly expect the same actors who have conspired to destroy the ecosystem for corporate profit not to do the same when commissioned to clean up their mess! Government's best use is to create a framework to allow moral individuals to clean up this mess, to take charge with personal responsibility as the paramount force, rather than its complete abdication to Big Climate Brother. Increasingly, informed environmentalists are raising the alarm against the Green New Deal, warning that "we need to stop the ongoing destruction being caused by so-called green energy projects."[59]

This book has documented the incremental agricultural destruction inflicted on America's soils, waters, food, and humans by the Green Revolution. The Green Revolution was never about "feeding the world" any more than the "climate emergency" is about saving the ecosystem—both are public relations spin, deceiving people into relinquishing personal sovereignty with the personal responsibility it demands. Just as the Green Revolution was really about selling chemicals, agricultural machinery, and engineered seeds (and plunging farmers into destructive debt), so is this climate-rescuing spin about peddling solar panels, EVs, and other technologies on which a handful of profiteers will make a quick bundle at the expense of true change. This is worse than inaction—it is misdirection, just as with federal organic food labeling, ethanol production, and Cash for Clunkers. All have been lying spin; all have been counterproductive; all have been orchestrated by big government aligned with big business and an uncritical big media.[60]

Big Ag and Big Food still preach the same lies about saving humanity while preying upon both humans and Creation with equal callousness.

Hope on the Horizon

An effort to survey potential positive regenerative agricultural policies has been offered here to open the door to greater conversation and understanding of just how much the despairing modern human condition is one of our own creation. We have painted ourselves into a corner that threatens the extinction of all life on Earth, most certainly the human strain. Instead of diverting trillions of shrinking dollars into manufacturing processes that benefit a handful of stakes-winning industrial manufacturing stakeholders, imagine if those Build Back Better funds were allocated to small farms.[61]

Another sensible idea is to diversify farming of staple food crops away from the rapidly depleting, environmentally vulnerable California agricultural oasis.[62] Shifting crops to more disparate, localized areas offers food security, economic growth, restored communities, preserved water and soil resources, and many other benefits. But most immediately and obviously, regenerative agricultural methods *reduce pollution*.[63]

Local farming is more productive than industrial methods and thus more economically beneficial (when artificial subsidies are extinguished) than EVs, solar panels, or chemical-dependent, genetically modified Frankenstein corn. It also disperses the wealth generated among small entrepreneurs and rural communities rather than a tiny cadre of devious hedge funds and their already-too-wealthy investors. Consumer awareness continues to increase via the food freedom movement. Americans have proved they will invest money wisely in their diets when they are aware of the truths about industrial foods. Tom Philpott notes:

> Overall, farm sales directly to consumers doubled between 1992 and 2007, reaching $3 billion by 2015, and holding steady since. . . . Locally grown food sold to wholesale markets and passed through to supermarkets and institutions like schools and hospitals has boomed, too, reaching $9 billion in 2017. . . .

> The boom in local food sales suggests a widespread yearning
> for something different; its leveling off in recent years suggests
> a blockage.[64]

That "blockage" is the ongoing federal subsidization of cheap foods, the regulatory burdens that make small-scale production cost-prohibitive and less competitive, and the implementation of unhealthy industrial practices that externalize pollution costs, including laws that allow genetically modified seed to contaminate heirloom organic alternatives. Organic and local food production and purchasing increased as Tom Philpott described—until those artificial impediments created an economic glass ceiling to more expanded sales to less wealthy consumers.

If there is to be hope for a sustainable food system in America—let alone any hope of reversing the climatic and environmental destruction Big Ag has wrought—it will come from erasing the perverse disincentives to responsible farming and from instructing our young people to return to farms and to learn better care for themselves and for the world.[65]

If Americans do not return to the land in significant numbers and cultivate it in ways of humble stewardship, the nation will have permanently abandoned any hope of reclaiming the ecosystem upon which it depends. But at the same time, it will have abandoned any hope to ever escape global enslavement, whether by conspiring governments or openly controlling multinational food conglomerates.

Any people that surrenders to total domination of their food supply by elitist technocrats and techno-mystical dreamers is doomed to totalitarian subjugation. It would be preferable, though, if they simply clutched tightly to the self-sufficiency that has ever been the foundation of human health, human prosperity, and human liberty. Americans ignore these warnings at their own grave peril.

CONCLUSION

A Beginning

Ultimately we are nothing without the soil.
—JOSH TICKELL, *Kiss the Ground*

Restoring the environment requires a seismic reorientation toward local and regenerative agriculture. Informed Americans must first and foremost advance a *politicization of the issue of agriculture*—to be touted by conservatives and liberals together as an environmental platform. The Left claims CO_2 is paramount. All evidence points to industrial agriculture as a chief culprit of both toxic chemical contaminants and greenhouse gas emissions. Republicans can embrace regenerative agriculture for the many other benefits offered that are consistent with conservative values. For a change, *everybody* should be able to agree!

The Republican Party's current official environmental policy is insipid. Most conservatives recognize that the party desperately requires a credible environmental policy platform to present to voters. Rising food inflation will motivate people to better investigate what they are eating and their economic, as well as nutritional, dependence on agriculture, presenting an opportunity to attract voters with an environmental policy that also nurtures human health and the economy. This would transform diets, agriculture, economies, and carbon dioxide levels, all at the same time.

Because COVID-19 restrictions prevented the drafting of a 2020 platform, the official National Republican Party platform on environmental policy remains that of 2016, which is far from a regenerative agricultural proposal. The proposals of this book are specifically advanced for conservatives to embrace but are incompatible with a number of provisions of the grossly outdated GOP platform. The regenerative agricultural policies and return-to-local advocacy touted in these pages do not seek to address *all* global environmental issues in toto, but narrow focus to an achievable shift in subsidies and policies relating to food and agriculture. This effort does not aspire to comprise the entirety of the national GOP environmental policy platform, but merely one component or plank.

The 2016 National Republican Party platform specifically condemns the aggressive regulatory overreach by the federal government under the Obama administration. But in its opening salvo related to environmental policy, the party applauds past "bipartisan consensus in government" that "valued the role of extractive industries and rewarded their enterprise by minimizing its interference with their work."[1] This is not a good footing for appealing to today's electorate. For example, there has been little government interference with identifying the "patented" ingredients in fracking injection water (later "recycled" and dumped back into aquifers used for crop irrigation). "Minimizing interference" with the "important work" of industrial polluters is a dodgy position and completely untenable in 2023 and beyond.

As recounted in this book, government has protected companies from disclosing the secret ingredients in their food "flavorings" and "additives," from testing novel manmade chemicals for toxicity, and from responsibility for spilling their GMO seed into organic fields. Instead, it has helped industry patent seeds and dominate natural varieties of plants with genetically modified government favorites. That simply does not accord well with the GOP's stated values. Republicans must choose between human versus corporate loyalty. Neither should vaccine components or the secret ingredients of Roundup be protected from the awareness of the public subjected to potential harms.

Regulatory favoritism of industry over humans extends also to federal telecommunications laws that shield corporations in perpetuity from any liability for damage to human health caused by electromagnetic radiation, including novel 5G technology. Federal laws insulate pharmaceutical companies from liability for vaccine injuries and deaths and shield medical providers who have been agents of that infliction. These conflicts of interest form a pattern in which human health is subservient to the health of corporate profits.

And so, when the 2016 Republican Party platform openly endorses GMOs, it is standing for corporate over human and environmental health. The platform vapidly claims that GMO food "has proven to be safe, healthy, and a literal life-saver for millions in the developing world." This is untrue, and to say so undermines trust and credibility for conservatives. Most GMOs depend on glyphosate and other chemical applications for their use and contribute to both water and soil deterioration. How is that "safe" and "healthy"? How are the agricultural methods these technologies employ lifesaving when they are washing away soil at world-destroying rates with precious, dwindling water sources?

The claim that GMO crops have been the salvation of the developing world reflects ignorance and gall—not at all swing-voter attractive. Perhaps the National GOP is unfamiliar with the work of Vandana Shiva showing the impact of these technologies in her home country of India or the impact on Mexico's corn farmers when that nation was flooded with cheap GMO NAFTA corn. If Americans want to examine the chief reasons for the poverty south of the border that leads to such desperate efforts to emigrate to the United States, they may want to follow the corn—and then follow the money.

The 2016 GOP platform must have been written by Monsanto executives, as it declares "the expansion of agricultural exports through the vigorous opening of new markets around the world is the surest path to farm security."[2] The industrial Siren so sweetly sings her lies: feed the world, save the starving millions, secure the profits of corporations masquerading as farms, and conquer new colonial frontiers to stain with GMOs and chemical applications. This is the game plan for corporate-industrial hegemony, not sensible agriculture policy. This plank of the 2016 GOP platform must be shredded—GMOs can be tolerated without exalting them as world-saving.

The church-like techno-mysticism continues in the scandalous 2016 GOP platform:

> Modern farm practices and technologies supported by programs from the Department of Agriculture have led to reduced erosion, improved water and air quality, increased wildlife habitat, all the while maintaining improved agricultural yield. This stewardship of the land benefits everyone.[3]

What balderdash! The US Department of Agriculture has been the Trojan horse employed to *destroy* generations of small family farms. The technologies that innovated unprecedented new ways to destroy water, soil, and air have been "improved" so that they produce less pollution and use less water—but they still produce waste and suck down water supplies on ever more acres. How much increased wildlife habitat can be created when 91.7 million acres of corn are planted to be in part wasted on ethanol? And it is well documented that yields are *dropping* for GMO crops, as super-weeds and superbugs that resist Roundup proliferate. Overall, drought and soil loss have *worsened*.

Instead of presenting environmental solutions, the GOP platform claims there is no need to be concerned about "the illusion of an environmental crisis," that the problem is already solved:

> The central fact of any sensible environmental policy is that, year by year, the environment is improving. Our air and waterways are much healthier than they were a few decades ago. . . . As a nation, we have . . . avoided environmental degradation.[4]

It is clear that this is embarrassingly untrue. There are other aspects of the agricultural content of the 2016 platform that are quite sound, including the importance of reducing oppressive federal regulations. Sadly, the Farm Bill is endorsed, though the GOP position at least recognizes the problems created by tying SNAP payments (which comprise more than 70 percent of the Farm Bill!) to agriculture and proposes to separate the administration of SNAP from the Department of Agriculture. To the extent the Farm Bill has addressed agriculture, it has historically served as conduit for handouts to huge agricultural interests. This is a legacy well soiled with Democrat hands.[5]

Covid has revealed numerous food distribution vulnerabilities unaddressed by the 2016 platform, which also does not present a plan for the steady inflation in food prices that will be the new normal. Layers of price-inflated fossil fuels and (fossil-fuel-based) fertilizers and other agriculture inputs will compound inflationary impacts in foods. Americans could be suffering severe economic hardship, malnutrition, and even starvation if and when food costs comprise 20 percent or 30 percent of their monthly budgets instead of the 10 percent to which they are accustomed. There is a very real risk of a jump to 50 percent or more of household budgets for basic groceries and even widespread food *shortages*—aggravated by hoarding and theft.

The Republican Party must steer its policies with foresight toward responding to these very real problems rather than wait until 2024 to dabble with another quixotic, disconnected, faux environmental policy prescription. America's conservatives must stake their political futures with working-class rural Americans, not corporate elites and billionaires. Regenerative agricultural policies, reduced regulation, and support for rural farming communities and family farms offer an agricultural policy pathway to economic, human, and environmental health—but also *political success* for conservatives. These proposals affirm traditional conservative values that include supporting small businesses and their economic importance for America. The widely dispersed smallholdings favored by Jefferson and the distributists remain the strongest bulwark against industrial domination and government totalitarianism. This foundation resists the vagaries of both capitalism and communism.[6] But more, it rests on traditionally espoused conservative values. Republicans must return to that legacy from which they have strayed.

The past century witnessed a relentless tightening of government regulatory control of nearly every morsel of food grown locally while rapidly and recklessly expanding access to dubiously labeled foreign-sourced foods that often lack thorough regulatory oversight. Family farms have all but vanished and local landscapes grown back in scrub brush and woods, or worse—"development." And the citizenry is being made ill by it all.

Republicans must get food and sustainable agriculture right. Prices of basic foods have already risen much faster than base inflation rates, and this will worsen as the Biden post-Covid spending infusions dilute the money supply. It is likely the government will issue more debt-fueled "relief," but this will instead fuel yet more inflation. There may well be food riots in American streets such as have not been seen since revolutionary times, when more than thirty local food riots occurred from 1775 to 1779, fueling the American Revolution.[7]

Restoring rural communities begins with subsidies for small-scale and regenerative farming practices instead of for monocultures and Chinese solar panels. When small families can afford to live in rural areas—*and wish to*—businesses that serve farmers and also these rural consumers will also return to rural towns, schools will grow in enrollment, and rural communities will thrive. The family farm is the foundation of soil stewardship as well as community, and that merits saving.

Eliminating subsidies over time for large-scale, soil-wrecking monoculture production is a necessity, along with paring back overly burdensome agriculture regulations. Targeted credits and subsidies will profoundly motivate Americans to consider an economically viable, healthy living in the diverse and beautiful landscapes that crave human nurturing and regeneration.

Humans rebel against being converted to a CAFO life. Just like cows, they are happier, healthier, and more balanced with the ecosystem only when they are *out on the land*. The policies proposed will do more than just restore fair opportunities for small-scale farmers; they will help all Americans weather future storms of inflation or food scarcity, as growing one's own food is the strongest possible hedge fund against a weak currency.

There are a number of potential food supply crises that face America linked to soil erosion and water supplies, but also to currency strength, fossil fuel market volatility, world war, and other potential threats. A land-based (agrarian) rural population is more resilient to such blows and serves as a resource for urban as well as rural Americans.

Conservatives and liberals must unite to support small farms and local food production. There is no need to embrace global warming or even carbon dioxide as culprit for conservatives to see the many benefits that follow. Democrats can fight the climate change battle separately while concurring on the many benefits proffered by a Republican policy initiative favoring regenerative practices and local agriculture. Should the nation quickly achieve consensus on chemical reduction and regenerative agriculture, the benefits would soon prove themselves: rural economic growth; healthier food supplies, and thus healthier people and less-costly healthcare; improved soil retention and healthier soils; cleaner water and reduced stress on aquifers; reduced overall government spending on agriculture subsidies; reduced fossil fuel, fertilizer, and other chemical inputs; and reduced dependency on foreign food, fuels, fertilizers, and other agricultural inputs. Additionally, carbon dioxide in the atmosphere could be measurably reduced (offsetting the surge of its production via solar panel and EV manufacturing!).

The political import of these proposals is to unite Americans strongly along policy priorities on the eve of a growing crisis of sustained food-price inflation and in the midst of a highly polarized political climate. This makes the proposal urgent, but no less political. More people could die in a month in America from an abrupt interruption in commerce than have succumbed to Covid through the entire pandemic.

A local food supply is also the best defense against tyranny. That was as true for the American colonists against the British Crown as it is for today's patriots. And once again, it's a win-win. Trustworthy government should encourage self-reliance and food security for its populace, not compel servitude to corporate hegemony.

The food movements rising around the nation have been gaining steam for some years for good reason—nutrition levels and trustworthiness have declined, and Americans' food supply has never been more vulnerable. This is a rising political movement—millions of people waking from the Food Matrix and refusing to remain plugged into its deadly artificiality.

As many of the titles referenced in this book attest, there is related environmental activism surrounding regenerative agriculture, particularly the tremendous potential of carbon sequestration from increasing soil health. Food liberties, healthy foods, domestic foods, and climate change are unavoidably connected. All awakened Americans must elevate this concern to the forefront of thought and action.

The undertaking of this book has been to connect the various food-supply dots to their environmental and political implications and form a policy that addresses these issues. As food prices continue to inflict the damaging realities of these long-stewing problems, Americans will seek political leadership that offers confident, sensible solutions, without tanking the economy or imposing martial environmental law. Voters will favor candidates who comprehend the increasingly dire threats of industrial food dependency and will prioritize securing healthy, affordable, abundant *local* food for We the People. This can be achieved while boosting economic growth, reducing federal deficits, and blossoming a host of additional positive benefits.

Improving water and soils and reversing the errors of industrial agriculture are just the beginning of what can be accomplished. Americans must reclaim a healthier agriculture, and conservatives hold an unusual opportunity to lead the way with common-sense economic, health, and environmental policies.

ACKNOWLEDGMENTS

This book is a product of my journey to bridge my own modern alienation from food and soil. In that decades-long transition, I have been guided and nurtured by the powerful, informed voices of Wendell Berry, Joel Salatin, Wes Jackson, Aldo Leopold, and others referenced in these pages.

Equally supportive have been my wife, Jacqueline, and my three wonderful children, who have endured decades of my ranting against industrial food production, as well as my stubborn determination to persist in animal husbandry as a way of life. Jacqueline has also been an invaluable constructive critic of my writing efforts and has helped improve the arguments and ideas in these pages.

The editors and designers at Chelsea Green Publishing are due a special thanks. Margo Baldwin has encouraged me at many turns; my guiding editor Ben Trollinger helped shape the manuscript greatly; Rebecca Springer devoted intense energy helping improve the book for clarity and style, as well as substantively.

I thank Joel Salatin and Wendell Berry with deep humility. Both of these writers have informed and expanded my knowledge of farming, both encouraged my personal battles to preserve on-farm slaughter traditions in Vermont, and both contributed suggestions for improved policies to nurture local farms and Earth-respecting practices. Joel Salatin deserves special thanks for helping me shape the specific strategy of targeting conservatives to become better informed about what is in their food and where it comes from.

I am also profoundly grateful for the many Vermont farmers who have patiently taught me how to farm and shared the rich cultural heritage of Vermont's shrinking farm community. From making hay to rearing calves to farrowing pigs, learning from their passion for agriculture has been a priceless experience.

NOTES

Introduction

1. John Klar, "The Myth of GMOs Saving the Planet," *Global Research*, January 9, 2023, http://www.globalresearch.ca/myth-gmos-saving-planet/5804013.
2. Wendell Berry, *What Are People For?* (Berkeley, CA: Counterpoint, 1990, 2010), 146.
3. For example, *Western Journal* reported, "The latest taxpayer-funded boondoggle involves a program that encourages farmers to grow 'carbon-capturing' crops that remove carbon dioxide from the air and divert it into the soil." Samantha Chang, "As World Faces Food Shortage, Biden Pushed American Farmers to Take Fields Out of Production," *Western Journal*, September 1, 2021, http://www.westernjournal.com/world-faces-food-shortage-biden-pushes-american-farmers-take-fields-production.
4. "A small but growing movement of millennials are seeking out a more agrarian life but the reality of life on the land is not always as simple as they hoped." Lucia Graves, "Back to the Land: Are Young Farmers the New Starving Artists?" *Guardian*, September 7, 2018, http://www.theguardian.com/environment/2018/dec/17/young-farmers-millennials.
5. "Congressional Democrats and Republicans say ensuring a younger generation of farmers can enter the business is key to upholding local and regional supply chains needed for emergencies, for general domestic food production and to meet the growing demand of local food." Ximena Bustillo, "There Aren't Enough Young Farmers. Congress Is Looking to Change That," National Public Radio, September 1, 2022, http://www.npr.org/2022/09/01/1120100449/farm-bill-not-enough-young-farmers-congress.
6. "On Aug. 24, [2022,] the USDA unveiled new pandemic aid dollars aimed at getting younger and more diverse people interested in jobs within agriculture—both farming and at the government level." Bustillo, "There Aren't Enough Young Farmers."
7. "When food, in the minds of eaters, is no longer associated with farming and with the land, then the eaters are suffering a kind of cultural amnesia that is misleading and dangerous." Berry, *What Are People For?*, 146.

Chapter 1. A Conservative Environmental Strategy

1. "I believe we have got to understand how the great one-cause, fear-motivated climate movement . . . can become a major distraction, not only from better ways of problem-solving and better ways of thinking and working, but also from the local causes of climate change—which has, after all, only local causes." Wendell Berry, *The Art of Loading Brush* (Berkeley, CA: Counterpoint, 2017), 71–72.
2. Wendell Berry, *Another Turn of the Crank* (Berkeley, CA: Counterpoint, 2011), 15.
3. Wes Jackson, *Nature as Measure* (Berkeley, CA: Counterpoint, 2011), 149.
4. "The Green New Deal is the ultimate wish list of the progressive environmental agenda. And it has almost nothing to do with science or 'saving the planet.'" Mark Morano, *Green Fraud:*

Why the Green New Deal Is Even Worse Than You Think (Washington, DC: Regnery, 2021), 1.

5. "This rash rush to ration ruminants is spurious. Once destroyed, Dutch agricultural economies and systems cannot be reclaimed, and there is no plan to replace either the lost income to the Netherlands, or the lost food supplies to the humans that 'feed on them." John Klar, "Glimpsing Armageddon in Dutch Cow Culling," *American Thinker*, December 9, 2022, http://www .americanthinker.com/blog/2022/12/glimpsing_armageddon_in_dutch_cow_culling.html.

6. "The national political malaise is not going to be corrected until there is a devolution of power from the state to the locality and a decentralization of institutions to the point where individuals may in fact control them. A return to the power and sovereignty of the community: this is politics on a human scale." Kirkpatrick Sale, *Human Scale Revisited* (White River Junction, VT: Chelsea Green, 2017), 277–78.

7. Sale, *Human Scale Revisited*, 190.

8. "We can conclude at the very least that what's wrong with infatuation with bigness is that it leads us to assumptions that are often unsupportable and hence to practices and policies that are often detrimental." Sale, *Human Scale Revisited*, 39.

9. Gene Logsdon, *Letter to a Young Farmer: How to Live Richly Without Wealth on the New Garden Farm* (White River Junction, VT: Chelsea Green, 2017).

10. "The great question now needing to be asked is how to get from protest, or fear or anger or guilt, to the actual accomplishment of good work." Berry, *The Art of Loading Brush*, 71.

11. "Perhaps the most unfortunate aspect of the centralized approach to environmental problems is that, while advancing a non-compromising agenda, it ignores the need to provide ordinary people with a motive for adopting it." Roger Scruton, *How to Think Seriously About the Planet: The Case for an Environmental Conservatism* (Oxford: Oxford University Press, 2012), 101.

12. "If we run out of cheap sources of commercial fertilizer, there will be no way to avoid a precipitous decline in crop yields, no matter how rapidly all farmers try to switch to all-organic methods. . . . It has taken us about one hundred years to reduce soil organic matter to dangerously low levels—from about 5 percent, on average, to below 2 percent—and experts say it might take at least that long to build them back up again using organic methods on a large scale." Logsdon, *Letter to a Young Farmer*, 2–3.

13. "One expression of the called-for evolution to local self-reliance is the Transition movement. . . . The movement is part of a convergence of thinking towards the principle that, if areas and communities are to be prepared for the shocks of the climacteric, it will not be government and regulatory agencies that do it." David Fleming, *Surviving the Future: Culture, Carnival and Capital in the Aftermath of the Market Economy* (White River Junction, VT: Chelsea Green, 2016), 170.

14. David Fleming emphasized this case for "limited aims" and "incremental improvement" as part of a realistic action plan toward this problem, which he described as "lean thinking." "Set people up the necessary resources, the skills and equipment, a common purpose, and the freedom to apply their judgment. This has advantages: it brings to life the imagination and tenacity of the people; it transforms the quality of decisions; it is flexible; it sets up conditions for alert observation and quick responses, responding to the local and real needs of the system, rather than to a distant caricature." Fleming, *Surviving the Future*, 203.

15. Scruton, *How to Think Seriously About the Planet*, 102.

16. "The anxiety and stress of chronic poverty do not make people green. Green is what people become when they feel personally secure, when their own appetites have been satisfied, when they do not fear for the future, or for their own survival, or their children's." Peter Huber, *Hard Green: Saving the Environment from the Environmentalists: A Conservative Manifesto* (New York: Basic Books, 1999), 151.

17. This is the subject of one of Wendell Berry's more influential early books, *The Unsettling of America* (San Francisco, CA: Sierra Club Books, 1977).

18. Joel Salatin, *The Sheer Ecstasy of Being a Lunatic Farmer* (Swoope, VA: Polyface, 2010), xvi, 250.

19. "All of these issues stem from industrial agriculture's marriage to high-yield monoculture, which in every way runs counter to the way nature establishes things." Mark Bittman, *Animal, Vegetable, Junk: A History of Food, from Sustainable to Suicidal* (Boston: Houghton Mifflin Harcourt, 2021), 251.

20. "It is of course unrealistic to expect to feed the entire population without the large farms that currently provide such staples as potatoes and corn, but the rebirth of local markets will change the ways that those farms produce and distribute what they grow." Scruton, *How to Think Seriously About the Planet*, 399.

21. Liberal commentator Thomas Frank has stridently warned the Democrats of the risks of abandoning the working class they once claimed to represent. See Thomas Frank, *Listen, Liberals: Or, Whatever Happened to the Party of the People?* (New York: Henry Holt, 2016). To date he appears to have gone unheeded.

22. Michael Pollan has predicted that "it is only a matter of time before politicians seize on the power of the food issue, which besides being increasingly urgent is also almost primal, indeed is in some deep sense proto-political. For where do all politics begin if not in the high chair?" Michael Pollan, "The Food Movement, Rising," *New York Review of Books*, May 20, 2010, http://www.nybooks.com/articles/2010/06/10/food-movement-rising.

23. Chris Smaje, *A Small Farm Future* (White River Junction, VT: Chelsea Green, 2020), 269.

24. "There's much to be gained from connecting a land-based peasant politics with progressive populism in the Global North. Progressive populism shares some aspects of its thinking with the traditional left but also with conservative Main Street populism in honouring the lives and struggles of ordinary people. It differs from most other political doctrines in lacking a utopia or a vision of an ultimately perfected political society. . . . Perhaps if we placed more emphasis on a politics of practical local livelihood rather than a politics of emotional identity at the level of the nation-state, we'd improve it." Smaje, *A Small Farm Future*, 250, 266–67.

25. Berry, *The Art of Loading Brush*, 152–53. Berry also notes: "The high must descend to learn, not what it would choose to learn, but what is indispensable to high and low alike." Wendell Berry, *Standing by Words* (Washington, DC: Shoemaker & Hoard, 1983), 197.

26. Smaje, *A Small Farm Future*, 270.

Chapter 2. Reclaiming a Republican Legacy

1. "Unlike most of his Republican successors, Nixon was not hostile to environmental measures, and signed most of the ones that came to his desk. . . . Nixon aide John C. Whitaker [wrote], 'He grasped the issue quickly and presented a comprehensive and broad legislative environmental agenda.'" Gregg Coodley and Davis Sarasohn, *The Green Years, 1964–1976:*

When Democrats and Republicans United to Repair the Earth (Lawrence: University Press of Kansas, 2021), 252.

2. Wendell Berry, *Bringing It to the Table: On Farming and Food* (Berkeley, CA: Counterpoint, 2009), 101.

3. See also David Gumpert, *Life, Liberty and the Pursuit of Food Rights* (White River Junction, VT: Chelsea Green, 2013); Baylen J. Linnekin, *Biting the Hand That Feeds Us: How Fewer, Smarter Laws Would Make Our Food System More Sustainable* (Washington, DC: Island Press, 2016); Joel Salatin, *Everything I Want to Do Is Illegal* (Swoope, VA: Polyface, 2007).

4. "Three characteristics distinguish the Republican reversal on the environment. Through the 1970s, the Republican Party (1) viewed environmental issues with a sense of urgency that demanded action; (2) put faith in scientific research and professional expertise; and (3) embraced an essential role for government in regulating business and industry to safeguard the public and environmental health. But such a strategy stands in sharp contrast to the party's 2016 agenda. Since the 1980s, the Republican Party has increasingly (1) viewed environmental concerns as alarmist and exaggerated; (2) cast doubt on scientific research and dismissed professional expertise; and (3) viewed many environmental regulations as unnecessary burdens on the economy and as threats to individual freedom and the free enterprise system." James Morton Turner and Andrew C. Isenberg, *The Republican Reversal: Conservatives and the Environment from Nixon to Trump* (Cambridge, MA: Harvard University Press, 2018), 6–7.

5. There is strong consensus of these benefits aside from climate change remediation. For example, in "Regenerative Agriculture: Good for Soil Health, but Limited Potential to Mitigate Climate Change," the World Resources Institute claims, "There is broad agreement that most regenerative agriculture practices are good for soil health and have other environmental benefits. No-till reduces soil erosion and encourages water to infiltrate soils (although it can require greater use of herbicides). Cover crops do the same, and can also reduce water pollution." https://www.wri.org/insights/regenerative-agriculture-good-soil-health -limited-potential-mitigate-climate-change.

6. "The 1970s and '80s sent us an unmistakable message: We can always count upon Republican administrations to support maximum fossil-fuel and nuclear energy, whatever ecological destruction results, and we cannot count on Democratic administrations to resolve energy or ecological issues if they aren't being pushed to do it by a grassroots rebellion." Stan Cox, *The Green New Deal and Beyond: Ending the Climate Emergency While We Still Can* (San Francisco: City Lights Books, 2020), 26.

7. Kristin Ohlson, *The Soil Will Save Us: How Scientists, Farmers, and Foodies Are Healing the Soil to Save the Planet* (Emmaus, PA: Rodale Books, 2014), 196.

8. Reagan notoriously dismissed the evidence of acid rain damage.

9. "Ponzi schemes" refer to fraudulent arrangements such as the 1920s, operations of Charles Ponzi, in which investors are deceived into pouring funds into fronts in which fake dividends or interest are distributed to prior investors while the fraudster spends the capital and it eventually implodes. Similarly, programs that increase CO_2 generation while pretending to do the opposite will eventually bankrupt the environment. The Green New Deal is the biggest industrial pollution Ponzi scheme ever!

10. "The election of President Joseph Biden marked a revived federal recognition of the problem of climate change. Whether the clear progress in reducing the cost of renewable energy

and its increasing adoption can occur fast enough to prevent the worst scenarios of climate change remains to be answered." Coodley and Sarasohn, *The Green Years, 1964–1976,* 244.

11. "The Republican reversal is a profound reorientation of the Republican Party's political agenda." Turner and Isenberg, *The Republican Reversal,* 13.

12. As proposed in the Green New Deal.

13. David Wallace-Wells, *The Uninhabitable Earth: Life After Warming* (New York: Tim Duggan Books, 2020), 258.

14. "Conservatives have succeeded in transforming environmental politics from a process that was once largely driven by science and expert information into one that has become, increasingly, a messy and lengthy debate over values." Turner and Isenberg, *The Republican Reversal,* 204. Readers will note again the common misjudgment here, that conservatives eschew "science and expert information," when in fact the opposite is true. Nowhere is this easier to demonstrate than by conservative acceptance of the less controversial (because less politicized and less novel) science of soil health, erosion, water depletion, and fossil fuel consumption.

15. Wallace-Wells, *The Uninhabitable Earth,* 261.

16. "The planetary sovereign the world is likeliest to turn to ... is the one that sold us climate change in the first place—that is neoliberalism." Wallace-Wells, *The Uninhabitable Earth,* 212–13.

17. "What inspires me about the Green New Deal ... is its theory of politics. The Green New Deal document introduced by Ocasio-Cortez and Markey doesn't aim to be a set of policies ready to sail through the current Congress. Rather, it sets ambitious policy goals—including to achieve 'net-zero greenhouse gas emissions through a fair and just transition for all communities and workers' and 'to create millions of good, high-wage jobs and ensure prosperity and economic security for all people of the United States'—that are almost impossible to imagine in the current political economy." Tom Philpott, *Perilous Bounty: The Looming Collapse of American Farming and How We Can Prevent It* (New York: Bloomsbury, 2020), 190.

18. Philpott, *Perilous Bounty,* 190.

Chapter 3. A Regenerative Farm Policy

1. "Solving the problem of land degradation is devilishly simple from a practices standpoint. The difficulty lies in marshalling the political wherewithal to stop subsidizing conventional farming and start promoting practices that build soil fertility." David Montgomery, *Growing a Revolution: Bringing Our Soil Back to Life* (New York: W. W. Norton, 2017), 267.

2. "Localization means shortening the distance between producers and consumers wherever possible and striking a healthier balance between local and global markets." Helena Norberg-Hodge, *Local Is Our Future: Steps to an Economics of Happiness* (East Hardwick, VT: Local Futures, 2019), 45.

3. "A shift to better farming practices is possible, but Sri Lanka's abrupt switch to organics offers a bitter lesson in how to change food systems in a sustainable way." Kenny Torrella, "Sri Lanka's organic farming disaster, explained," *Vox,* July 15, 2022,, https://www.vox.com/future -perfect/2022/7/15/23218969/sri-lanka-organic-fertilizer-pesticide-agriculture-farming.

4. Ohlson, *The Soil Will Save Us,* 64–65.

5. "In spite of all our scientific and technological cleverness in recent decades, *not one significant breakthrough* has been advanced for a truly *sustainable* agriculture that is at once *healthful* and sufficiently *compelling* to be employed by a stable population, let alone an exploding

one. Even when we do think deeply about the problem, we are inclined to accept the eventual decline of agriculture as being in the nature of a tragedy in drama—inevitable." Jackson, *Nature as Measure*, 5.

6. "In 2020, greenhouse gas emissions from the agriculture economic sector accounted for 11% of total US greenhouse gas emissions. Greenhouse gas emissions from agriculture have increased by 6% since 1990. This increase is largely driven by a 62% growth in combined CH_4 and N_2O emissions from livestock manure management systems, reflecting the increased use of emission-intensive liquid systems over this time period. Emissions from other agricultural sources have generally remained flat or changed by a relatively small amount since 1990." United States Environmental Protection Agency, "Sources of Greenhouse Gas Emissions," last updated on August 5, 2022, http://www.epa.gov/ghgemissions/sources-greenhouse-gas-emissions.

7. Montgomery, *Growing a Revolution*, 227.

8. "Our biggest opportunity is to sequester carbon in soil, which actually benefits biodiversity and can feed us with nutrient-dense food. . . . Some exciting new research is being done looking at the impact and carbon cycle of well-managed cattle. . . . [One] meta-analysis . . . showed that grazing lands not only sequester carbon but also that the amount sequestered could partially or totally offset urban emissions. . . . The real threat to human health and the planet is industrially produced food." Diana Rodgers and Robb Wolf, *Sacred Cow: Why Well-Raised Meat Is Good for You and Good for the Planet* (Dallas: BenBella Books, 2020), 143, 145, 265.

9. "Knowing as we do that diversity is invaluable to ecosystems, how can anyone seriously propose that it's in our best interests to stop raising and eating animals and instead cover every inch of farmable land with the same three crops? . . . One must wonder how a row-crop-centric food system, which hinges on the use of these unsustainable inputs, can be put forward as a solution to global food security." Rodgers and Wolf, *Sacred Cow*, 127–29.

10. Cox, *The Green New Deal and Beyond*, 116.

11. "[S]mall-scale, diversified farms have a higher total output per unit of land than large-scale monocultures, based on studies carried out all over the world. . . . At the same time, our taxes are subsidizing a dramatic increase in the use of energy and scarce natural resources. We have a system that is simultaneously creating mass unemployment, poverty and pollution." Norberg-Hodge, *Local Is Our Future*, 13, 89.

12. *The Andromeda Strain* was a 1969 techno-thriller in which scientists battle a fast-growing extraterrestrial microorganism.

13. "The enemy is industrial agriculture and hyperpalatable infinite-shelf-life junk food, not the family of farmers down the street who want to raise their animals on grass. Let's unify the real food community." Rodgers and Wolf, *Sacred Cow*, 216.

Chapter 4. Escaping the Carbon Cult

1. Joel Salatin, *The Sheer Ecstasy of Being a Lunatic Farmer*, 29. Kristin Ohlson agrees: "We need to do everything we can to stop losing historic soil carbon, and we also need to do everything we can to build and retain more carbon in the soil." Ohlson, *The Soil Will Save Us*, 5.

2. "And this entire cycle depends on the herbivore, both its eating and pooping, to synergize it. . . . One of the most environmentally-enhancing things you can do is to eat grass-finished beef. That sequesters more carbon than soybeans or corn or any other annual. And yet how many radical environmentalists have turned to soy milk and veganism in order to be earth friendly." Ohlson, *The Soil Will Save Us*, 28.

3. "Some of these [new, regenerative] farmers don't care a whit about global warming; they're influenced by the industry-connected American Farm Bureau, which claims that 70 percent of farmers don't believe in human-induced climate change. But many other farmers are thrilled to find out that their humus is helping to keep excess carbon dioxide out of the atmosphere." Ohlson, *The Soil Will Save Us*, 19.

4. "The prescription for climate change mitigation is pretty much identical to the prescription for more productive working lands, clean water, better air quality, bountiful wildlife habitat, and so on." Ohlson, *The Soil Will Save Us*, 197–98.

5. Vandana Shiva, *Stolen Harvest: The Hijacking of the Global Food Supply* (Cambridge, MA: South End Press, 2000), 95.

6. "The monoculture paradigm focuses on yields of single commodities and externalizes the costs of chemicals and energy. Inefficient and wasteful industrial agriculture are hence presented as efficient and productive." Shiva, *Stolen Harvest*, 113. This is what is being done now by those who advocate for manufacturing renewable energy products as salvific while ignoring water, air and soil pollution, and impacts by chemicals on human and environmental health.

7. "Highly soluble chemicals, though readily taken up by plants, can inhibit or kill soil microbes, and be washed away to pollute groundwater. Moreover, plants are also able to absorb and benefit from complex bio-chemicals such as vitamins and antibiotics, which are not present in artificially-synthesized fertilizers." Grace Gershuny and Joseph Smillie, *The Soul of Soil*, 3rd ed. (Davis, CA: AgAccess, 1995), 22.

Chapter 5. The Soil of a Nation

1. Philip Lymbery and Isabel Oakenshott, *Farmageddon: The True Cost of Cheap Meat* (London: Bloomsbury, 2014), 341.

2. "Land, then, is not merely soil; it is a fountain of energy flowing through a circuit of soils, plants, and animals. Food chains are the living channels which conduct energy upwards; death and decay return it to the soil.... It is a sustained circuit, like a slowly augmented revolving fund of life." Aldo Leopold, *The River of the Mother of God: and Other Essays* (Madison: University of Wisconsin Press, 1992), 268–69.

3. "True stewards of the land understand that more living organisms are in a double-handful of healthy soil than there are people on the face of the earth.... And this precious resource of mineral, decaying biomass, gasses, water, and critters is the only protective veil between humanity and starvation.... Utterly dependent on this most precious resource, we arrogantly dismiss it as dirt." Salatin, *The Sheer Ecstasy of Being a Lunatic Farmer*, 6, 7.

4. "The agricultural-chemical experiment results in ruined land, poisoned waters, and an array of debilitating health conditions. That leaves us with just one way to put nutrients and microbes back into the soil." Josh Tickell, *Kiss the Ground: How the Food You Eat Can Reverse Climate Change, Heal Your Body & Ultimately Save Our World* (New York: Enliven Books, 2017), 168–69.

5. "The organic fraction of the soil is a dynamic substance, constantly undergoing change. It consists of living organisms, including plant roots and bacteria, as well as dead plant residues and other wastes. The total weight of the living organisms in the top six inches of an acre of soil can range from 5,000 to as much as 20,000 pounds." Gershuny and Smillie, *The Soul of Soil*, 19.

6. "Soil is a placenta or matrix, a living organism which is larger than the life it supports, a tough elastic membrane which has given rise to many life forms and has watched the thousands of species from their first experiments at survival, many of them through millennia-long roaring successes and even dominion before their eventual decline and demise.... The human agricultural enterprise and all of civilization has depended upon fighting that succession. The human purpose has so dominated our thinking that those in high places are out of touch." Jackson, *Nature as Measure*, 19.

7. Shiva, *Stolen Harvest*, 71.

8. "Agriculture ... has emerged as a machine for sacrificing soil, at a time when farms need to be building soil to prepare for coming weather shocks." Philpot, *Perilous Bounty*, 6.

9. "Soil erosion is already reported at record rates in many parts of the US, and topsoil is being depleted in temperate zones worldwide by an estimated 23 billion tons a year, an unprecedented toll." Sale, *Dwellers in the Land: The Bioregional Vision*, 36. See also Jackson, *Nature as Measure*, 29.

10. Kurt Lawton, "Economics of Soil Loss," *Farm Progress*, March 13, 2017, http://www.farmprogress.com/soil-health/economics-of-soil-loss.

11. Joel Salatin, *Folks, This Ain't Normal* (New York: Center Street, 2011), 32.

12. "Since the start of mechanized agriculture, North America's tilled fields have lost more than 40 percent of their original soil organic matter.... Today, most croplands have been under conventional practices for long enough to have reduced soil organic matter by more than half.... It would take fundamental changes in agricultural practices to restore soil carbon to near-historic levels." Montgomery, *Growing a Revolution*, 224–25.

13. Jackson, *Nature as Measure*, 5.

14. Albert Howard, *An Agricultural Testament* (Naples, Italy: Albatross, 1940, 2018), 20.

15. "Topsoil degradation makes future harvests uncertain at best.... Although difficult to predict, it is reasonable to assume that as topsoil degrades, harvests may be negatively affected, which generally involves a 'doubling down' on things like synthetic fertilizer, which may accelerate this process." Rodgers and Wolf, *Sacred Cow*, 128.

16. "If large amounts of nitrate fertilizer flood the soil system, the bacteria responsible for converting protein fragments into nitrates will be suppressed, in turn 'backing up' the whole organic decomposition process.... If this process is repeated year after year, the capacity of that soil to digest fresh organic matter will be seriously damaged." Gershuny and Smillie, *The Soul of Soil*, 16.

17. "Soils contain more carbon than the combined amount in the atmosphere and all of the plant and animal life on earth. Most soil carbon is held in the top several feet, due to surficial inputs of organic matter and the carbon-rich exudates that shallow roots push out into the soil. This means that changes in the organic-matter content of topsoil can significantly impact the amount of carbon in the atmosphere, and therefore global climate." Montgomery, *Growing a Revolution*, 224.

18. Montgomery, *Growing a Revolution*, 223.

19. Montgomery, *Growing a Revolution*, 195.

20. "The cycles that permit nutrients to flow from soil to plant are all interdependent, and proceed only with the help of the living organisms that constitute the soil community. Soil microorganisms are the essential link between mineral reserves and plant growth. Animals and people are also part of this community. Unless their wastes are returned to the soil—for

the benefit of the organisms that live there—the whole life-supporting process will be undermined." Gershuny and Smillie, *The Soul of Soil*, 37.

21. "Nature has provided in the forest an example which can be safely copied in transforming wastes into humus—the key to prosperity." Howard, *An Agricultural Testament*, 223. There is no technological method to surpass this natural cycle.

22. "Over the past half-century, many farm animals have disappeared from fields and been confined in sheds, in an agricultural system that has become divorced from the land and separated from the so-called 'nutrient cycle.' The natural cycle in which sun and rain fed grass, which fed animals, whose manure enriched the soil, has been replaced by a new system dependent on fossil-fuel based synthetic fertilisers." Lymbery and Oakenshift, *Farmageddon*, 341–42.

23. Montgomery, *Growing a Revolution*, 226.

24. "Soil scientist Dr. Rattan Lal states, 'A mere 2 percent increase in the carbon content of the planet's soils would offset 100 percent of all greenhouse gas emissions going into the atmosphere. Remember that all tillage agriculture contributes to global warming—indeed, agriculture marks the beginning of it. . . . Growing soil, combined with stopping fossil fuels, is our one and only hope—and it's also not too late.'" Derrick Jensen, Lierre Keith, and Max Wilbert, *Bright Green Lies: How the Environmental Movement Lost Its Way and What We Can Do about It* (Rhinebeck, NY: Monkfish, 2021), 454.

25. "If we continue to lose soil, if our soils and groundwater supplies continue to be polluted because of our single-vision focus on production, the day will come when few will care whether molecular biology ever existed as a discipline." Jackson, *Nature as Measure*, 114, 136.

26. "What our farmers have had to learn with surprise and pain and to their cost, and what most politicians and businessmen have never learned: it is not the area of a country that makes its value, but its life, the depth and richness of its topsoil." Wendell Berry, *A Continuous Harmony: Essays Cultural and Agricultural* (San Diego: Harcourt Brace Jovanovich, 1972), 13.

27. "We might succeed on the energy front, but once soil has eroded, its restoration comes in geologic time, and no technological substitute will do. And in spite of our efforts so far, soil erosion and other landscape degradations are increasing globally." Wes Jackson, *Hogs Are Up: Stories of the Land, with Digressions* (Lawrence: University Press of Kansas, 2021), 102.

Chapter 6. The Looming Water Crisis

1. "We are losing the easily irrigable land and 'replacing' it by land reclaimed at great expense. The significant fact that is not understood is that this 'replacement' is no replacement at all, but rather slicing at one end of our loaf while the other end sloughs away in waste. Some day the slicing and sloughing will meet. Then we shall realize that we needed the whole loaf." Leopold, *The River of the Mother of God*, 87.

2. "While people are ingenious at replacing many depleting material feedstocks with new ones, we haven't been so successful at finding substitutes for water. . . . One estimate suggests that two-thirds of the global population may be living in water-stressed conditions by 2025. Civilization sprouted from agriculture, and there has never been a successful agricultural practice without adequate water." Bittman, *Animal, Vegetable, Junk*, 20.

3. "Globally, between 70 and 80 percent of freshwater is used for food production and agriculture, with an additional 10 to 20 percent set aside for industry." Wallace-Wells, *The Uninhabitable Earth*, 94.

4. Smaje, *A Small Farm Future*, 41.

5. "Nebraska had the most irrigated land among all U.S. states, with 8.6 million acres of irrigated cropland, accounting for 14.8 percent of all irrigated cropland in the United States. The prevalence of irrigated acreage in Nebraska relates to the abundance of groundwater resources as much of the state overlies the High Plains (Ogallala) aquifer. California ranked second, with 7.8 million acres, or 13.5 percent of all U.S. irrigated cropland; Arkansas, Texas, and Idaho rounded out the top 5 states in total irrigated cropland acreage in 2017. Since 1890, irrigated acreage nationwide has grown from less than 3 million acres to over 58 million acres in 2017." United States Department of Agriculture Economic Research Service, "Irrigation & Water Use," http://www.ers.usda.gov/topics/farm-practices-management/irrigation-water-use.

6. "Nonrenewable groundwater extraction in the U.S. is estimated to have more than doubled since 1960 and is projected to at least double again by the end of the century. Excessive nonrenewable groundwater extraction has several negative impacts to the local environment including land subsidence, water quality degradation, and sea level rise. Nevertheless, for many parts of the U.S., nonrenewable groundwater pumping is a necessity. In these areas, nonrenewable groundwater use for irrigation is increasing to meet domestic and international food demands. This practice is projected to continue into the future." Neal T. Graham et al., "Agricultural Impacts of Sustainable Water Use in the United States," *Nature Scientific Reports* 11 (2021), http://www.nature.com/articles/s41598-021-96243-5.

7. "[E]xploding demand for food with high environmental footprints, such as meat from industrial farms, is contributing to unsustainable agricultural intensification and to water-quality degradation. This growth in crop production has been achieved mainly through the intensive use of inputs such as pesticides and chemical fertilizers." Food and Agriculture Organization of the United Nations, "Agriculture: Cause and Victim of Water Pollution, but Change Is Possible," http://www.fao.org/land-water/news-archive/news-detail/en/c/1032702.

8. "The food system doesn't bear the long-term—or even short-term—costs of local water depletion, leading it to over-produce water-intensive crops, particularly cash export crops. This is particularly so in the case of non-renewable water from aquifers such as the Ogallala aquifer, which transects several Midwestern states in the United States and holds 'fossil' meltwater from the Ice Age. The depletion of such aquifers has major consequences for future crop selection and yield." Smaje, *A Small Farm Future*, 41–42.

9. "Farmers are pulling water out of the Ogallala [Aquifer] faster than rain and snow can recharge it. Between 1900 and 2008 they drained some 89 trillion gallons from the aquifer—equivalent to two-thirds of Lake Erie. . . . But our research . . . shows that farmers are draining the Ogallala because state and federal policies encourage them to do it. . . . Government payments create a vicious cycle of overproduction that intensifies water use. Subsidies encourage farmers to expand and buy expensive equipment to irrigate larger areas." Matthew R. Sanderson et al., "Farmers Are Depleting the Ogallala Aquifer Because the Government Pays Them to Do It," *The Conversation*, November 9, 2020, http://www.theconversation.com/farmers-are-depleting-the-ogallala-aquifer-because-the-government-pays-them-to-do-it-145501.

10. Timothy Egan, *The Worst Hard Time* (Boston: Houghton Mifflin Harcourt, 2006), 310.

11. David Condos, "How Kansas Could Lose Billions in Land Values as Its Underground Water Runs Dry," High Plains Public Radio, April 1, 2022, https://www.hppr.org/hppr-news/2022-03-31/how-kansas-could-lose-billions-in-land-values-as-its-underground-water-runs-dry.

12. "California's mounting water scarcity will be impossible to ignore when drought recurs, as it inevitably will." Philpott, *Perilous Bounty*, 167.

13. Bittman, *Animal, Vegetable, Junk*, 247.

14. Philpott, *Perilous Bounty*, 168–69.

15. United States Geographical Survey, "California's Central Valley," https://ca.water.usgs.gov/projects/central-valley/about-central-valley.html.

16. Philpott, *Perilous Bounty*, 173. Josh Tickell notes of the Central Valley that "In most locations, it's only fallen a foot over the past few decades. But in other locations, it has fallen as much as twenty-nine feet, about a foot a year." (Tickell, *Kiss the Ground*, 106.) Meanwhile, Mexico and Chile, both of which supply food crops to the United States, are also grappling with serious water overdrafts from underground aquifers. (Philpott, *Perilous Bounty*, 174–75.) This creates direct dependence for those crops on distant, threatened aquifers.

17. County of Monterey Agricultural Commissioner, "Monterey County 2019 Crop Report: Invasive Species," http://www.co.monterey.ca.us/home/showdocument?id=92362.

18. "Climate change does indeed play a role in tightening water supplies, but the type of change that took the greatest toll was the initial alteration of the land." Tickell, *Kiss the Ground*, 100–101.

19. Tickell, *Kiss the Ground*, 100.

20. Ohlson, *The Soil Will Save Us*, 66.

21. "ARkStorm Scenario," USGS, https://www.usgs.gov/programs/science-application-for-risk-reduction/science/arkstorm-scenario.

22. Xingying Huang, "Climate Change Is Increasing the Risk of a California Megaflood," *Science Advances* 8, no. 32 (August 12, 2022), https://doi.org/10.1126/sciadv.abq0.

23. Smaje, *A Small Farm Future*, 43.

24. "The net effect of cattle in the food system is to benefit the world's waters. There is simply nothing better at absorbing, holding and filtering water than lands densely covered by grass, and there is no better way to keep those lands biologically diverse, hydrated and vibrant than by periodically grazing them." Nicolette Hahn Niman, *Defending Beef: The Case for Sustainable Meat Production* (White River Junction, VT: Chelsea Green, 2014), 92.

25. Joel Salatin, *You Can Farm: The Entrepreneur's Guide to Start and Succeed in a Farming Enterprise* (Swoope, VA: Polyface, 1998), 294.

Chapter 7. A Matter of National (and Local) Security

1. "The seed, for the farmer, is not merely the source of future plants and food; it is the storage place of culture and history. Seed is the first link in the food chain. Seed is the ultimate symbol of food security." Shiva, *Stolen Harvest*, 8.

2. Tickell, *Kiss the Ground*, 188.

3. Wendell Berry, *The Art of the Commonplace: The Agrarian Essays of Wendell Berry* (Berkeley, CA: Counterpoint, 2002), 288.

4. Salatin, *The Sheer Ecstasy of Being a Lunatic Farmer*, 297–98.

5. "We have reached a point at which we must either consciously desire and choose and determine the future of the earth or submit to such an involvement in our own destructiveness that the earth, and ourselves with it, must certainly be destroyed." Wendell Berry, *The Long-Legged House* (Washington, DC: Shoemaker & Hoard, 1969), 46.

6. "It would be foolish to deny the mounting evidence that an ecological crisis of some magnitude seems to be at hand. . . . There is simply no escaping the rock-hard truths of the overall

evidence of environmental peril in which our human society has plunged itself." Kirkpatrick Sale, *Dwellers in the Land: The Bioregional Vision* (Athens: University of Georgia Press, 2000), 36–37.

7. "The collapse of the western Roman Empire was … a catabolic collapse driven by a combined maintenance and resource crisis." John Michael Greer, *The Long Descent: A User's Guide to the End of the Industrial Age* (Gabriola Island, BC: New Society, 2008), 234.

8. "North America is unusually vulnerable to a descent into rural anarchy because of its size, its dependence on automobiles, and its lack of pre-petroleum infrastructure." Greer, *The Long Descent*, 121.

9. Smaje, *A Small Farm Future*, 152–53.

10. "Just a few clusters of water-stressed counties in a single state provide 81 percent of U.S.-grown carrots, 95 percent of broccoli, 78 percent of cauliflower, 74 percent of raspberries, 91 percent of strawberries, 66 percent of lettuce, 63 percent of tomatoes, and on and on." Philpott, *Perilous Bounty*, 176.

11. Maxim Lott, "10 Times 'Experts' Predicted the World Would End by Now," FoxNews, March 19, 2019, https://www.foxnews.com/science/10-times-experts-predicted-the-world -would-end-by-now.

12. "Here's What the World Will Look Like in 2030 … Right?," *Wired*, January 1, 2020, https://www.wired.com/story/heres-what-the-world-will-look-like-in-2030-right.

13. Lott, "10 Times 'Experts' Predicted the World Would End by Now."

14. Artem Milinchuk, "Is Regenerative Agriculture Profitable?," *Forbes*, January 30, 2020, https:// www.forbes.com/sites/forbesfinancecouncil/2020/01/30/is-regenerative-agriculture-profitable /?sh=5e8e9329cdf2.

15. "The standard sets of time-dependent scenarios used by the climate modeling community as input to global climate model simulations provide the basis for the majority of the future projections presented in IPCC assessment reports and U.S. National Climate Assessments (NCAs)." USGCRP, 2017: Climate Science Special Report: Fourth National Climate Assessment, Volume I [D.J. Wuebbles, D.W. Fahey, K.A. Hibbard, D.J. Dokken, B.C. Stewart, and T.K. Maycock (eds.)]. U.S. Global Change Research Program, Washington, DC, https:// science2017.globalchange.gov/chapter/4/.

16. "Climate Models," MIT Climate Portal, January 8, 2021, https://climate.mit.edu/explainers /climate-models.

17. Umair Irfan, "What's the Worst That Could Happen?," *Vox* (September 10, 2021), https://www .vox.com/22620706/climate-change-ipcc-report-2021-ssp-scenario-future-warming.

18. Steven E. Koonin, *Unsettled: What the Climate Science Tells Us, What It Doesn't, and Why It Matters* (Dallas: BenBella Books, 2021), 248.

19. Paul Voosen, "The Hunger Forecast: How a Team of Scientists Studying Drought Helped Build the World's Leading Famine Prediction Model," *Science* (April 15, 2020), https://www.science .org/content/article/how-team-scientists-studying-drought-helped-build-world-s-leading -famine-prediction.

20. Maria Paula Rubiano, "How Scientists Predict Famine Before It Hits," UC Santa Barbara, *Geography* (May 30, 2022), https://www.bbc.com/future/article/20220525-how-scientists -predict-famine-before-it-hits.

21. World Food Programme, "A Global Food Crisis," https://www.wfp.org/global-hunger-crisis.

22. Greta Thunberg, *No One Is Too Small to Make a Difference* (New York: Penguin Books, 2019).

NOTES

23. John Klar, "The Worst Shortage You Haven't Heard Of," *American Thinker* (June 4, 2022), https://www.americanthinker.com/blog/2022/06/the_worst_shortage_you_havent_heard_of.html.

24. Lili Xia et al., "Global Food Insecurity and Famine from Reduced Crop, Marine Fishery and Livestock Production Due to Climate Disruption from Nuclear War Soot Injection," *Nature Food* 3 (August 15, 2022): 586–96, https://www.nature.com/articles/s43016-022-00573-0.

25. "In 1934, nearly 30 percent of all Americans still lived on farms, and a good part of how the nation viewed itself was rooted in its agricultural traditions and experience." T. H. Watkins, *The Great Depression: America in the 1930s* (Boston: Little, Brown, 1993), 189–90. "The Democratic Party's platform of 1932 had called for help to the farmers, and in Roosevelt's acceptance speech he had emphasized their plight. He pointed out that 50,000 Americans, or more than half the nation's population, depended on agriculture—directly or indirectly—for a livelihood." Edward Robb Ellis, *A Nation in Torment: The Great American Depression 1929–1939* (New York: Coward-McCann, 1970), 311.

26. Bittman, *Animal, Vegetable, Junk*, 247.

27. "The binge the developed world has enjoyed is about over. It's time to find our way home and use what little time is left for partial redemption of this prodigal generation." Jackson, *Becoming Native to This Place* (Washington, DC: Counterpoint, 1996), 5.

28. "More than half of U.S.-consumed fruit and about a third of fresh vegetables were grown in other countries [as of 2017], and the proportions are growing." Philpott, *Perilous Bounty*, 174.

29. Bittman, *Animal, Vegetable, Junk*, 245. See also Fleming, *Surviving the Future*, 155: "Concentration into just a few giant food production centres removes all defences against the spread of trouble, which will ripple through the entire industry, giving our security against famine the resilience of a house of cards."

30. "If allowed to proceed, globalization will continue to have wide-ranging negative impacts that point towards the collapse of human communities and Earth's living systems." Norberg-Hodge, *Local Is Our Future*, 26; "We are . . . in a crisis wrought by the excesses of an industrial civilization knowing no limits or proportion that seems certain, if there is no change in its current course, to bring that civilization to ruin." Sale, *Human Scale Revisited*, 355.

31. "Much will have to change if the ongoing overshoot is not to be followed by collapse during the twenty-first century. . . . The collapse will arrive very suddenly, much to everyone's surprise." Donella Meadows, Jorgen Randers, and Dennis Meadows, *Limits to Growth: The 30-Year Update* (White River Junction, VT: Chelsea Green, 2004), xvi, xxi.

32. "The problem modern civilisation faces isn't just finding substitutes for a few resource inputs but for many, at a time when demand is growing and pollution sinks are shrinking." Smaje, *A Small Farm Future*, 40.

33. "The outlook is grim. Most economists and agricultural experts who have examined the evidence believe that the era of food surpluses is over and that high food prices are here to stay. . . . It seems clear that food scarcity will increasingly shape modern politics; even trigger wars." Plymbery and Oakeshott, *Farmageddon*, 252.

34. "The key to all this is to recognise that the driving force behind industrial agriculture is not (as is usually claimed) the need to feed the world's population of 7 billion or more." Fleming, *Surviving the Future*, 156.

35. Shiva, *Stolen Harvest*, 11. See also Aldo Leopold: "Agricultural science is largely a race between the emergence of new pests and the emergence of new technologies for their control." Leopold, *The River of the Mother of God*, 269.

36. "Fifty-four percent of the increase in transgenic crops is for those engineered for herbicide resistance, or, rather, the increased use of herbicides, not increased food.... The myth of increasing yields is the most common justification for introducing genetically engineered crops in agriculture. However, genetic engineering is actually leading to a 'yield drag.'" Shiva, *Stolen Harvest*, 103, 113.

37. "Where genetically modified crops have been used, the feasibility of converting from industrial agriculture to a less input-intensive regime will be reduced by impoverished soil and super-persistent weeds; since genetic changes persist, it may even be impossible on any relevant timescale." Fleming, *Surviving the Future*, 153.

38. "We spend only ten percent of our budget on food, compared to 40 percent by our great-grandparents in 1900, and 30 percent by our grandparents in the 1950s. It is a number that has been decreasing the entire century along with the rise of mass supply chains.... The fact is we spend less money than almost every other country in the world on food and we spend less time gathering that food than at any time in history." Benjamin Lorr, *The Secret Life of Groceries: The Dark Miracle of the American Supermarket* (New York: Avery, 2020), 5–6.

39. Berry, *What Are People For?*, 124.

40. "Indeed, so regularly does one encounter this phenomenon in the reading of history that I am emboldened to advance this as a full-blown maxim, what we may call the Law of Government size: Economic and social misery increases in direct proportion to the size and power of the central government of a nation or state." Sale, *Human Scale Revisited*, 64.

41. Ironically, overuse of phosphates has polluted the oceans and American rivers, including Vermont's waterways—the phosphorus from synthetic fertilizers dispersed on midwestern fields is passed into grains (feed) and trucked to cows in Vermont, where it flows in manure onto the wet slopes and fields of the Green Mountains.

42. USDA Economic Research Service, "Recent Volatility in US Fertilizer Prices," March 1, 2009, http://www.ers.usda.gov/amber-waves/2009/march/recent-volatility-in-us-fertilizer-prices.

43. "The present world-historical moment ... involves impending food and political-economic crises, sharpening the relevance of bygone peasant assertions. What will you do when you can no longer rely on the centralised state that you're familiar with to keep supplying you with eggs and other forms of welfare?" Smaje, *A Small Farm Future*, 269.

44. "It sounds dramatic, given how far removed we are from our food sources, but civilizations live or die by the strength and resilience of their food systems. And these depend on healthy soil.... Soil and the people who work it are the foundation of a thriving society." Bittman, *Animal, Vegetable, Junk*, 22, 21.

45. Robert Malone, *Lies My Gov't Told Me, and The Better Future Coming* (New York: Skyhorse, 2022), 412.

46. "The world crunch will come, for land really is finite while population is not, for the earth does at last say no to generations of chemicals. The squeeze will come vengeful and cruel; but it will also come too late, I think, for the last cohort of American family farmers who were born this century, who alone would have welcomed the enormity of that epic and last struggle against nature to save their kindred." Victor Davis Hanson, *Fields Without Dreams: Defending the Agrarian Idea* (New York: Simon & Schuster, 1996), 182.

47. Wendell Berry, *Sex, Economy, Freedom & Community* (New York: Pantheon Books, 1993), 50–51.

Chapter 8. A Regenerative Economics

1. Leopold, *The River of the Mother of God*, 269–70.

2. Berry, *Another Turn of the Crank*, 15–16.

3. "One of the strangest assumptions of present-day mental models is the idea that a world of moderation must be a world of strict, centralized government control. For a sustainable economy, that kind of control is not possible, desirable, or necessary. (From a systems point of view, it has serious deficiencies, as the former Soviet Union amply demonstrated.)" Meadows, Randers, and Meadows, *Limits to Growth*, 257.

4. "Even in a democratic society ... the evidence is that state bureaucracies become a danger to the environment as soon as they acquire the role of controlling rather than containing what is done." Scruton, *How to Think Seriously About the Planet*, 93–94.

5. "If conservationists are serious about conservation, they will have to realize that the best conserver of land in use will always be the small owner or operator, farmer or forester or both, who lives within a securely placed family and community, who knows how to use the land in the best way, and who can afford to do so." Berry, *Another Turn of the Crank*, 59.

6. "The more dependent we become on the industries of eating and drinking, the more waste we are going to produce. The mess that surrounds us, then, must be understood not just as a problem in and of itself but as a symptom of a greater and graver problem: the centralization of our economy, the gathering of the productive property and power into fewer and fewer hands, and the consequent destruction, everywhere, of the local economies of household, neighborhood, and community." Berry, *What Are People For?*, 128.

7. Scruton, *How to Think Seriously About the Planet*, 398–99.

8. "One big reason for surging fertilizer prices is surging prices of coal and natural gas. The urea in your urine is produced in the liver. The industrial kind is made through a century-old process that uses natural gas or gas derived from coal to produce ammonia, which is then used to synthesize urea." Raymond Zhong, "This Chemical Is in Short Supply, and the Whole World Feels It," *New York Times*, December 6, 2021.

9. "Facing short supplies, China increased its export taxes on fertilizers from 35 percent in 2007 to 135 percent in 2008 to ensure that domestic production remained in the country." USDA Economic Research Service, "Recent Volatility in U.S. Fertilizer Prices."

10. USDA Economic Research Service, "Fertilizer Prices Spike in Leading U.S. Market in Late 2021, Just Ahead of 2022 Planting Season," February 9, 2022, https://www.ers.usda.gov/data-products/chart-gallery/gallery/chart-detail/?chartId=103194.

11. Markets Insider, Natural Gas PRICE Today, Natural Gas Price Chart, https://markets.businessinsider.com/commodities/natural-gas-price.

12. E. F. Schumacher, *Small Is Beautiful: Economics as If People Mattered* (New York: Harper Perennial, 1973, 2010), 7. Also note Norberg-Hodge, *Local Is Our Future*, 35: "In addition to a host of social problems, urbanization contributes to a substantial increase in resource use and pollution. Nearly every material need of urbanized populations must be shipped in from elsewhere, while the resulting waste—much of which could be put to use in a rural setting—becomes a highly concentrated source of pollution."

13. Shiva, *Stolen Harvest*, 13. See also Montgomery, *Growing a Revolution*, 167–68 (quoting North Dakota rancher Gabe Brown): "The trick is to maintain yields while slashing input costs."

14. "Our farm is a rural revitalization engine. Money flows into the rural area, not away from it. That's money that stays here in local banks to lend out to local businesses and people who

NOTES

want to buy houses." Salatin, *The Sheer Ecstasy of Being a Lunatic Farmer*, 297. As Salatin explains on page 246: "An economy can only be as healthy as its farmers. Farmers drive the lion's share of landscape stewardship. Ultimately, if the landscape ecology fails, the economy will fail. Farmers drive food quality. Ultimately, if health fails, the economy will fail."

15. Artem Milinchuk, "Is Regenerative Agriculture Profitable?", *Forbes*, January 30, 2020, https://www.forbes.com/sites/forbesfinancecouncil/2020/01/30/is-regenerative-agriculture-profitable/?sh=5e8e9329cdf2.

16. "The closer we live to the ground that we live from, the more we will know about our economic life; the more we know about our economic life, the more able we will be to take responsibility for it." Berry, *Sex, Economy, Freedom & Community*, 39.

17. Montgomery, *Growing a Revolution*, 228–29.

18. "These products of the land, and not the detritus of financial speculations, represent real wealth." Allan C. Carlson, "Distributism: A Short History," *Local Culture: A Journal of the Front Porch Republic* 2, no. 1 (March 2020): 7.

19. "[Pulitzer Prize winner Herbert] Agar held that the United States had been founded as a healthy land of family farmers, independent artisans, and small-scale merchants. However, as early as the presidency of Thomas Jefferson, political elites surrendered to 'a greedy middle-class Hamiltonian capitalism.' By 1900, Agar held, this Hamiltonian shift had produced the industrial plutocrats of the Gilded Age, along with a 'mass of property-less wage slaves' in the cities and desperate tenants in the countryside. Thirty years later American democracy was no more than 'a soiled screen for plutocracy,' as 'the politics of Big Business' destroyed America." Carlson, "Distributism: A Short History," 7.

20. Berry, *Another Turn of the Crank*, 49. Berry also remarks that "the good use of property requires the widest possible distribution of ownership." Wendell Berry, *Home Economics: Fourteen Essays* (Berkeley, CA: Counterpoint, 1987), 106.

Chapter 9. Culture and Agriculture

1. Berry, *The Art of the Commonplace*, 301.
2. Berry, *A Continuous Harmony*, 8–9.
3. Berry, *The Art of the Commonplace*, 288.
4. Berry, *The Art of the Commonplace*, 285.
5. Salatin, *The Sheer Ecstasy of Being a Lunatic Farmer*, 8.
6. "Food is a cultural product: it cannot be produced by technology alone." Berry, *The Unsettling of America*, 41.
7. "Since our break with nature came with agriculture, it seems fitting that the healing of culture begins with agriculture, fitting that agriculture take the lead." Jackson, *Nature as Measure*, 57.
8. Quoted in Jackson, *Nature as Measure*, 84.
9. Jackson, *Nature as Measure*, 111, 113.
10. "If we brought livestock back out onto the land, rural America might be able to support a more dense human population. Re-integrating animal husbandry with crop production on smaller farms can bring life back to farm—and family farms back to life." Montgomery, *Growing a Revolution*, 195.
11. "As a culture we do a generally excellent to overzealous job thinking about food, a highly conflicted job thinking about its origins in the natural world as a living thing, and spend

almost no time thinking about our groceries as retail product." Benjamin Lorr, *The Secret Life of Groceries*, 11.

12. "By memory and association, men are made fit to inhabit the land. At present our society is almost entirely nomadic, without the comfort or the discipline of such memories, and it is moving about on the face of this continent with a mindless destructiveness, of substance and of meaning and of value, that makes Sherman's march to the sea look like a prank." Berry, *A Continuous Harmony*, 68–69.

13. Smaje, *A Small Farm Future*, 232.

14. Jackson, *Nature as Measure*, 114–15.

15. Berry, *What Are People For?*, 157, 166.

16. Berry, *Sex, Economy, Freedom & Community*, 119.

Chapter 10. A Cry for Food Freedom

1. "America was founded on food.... The Revolution was, by and large, a direct response to British taxation (without representation), and specifically British taxes on food. Sam Dean, "Was the American Revolution Fought for Food Freedom?", *Bon Appetit*, July 4, 2013, http://www .bonappetit.com/trends/article/was-the-american-revolution-fought-for-food-freedom.

2. "Jefferson saw food as the linchpin of a free society, and the self-sufficient farmer as the ideal citizen, the freest of all men." Dean, "Was the American Revolution Fought for Food Freedom?"

3. James E. McWilliams, *A Revolution in Eating: How the Quest for Food Shaped America* (New York: Columbia University Press, 2005), 297.

4. Wickard v. Filburn, 317 U.S. 111 (1942).

5. Wickard v. Filburn, 317 U.S. 111 (1942), 118, 127.

6. Wickard v. Filburn, 317 U.S. 111 (1942), 128.

7. Gonzales v. Raich, 545 U.S. 1 (2005).

8. Constitution of the State of Maine, Article 1, Section 25, https://legislature.maine.gov/ros /LawsOfMaine/#Const.

9. "This massive ascendancy of corporate power over democratic process is probably the most ominous development since the end of World War II, and for the most part 'the free world' seems to be regarding it as merely normal." Berry, *Bringing It to the Table*, 67.

10. "Everyday patriots responded as much to abstract principles as they did to the concrete reality of their material lives. The connection among food, local trade, and Revolutionary activity mattered so deeply because if there was one single customary right that white colonists throughout the colonies universally and passionately valued it was their ability to produce and consume their own food and gain access to those foods that they didn't produce. In a very real sense, food was freedom." McWilliams, *A Revolution in Eating*, 283–84.

11. Bowman v. Monsanto Co., 569 U.S. 278 (2013).

12. Salatin, *Everything I Want to Do Is Illegal*, chapter 11.

13. Berry, *Bringing It to the Table*, 101.

14. "Corporate control of food and globalization of agriculture are robbing millions of their livelihoods and their right to food.... This phenomenon of the stolen harvest ... is being experienced in every society, as small farms and small farmers are pushed to extinction, as monocultures replace biodiverse crops, as farming is transformed from the production of nourishing and diverse foods into the creation of markets for genetically engineered seeds, herbicides, and pesticides." Shiva, *Stolen Harvest*, 7.

15. See Charles MacFarlane, "Why Is the USDA Buying Submachine Guns?" *Modern Farmer*, September 19, 2014, http://www.modernfarmer.com/2014/09/usda-buying-submachine-guns.

16. Linnekin, *Biting the Hand That Feeds Us*, 9. Similar warnings are sounded in Dr. Sina McCullough's *Hands Off My Food! How Government and Industry Have Corrupted Our Food and Easy Ways to Fight Back* (Columbia, SC: Watchdog Works, 2017).

17. Salatin, *Folks, This Ain't Normal*, 306.

18. John Lukacs, *Last Rites* (New Haven, CT: Yale University Press, 2009), 68.

19. "We must ask again whether or not we really want to be a free people. We must consider again the linkages between land and landownership and land use and liberty." Berry, *Another Turn of the Crank*, 23, 35.

20. In 2011, John Fonte foresaw the rise of these same neo-liberal forces as a threat to American sovereignty: "The ideology of global governance challenges the major premises of liberal democracy: individual over group rights, free speech, majority rule, democratic accountability, national identity, the primacy of the nation-state." John Fonte, *Sovereignty or Submission: Will Americans Rule Themselves or Be Ruled by Others?* (New York: Encounter Books, 2011), 185.

21. Shiva, *Stolen Harvest*, 17–18.

22. Note that large meat processors are self-regulating and issue their own recalls when their tainted products are unleashed on consumers. Not so for small producers, who are persistently hounded by the USDA and other regulatory behemoths.

23. Salatin, *Folks, This Ain't Normal*, 258, 305–306. After critiquing federal policies that deliberately lowered commodity prices in order to drive rural farmers into the cities, Wes Jackson remarks: "In our universities, there is good reason to believe that the Declaration of Independence would not be passed by university professors if it were brought to a vote today. Unlike those who signed that document, most modern scholars are less servants of the people." Jackson, *Nature as Measure*, 82.

24. Philpott, *Perilous Bounty*, 7.

25. Rodgers and Wolf, *Sacred Cow*, 132.

26. Sale, *Human Scale Revisited*, 256, 276.

27. Sale, *Human Scale Revisited*, 255. Berry, *A Continuous Harmony*, 129.

28. See Monica M. White, *Freedom Farmers: Agricultural Resistance and the Black Freedom Movement* (Chapel Hill: University of North Carolina Press, 2018). See also Bittman, *Animal, Vegetable, Junk*.

29. "Private farming was banned and those who dared engage in it were persecuted as counter-revolutionaries. . . . The ban on private smallholdings ruined peasant life at the most basic level. Villagers simply could not make a living, because they were no longer able to exploit their own land. The result was huge-scale famine." Lymbery and Oakeshott, *Farmageddon*, 289–90.

30. Berry, *Sex, Economy, Freedom & Community*, 38.

31. Berry, *The Art of Loading Brush*, 17.

32. Greer, *The Long Descent*, 204.

33. Cox, *The Green New Deal and Beyond*, xviii.

34. "Using the specter of mass extinction as a fear tactic to scare the public into compliance." Morano, *Green Fraud*, 11.

35. Morano, *Green Fraud*, 2.

36. Morano, *Green Fraud*, 3.

37. "The food police don't think we should have the freedom to eat something that might hurt us—as if their sanctioned factory-farmed supermarket fare is good." Salatin, *Folks, This Ain't Normal*, 306.

38. Joseph Mercola and Ronnie Cummins, *The Truth About COVID-19: Exposing the Great Reset, Lockdowns, Vaccine Passports, and the New Normal* (White River Junction, VT: Chelsea Green, 2021), 157.

39. "We have neglected to understand that we cannot be free if our food and its sources are controlled by someone else. The condition of the passive consumer of food is not a democratic condition. One reason to eat responsibly is to live free." Berry, *What Are People For?*, 147.

40. Berry, *Home Economics*, 108–109.

41. "Food sovereignty emphasizes 'growers and eaters' allying politically at the local level rather than 'producers and consumers' relating to each other only by seeking the best price in the market." Smaje, *A Small Farm Future*, 257.

42. Berry, *A Continuous Harmony*, 103–104, 130. Also see Berry, *Another Turn of the Crank*, xi: "Underlying all that I have written here is the assumption that a people who are entirely lacking in economic self-determination, either personal or local, and who are therefore entirely passive in dealing with the suppliers of all their goods and services, cannot be governed democratically—or not for long."

Chapter 11. The Illusion of "Renewables"

1. "If we apply those questions to bright green technology—where its materials came from, how it impacts the Earth, and what happens when it wears out—and answer them honestly: not one bright green technology helps the planet. All of them destroy what's left of the living." Jensen, Lierre, and Wilbert, *Bright Green Lies*, 455–56.

2. Greer, *The Long Descent*, 18.

3. Leopold, *The River of the Mother of God*, 197.

4. "The study finds that customer generation costs per solar MWh are estimated to be more than twice as high for residential-scale systems than the equivalent amount of utility-scale PV systems." Bruce Tsuchida et al., "Comparative Generation Costs of Utility-Scale and Residential-Scale PV in Xcel Energy Colorado's Service Area," July 2015. See also John Klar, "Taking from the Poor to Fund Solar Panels," *True North Reports*, April 1, 2021, https://www.truenorthreports.com/john-klar-taking-from-the-poor-to-fund-solar-panels.

5. Hal Harvey, Robbie Orvis, and Jeffrey Rissman, *Designing Climate Solutions: A Policy Guide for Low-Carbon Energy* (Washington, DC: Island Press Books, 2018), 64.

6. "The determination by activist journalists and TV producers to paint deforestation in the Amazon as apocalyptic was inaccurate and unfair." Michael Shellenberger, *Apocalypse Never: Why Environmental Alarmism Hurts Us All* (New York: HarperCollins, 2020), 43.

7. "Great emergencies require top-down solutions. They can be met only by mobilizing society as a whole, and establishing a command-structure that will unite the people around a single goal. And if you wish for such a command-structure, maybe with yourself and your friends (who will soon cease to be your friends) at the top of it, then you are well advised to invent the great emergency that will require it." Scruton, *How to Think Seriously About the Planet*, 82–83.

8. "All of this leaves only renewable resources such as solar power, wind, and biofuels to supply our energy. Some of these have net energies in the single figures, others are close to breakeven, and still others fall well below the breakeven point, making them useless once the energy

subsidy from oil runs out. Those that yield positive net energy have a valuable part to play in the world's energy future, but crippling problems of scale make it impossible to replace more than a small fraction of fossil fuels with renewable energy." Greer, *The Long Descent*, 17.

9. "Between January 2007 and mid-2008, corn prices increased 100 percent, wheat prices rose 83 percent, and soybean prices were up 112 percent. At the same time, growth in worldwide biofuel production diversified the use options of grains, sugarcane, soybeans, and rapeseed and contributed to higher prices for biofuel feedstocks, particularly corn.... High agricultural commodity prices encouraged producers to expand total crop acres, adjust the mix of crops planted, and increase fertilizer use to boost yields, all of which led to increased global fertilizer demand." USDA Economic Research Service, "Recent Volatility in U.S. Fertilizer Prices."

10. Greer, *The Long Descent*, 17.

11. "Continual removal of all crop residues to produce biofuels of biochar would lead back to soil degradation.... It makes no sense to cut down primary forest to produce biochar." Montgomery, *Growing a Revolution*, 218.

12. "The very concept of offsets is not only unjust but also incompatible with the sure, rapid elimination of fossil fuels.... [According to Kevin Anderson:] 'Offsetting is worse than doing nothing. It is without scientific legitimacy, is dangerously misleading, and almost certainly contributes to a net increase in the absolute rate of global emissions growth.'" Cox, *The Green New Deal and Beyond*, 118.

13. Harvey et al., *Designing Climate Solutions*, 237–38.

14. "A more direct way to reduce emissions from both manure and enteric fermentation would be to reduce the number of animals (particularly ruminants) in the agriculture system by reducing demand for meat and dairy products." Harvey et al., *Designing Climate Solutions*, 239.

15. "At the end of the day, the energy required for the process far exceeds any type of current livestock production model.... What's more, the row crops grown for this process, if not grown differently, destroy the topsoil. Ironically, if we were to try to produce the grain inputs for lab meat in a regenerative way, we'd need to use ruminant animals to do this—sort of defeating the purpose of nonanimal meat!" Rodgers and Wolf, *Sacred Cow*, 130–31.

16. Rodgers and Wolf, *Sacred Cow*, 132.

17. "The White House announced steps on Thursday to crack down on forced labor in the supply chain for solar panels in the Chinese region of Xinjiang, including a ban on imports from a silicon producer there.... A significant portion of the world's polysilicon, which is used to make solar panels, comes from Xinjiang, where the United States has accused China of committing genocide through its repression of Uyghurs and other Muslim minorities." Thomas Kaplan, Chris Buckley, and Brad Plumer, "U.S. Bans Imports of Some Chinese Solar Materials Tied to Forced Labor," *New York Times*, June 26, 2021.

18. "The technology necessary to satisfy ... [future] needs does not exist at present." Harvey et al., *Designing Climate Solutions*, 298.

19. Morano, *Green Fraud*, 22.

20. So-called incentives and mandates have turned energy markets upside down. In many states with very poor sunlight, these solar technologies are abysmally unprofitable without government intrusion: "less-valuable power is more profitable." Meredith Angwin, *Shorting the Grid: The Hidden Fragility of Our Electric Grid* (Wilder, VT: Carnot Communications, 2020), 5. These programs are both economically and environmentally counterproductive, but they produce guaranteed profits and industry growth for those ever-present industry stakeholders.

21. Jensen, Lierre, and Wilbert, *Bright Green Lies*, 465.

22. Cox, *The Green New Deal and Beyond*, xxvii.

23. Schumacher, *Small Is Beautiful*, 6.

24. Gershuny and Smillie, *The Soul of Soil*, 39.

25. Jeremy Bloom, "Here's the Full Text of Congress' Green New Deal, Introduced by Rep. Alexandria Ocasio-Cortez," *Clean Technica*, February 8, 2019, http://www.cleantechnica .com/2019/02/08/heres-the-full-text-of-congress-green-new-deal-resolution-introduced-by -rep-alexandra-ocasio-cortez.

26. "It is conceivable that energy sources such as solar or nuclear could make energy so abundant that the industrial food system could continue while largely ceasing to produce carbon dioxide. While this development is something to be hoped for, it will not solve the . . . looming threat of topsoil loss." Rodgers and Wolf, *Sacred Cow*, 127.

27. "The industrial age is a pulse waveform, a single, bell-shaped, nonrepeating curve centered on 1979. Since no renewable energy resource can provide more than a small fraction of the immense amounts of fossil fuel energy we've squandered in the recent past . . . the millennia of low tech cultures preceding the industrial pulse—before the fantastic treasure of fossil fuel was discovered and unlocked—will be balanced by millennia of low tech cultures after the industrial pulse—when the treasure will be gone forever." Greer, *The Long Descent*, 29.

Chapter 12. Regenerating Human Health

1. McCullough, *Hands Off My Food!*, 35. The more Americans investigate these food production and processing issues, the more they will awaken to a "well-earned distrust."

2. "For decades now the entire industrial food economy, from the large farms and feedlots to the chains of supermarkets and fast-food restaurants, has been obsessed with volume. . . . As capital replaces labor, it does so by substituting machines, drugs, and chemicals for human workers and for the natural health and fertility of the soil." Berry, *Bringing It to the Table*, 231.

3. McCullough, *Hands Off My Food!*, 17.

4. Mercola and Cummins, *The Truth About COVID-19*, 11.

5. "Globalization has created the McDonaldization of world food, resulting in the destruction of sustainable food systems." Shiva, *Stolen Harvest*, 70.

6. Mercola and Cummins, *The Truth About COVID-19*, 11.

7. "So much has happened to our food, and so quickly by evolutionary terms, that some scientists are now framing our disordered eating as a vast and terrible mismatch with our biology—because our brain and body, in their ability to size up and metabolize the calories in what we eat and drink, just haven't had time to adjust to the change in our diet." Michael Moss, *Hooked: Food, Free Will, and How the Food Giants Exploit Our Addictions* (New York: Random House, 2021), xxvi.

8. Shanna H. Swan and Stacey Colino, *Countdown: How Our Modern World Is Threatening Sperm Counts, Altering Male and Female Reproductive Development, and Imperiling the Future of the Human Race* (New York: Scribner, 2020), 108.

9. "Like the constant dripping of water that in turn wears away the hardest stone, this birth-to-death contact with dangerous chemicals may in the end prove disastrous. Each of these recurrent exposures, no matter how slight, contributes to the progressive buildup of chemicals in our bodies and so to cumulative poisoning. Probably no person is immune to contact with this spreading contamination unless he lives in the most isolated situation imaginable." Rachel Carson, *Silent Spring* (Boston: Houghton Mifflin Harcourt, 1962, 2002), 173–74.

10. Joseph Mercola, "New Study Links Phthalates to Cardiovascular Disease," *Epoch Times*, December 16, 2021.

11. "It appears that given the increasing number and volume of endocrine-disrupting chemicals and other toxins in our world, the damaging effects could be additive over time in descendants of the originally exposed person." Swan and Colino, *Countdown*, 139.

12. "This much is clear: The problem isn't that something is inherently wrong with the human body as it has evolved over time; it's that chemicals in our environment and unhealthy lifestyle practices in our modern world are disrupting our hormonal balance, causing varying degrees of reproductive havoc that can foil fertility and lead to long-term health problems even after one has left the reproductive years." Swan and Colino, *Countdown*, 2.

13. Leo Trasande, *Sicker Fatter Poorer* (Boston: Houghton Mifflin Harcourt, 2019), 136.

14. "Ultra processed foods, more akin to poison than actual food, are making us sick as surely as if we were vitamin deficient.... Even accounting for COVID-19, chronic disease is our country's and the world's leading killer." Bittman, *Animal, Vegetable, Junk*, 248.

15. "Curtailing the consumption of sugar is a public health priority, and it's likely that sugar will be thought of as the tobacco of the twenty-first century." Bittman, *Animal, Vegetable, Junk*, 187.

16. "Formula makers took over the education and caregiving process of young women throughout the world. Maternity wards were stocked with formula paraphernalia, coupons, and samples. Formula representatives dressed as nurses encouraged women to ignore nature, and doctors were bought off to become formula pushers." Bittman, *Animal, Vegetable, Junk*, 196.

17. This calls to memory the horrible side effects of the highly marketed drug thalidomide.

18. "Producers continue to distribute free formula samples in hospitals, to label their formula in languages other than that of the country in which they're selling, to pay health professionals to recommend formula, and to advertise recommendations that run counter to Code guidelines. Save the Children estimates that Code violations result in the preventable deaths of almost four thousand children a day." Bittman, *Animal, Vegetable, Junk*, 197.

19. Bittman, *Animal, Vegetable, Junk*, 198. (A discussion of the cereal industry and its influence follow.)

20. Sustainable Pulse, "A Short History of Glyphosate," *The Natural Farmer*, August 10, 2020.

21. "The ubiquity of insidiously harmful chemicals in the modern world is threatening the reproductive development and functionality of both humans and other species." Swan and Colino, *Countdown*, 9.

22. "The problem of plastic is one that we could solve, both nationally and globally. If no attempt is being made to solve it, this is in part because of the great climate 'emergency' upon which all our treaty-making energies are being uselessly expended." Scruton, *How to Think Seriously About the Planet*, 69.

23. McCullough, *Hands Off My Food!*, 59.

24. "In total, over 90 percent of all corn, soy and cotton planted in the United States is genetically engineered. The three government-subsidized crops take up roughly 169 million acres of farmland." McCullough, *Hands Off My Food!*, 62

25. Joel Salatin and Sina McCullough, *Beyond Labels: A Doctor and a Farmer Conquer Food Confusion One Bite at a Time* (Swoope, VA: Polyface, 2020).

26. Sally Fallon and Mary G. Enig, *Nourishing Traditions: The Cookbook That Challenges Politically Correct Nutrition and the Diet Dictocrats*, 2nd ed. (Washington, DC: NewTrends, 2001).

27. About 80 million pounds of atrazine are applied annually in the United States.

28. Stephanie Seneff, *Toxic Legacy: How the Weedkiller Glyphosate Is Destroying Our Health and the Environment* (White River Junction, VT: Chelsea Green, 2021), 10.

29. Seneff, *Toxic Legacy*, 14, 145.

30. Seneff, *Toxic Legacy*, 11.

31. Lymbery and Oakeshott, *Farmageddon*, 271–72.

32. "Nutritional density is a difficult thing to assess over time, but studies put the loss of nutrition in fruits and vegetables over the past sixty years at anywhere between 5 and 40 percent." Tickell, *Kiss the Ground*, 78.

33. "Since 1950, much of the good stuff in the plants we grow—protein, calcium, iron, vitamin C, to name just four—has declined by as much as one-third, a landmark 2000 study showed. Everything is becoming more like junk food." Wallace-Wells, *The Uninhabitable Earth*, 63.

34. Victor Davis Hanson relates the transformation of his family's grape harvest into a commercial operation in which industrial practices converted their fruit for market into "obscene balloons full of red sweet juice that never aged." Hanson, *Fields Without Dreams*, 140.

35. "China is undergoing a food-confidence crisis. . . . The public can no longer ignore the shady origins of much of China's food." Lymbery and Oakeshott, *Farmageddon*, 291.

36. Lymbery and Oakeshott, *Farmageddon*, 148.

37. "This steady diet of corn along with the cramped quarters in feedlots and confined dairies tends to keep cattle in chronic poor health, so the operators routinely mix antibiotics into their feed. Antibiotic-resistant bacteria can develop as a result and then be passed on to humans through beef consumption and leave us vulnerable when we're sick and need the intervention of antibiotics." Ohlson, *The Soil Will Save Us*, 210.

38. Jamie Metzl, "It's Time for a 'Moo Shot' to Disrupt Industrial Animal Agriculture," *The Hill*, October 20, 2021, https://thehill.com/opinion/energy-environment/577633-its-time-for-a-moo-shot-to-disrupt-industrial-animal-agriculture.

39. "Nationally, the United States should also create a food research agency as part of the Biden administration's Build Back Better initiative. It could be based on the model of the Defense Advanced Research Projects Agency—which spurred the creation of the internet, stealth technology, mRNA vaccines—backed with significant funding and a mandate to bring together academia, industry, government and civil society players. This agency—the Agriculture and Food Advanced Research Projects Agency—let's call it, could be co-sponsored by the U.S. Department of Agriculture and the Food and Drug Administration. This food research agency could help ensure American leadership in this critically important area and spark a transition away from industrial animal farming and toward alternative and cellular animal agriculture." Metzl, "It's Time for a 'Moo Shot.'"

40. Tickell, *Kiss the Ground*, 81.

41. Tickell, *Kiss the Ground*, 64–65.

42. Scruton, *How to Think Seriously About the Planet*, 398–99.

Chapter 13. America's Youth Are Our Small-Farm Future

1. Smaje, *A Small Farm Future*, 76. Joel Salatin similarly observes: "Maintaining a sense of awe and mystery toward the universe, cultivating a profound sense of dependency on something bigger than ourselves, seem to be a fundamental responsibility we adults should have toward our children. To abdicate this responsibility is to populate our culture with manipulators and dominion-thinkers on overdrive." Salatin, *Folks, This Ain't Normal*, 6.

2. Jackson, *Nature as Measure*, 113. Wendell Berry agrees: "An important source of instruction and pleasure to a child growing up on a farm was participation in the family economy. Children learned about the adult world by participating in it in a small way, by doing a little work and earning a little money—a much more effective, because pleasurable, and a much cheaper method than the present one of requiring the adult world to be learned in the abstract in school." Berry, *Bringing It to the Table*, 82.

3. McCullough, *Hands Off My Food!*, 17.

4. Salatin, *Folks, This Ain't Normal*, 17.

5. "Children are the real losers when it comes to the Farm Bill. They are stuck eating the highly-processed foods that the government has encouraged our farmers to overproduce.... To add insult to injury, as taxpayers, we are charged twice for the foods subsidized in our children's lunches. We pay farmers through the federal subsidies included in the Farm Bill. After these crops are processed into food-like substances, we pay another tax when the subsidized junk foods are in the nutrition programs at schools. In other words, first we subsidize the crops, like wheat and corn, and then we buy them back to be used in our children's lunches." McCullough, *Hands Off My Food!*, 69–70.

6. "The adoption of conservation agriculture will depend on how we instruct our youth. And the United States needs some kind of program to connect young farmers to older farmers who are looking for someone to eventually take over their farms.... We also need programs to put young people back on the land—and reward them if they build soil health. The average age of American farmers is about sixty. As the current generation of farmers retires, we need to encourage a new generation to return to the land—and train and equip them to adopt regenerative practices." Montgomery, *Growing a Revolution*, 236, 277.

7. "If we can get people trained in ecological agriculture, we could change the structure of American agriculture very fast, for in another ten to fifteen years many of these people would move into positions of responsibility." Jackson, *Nature as Measure*, 137.

Chapter 14. Policies That Let Small Farms Breathe

1. "But to solve the question of the storage of carbon, it's necessary that we have accompanying public policies. And we cannot succeed without farmers. Our farmers started this a long time ago." Tickell, *Kiss the Ground*, 31, quoting France's former Minister of Agriculture Stephane Le Foll.

2. "Many of those larger companies aren't the enemy but are, rather, part of the solution." Linnekin, *Biting the Hand That Feeds Us*, 199.

3. "Surplus production, which once kept peasants dependably and profitably poor, became in modern times a major impoverisher and bankruptor of farmers." Wendell Berry, *The Art of Loading Brush*, 95.

4. Wendell Berry and other seasoned veterans of farm markets are adamant that such an overarching structure is necessary: "The related problems of low prices and overproduction of a single but significant crop were solved for about sixty years ... in the only way they could be solved: by a combination of price supports and production controls." Berry, *The Art of Loading Brush*, 44.

5. "Carbon farming could have a big impact on both agricultural production and climate change." Tickell, *Kiss the Ground*, 219.

6. Norberg-Hodge, *Local Is Our Future*, 79.

7. "American [yeomen]...[are] the most clever and diligent of farmers in the world....American farmers come alive only when there are genuine shortages, when they are told people need them to produce food, when they are turned loose to pour labor and capital into the ground, guided by their own degree of expertise and daring." Hanson, *Fields Without Dreams: Defending the Agrarian Idea*, 182.

8. Seneff, *Toxic Legacy*, 170. See also Berry, *The Art of Loading Brush*, 152: "Most damaging has been the division between the field crop industry and the meat-animal industry. To remove the farm animals from farming is to remove more than half of the need for knowledge, skill, and intelligence, and nearly all of the need for sympathy."

9. Seneff, *Toxic Legacy*, 170.

10. "Under the right conditions, grazing ruminants can be beneficial to landscapes, keeping carbon, topsoil, and water in the ground while adding nutrients. But by confining these animals, by feeding them grain, we not only wreck their health but increase the amount of land used for monoculture of corn and soy, contributing to erosion and runoff problems, soil oxidation, and the release of carbon. Taken together, this may double the contribution of industrial animal production to greenhouse gas emissions." Bittman, *Animal, Vegetable, Junk*, 245. See also Philpott, *Perilous Bounty*, 176: "The factory-livestock farming system that requires such an enormous and inefficient allocation of corn and soybeans must be rethought from the ground up. The most viable solution is to ramp up pasture-based meat production, both within the Corn Belt and in regions across the country."

11. "Contrary to what many will assume, we do have the acreage to grass-finish all the beef cattle in the US. As soil health improves, so does water retention and the amount and quality of the pasture. With good management techniques like intensive grazing, the 'carrying capacity' of the land is increased, meaning more cattle can be placed on the same amount of land." Rodgers and Wolf, *Sacred Cow*, 167.

12. "What boosted numbers was not so much scientific miracles but massive price subsidies." Bittman, *Animal, Vegetable, Junk*, 205.

13. "The Farm Bill in the US gives out around $30 billion in the form of subsidies to farmers, with three-quarters going to just a tenth of farms—generally the wealthiest and biggest. Corn (maize) continues to be the most heavily subsidized crop, underpinning a cheap-meat culture based on the products of factory-farmed animals fed cereals and soya instead of grass and forage from the land." Lymbery and Oakeshott, *Farmageddon*, xiii.

14. Philpott, *Perilous Bounty*, 184.

15. "From direct payments to subsidized crop insurance, the system that has evolved since the 1980s keeps farmers just scraping by while delivering as much corn and soybeans as they can, typically way more crop than the market demands....These policies...keep the profits humming for the agribusiness industry, which in turn uses its financial muscle to keep it that way." Philpott, *Perilous Bounty*, 182.

16. McCullough, *Hands Off My Food!*, 56, 58, 71, 77.

17. "Welcome to the new 'circle of life' in modern day America, where taxpayers foot the bill to make cheap processed food. Then, taxpayers foot the bill again to heal the people who get sick from the subsidized food....In addition, while propping up a system that creates cheap junk food, our government drives up the price of fruits and vegetables." McCullough, *Hands Off My Food!*, 64–65. See also Bittman, *Animal, Vegetable, Junk*, 293: "Today, government subsidizes a destructive form of food and forces it into markets everywhere."

18. Bittman, *Animal, Vegetable, Junk*, 187.

19. According to the USDA: "Among major U.S. field crops, corn uses the most fertilizer, has the highest fertilizer costs per acre ($93 at average 2007 prices), and has the highest fertilizer costs as a share of operating costs for planting, growing, and harvesting (41 percent)." USDA Economic Research Service, "Recent Volatility in U.S. Fertilizer Prices."

20. Rodgers and Wolf, *Sacred Cow*, 164.

21. Bittman, *Animal, Vegetable, Junk*, 185–86.

22. "Federal crop insurance continues to do everything to support conventional agriculture and very little to support alternatives. Farmers pay a reduced rate for crop insurance when they plant seeds that are Roundup-ready or have some other genetic modification, because these crops are seen as being less risky than non-GMO crops. On the other hand, they pay a premium on their crop insurance if they farm organically." Ohlson, *The Soil Will Save Us*, 178.

23. "We in the United States have our subsidies backward. Changing crop insurance programs and subsidies to promote building soil health could better align farmers' short-term interests with society's long-term interests. Why not financially backstop farmers for the first couple of years, during the transition period? . . . From a societal perspective, it makes sense to restructure agricultural subsidies to reward farmers for improving soil fertility—it makes none to continue subsidizing practices that do the opposite." Montgomery, *Growing a Revolution*, 276.

24. Norberg-Hodge, *Local Is Our Future*, 52.

25. "Ending farm subsidies and other federal, state and local rules that favor big food producers over smaller ones means sustainable food producers need fewer rules—not more—to succeed." Scruton, *How to Think Seriously About the Planet*, 196.

26. "The U.S. leads the world in the production of grain-fed beef. This production advantage primarily exists because grains and soy are so heavily subsidized under the USDA federal farm program. Grassfed beef producers in America are unsubsidized. The subsidies on grain permits our domestic grain-fed beef products to be marketed below the pricing thresholds that would allow stiff competition from imported product. The big winners in the repeal of COOL are the multinational meat companies. This has allowed them to shop for meat in the cheapest markets in the world, and bring it into the best market in the world, and sell it to consumers as 'Product of the USA,' even though the animal had never drawn a single breath of air in the United States." Ronnie Cummins, "Do You Know Where Your Meat Comes From?" Organic Consumers Association, May 27, 2018, http://www.ecowatch.com/country-of-origin-labeling-meat-2572003641.html.

27. "Unsurprisingly, less expensive grass-fed beef from these countries has been rolling into the U.S. for some time. By value, 75 percent to 80 percent of grass-fed beef sold in the U.S. comes from abroad. . . . The labeling gets even trickier, since the designation 'grass-fed' doesn't have an official USDA definition. Unlike anything with an organic seal, which requires adherence to more definitive USDA rules, calling beef 'grass-fed' doesn't require an on-farm inspection or even mandate that animals live freely on a pasture." Deena Shanker, "Most Grass-Fed Beef Labeled 'Product of U.S.A.' Is Imported," *Bloomberg*, May 23, 2019.

28. Salatin, *The Sheer Ecstasy of Being a Lunatic Farmer*, 245.

29. Scruton, *How to Think Seriously About the Planet*, 241.

30. Wendell Berry has rightly complained about the excesses of these regulations: "Aside from the fashions of leisure and affluence—so valuable to corporations, so destructive of values—the

greatest destroyer of the small economies has been the doctrine of sanitation." Berry, *Bringing It to the Table*, 83.

31. "The path to promoting the return of livestock to smaller diversified farms lies in rebuilding decentralized infrastructure. Like small-scale slaughter facilities to make meat production and processing easier for small farms." Montgomery, *Growing a Revolution*, 278.

32. Linnekin, *Biting the Hand That Feeds Us*, 12.

33. Open Markets Institute and Friends of the Earth, "Agricultural Carbon Markets, Payments, and Data: Big Ag's Latest Power Grab," March 2023, https://foe.org/wp-content/uploads/2023/02/Carbon-Markets-Report_ExecutiveSummary_Final.pdf.

34. "In almost every country, tax regulations systematically discriminate against small and medium-scale businesses. . . . Reversing this bias in the tax system would help local economies and create more jobs by favoring people instead of machines." Norberg-Hodge, *Local Is Our Future*, 49–50.

35. Salatin, *The Sheer Ecstasy of Being a Lunatic Farmer*, 99.

36. "Amending federal farm credit rates could also slow the treadmill. Generous terms promote borrowing for irrigation equipment; to pay that debt, borrowers farm more land. Offering lower rates for equipment that reduces water use and withholding loans for standard, wasteful equipment could nudge farmers toward conservation. . . . The most powerful tool is the tax code. Currently, farmers receive deductions for declining groundwater levels and can write off depreciation on irrigation equipment. Replacing these perks with a tax credit for stabilizing groundwater and substituting a depreciation schedule favoring more efficient irrigation equipment could provide strong incentives to conserve water." Sanderson et al., "Farmers Are Depleting the Ogallala Aquifer Because the Government Pays Them to Do It."

37. "Taxing food drives us further from a free market and closer to serfdom." McCullough, *Hands Off My Food!*, 203.

38. Smaje, *A Small Farm Future*, 266.

39. "We already grow more than enough food for 9 billion people. . . . The problem is not one of production, but of distribution." Ohlson, *The Soil Will Save Us*, 171.

40. Bittman, *Animal, Vegetable, Junk*, 246.

41. This includes the indirect subsidization of large industrial food companies that inordinately benefit from public expenditures in roadways and other infrastructure. "Nothing will solve the problem of transport that does not redress the balance in favour of the local economy, not least the local food economy, which has been damaged by the hidden subsidies enjoyed by the supermarket chains and by the heavy hand of the state on the practice of agriculture." Scruton, *How to Think Seriously About the Planet*, 395.

42. "We should not be discouraged to find that local food economies can grow only gradually; it is better that they should grow gradually. But as they grow they will bring about a significant return of power, wealth, and health to the people." Berry, *Another Turn of the Crank*, 6–7. See also Smaje, *A Small Farm Future*, 192: "A good deal of effort in the alternative farming and alternative economics movement dedicates itself to opening out that concentrated middleman sector, for example by supporting direct farmer-to-consumer retailing or wholesale co-operatives that don't disproportionately extract value from producers."

43. Philpott, *Perilous Bounty*, 176.

44. Ohlson, *The Soil Will Save Us*, 212.

45. Emily Broad Leib, Introduction to Linnekin, *Biting the Hand That Feeds Us*, x. Other sources estimate the total for the developed world is 30 percent. See Ohlson, *The Soil Will Save Us*, 171.

46. "Real opportunities do exist for repurposing rural and urban organic wastes to produce energy, sequester carbon, and build soil fertility." Tickell, *Kiss the Ground*, 219. See also Berry, *The Gift of Good Land* (New York: North Point Press, 1981), 186: "One of the laws that the world imposes on us is that everything must be returned to its source to be used again." More controversially, human waste can also be repurposed for agricultural compost. David R. Montgomery outlines how these resources can be employed in agriculture in *Growing a Revolution*, 265.

47. "We could fully meet our national demand for phosphorus fertilizers for corn through recycling just over a third of the manure our livestock produce. Yet, at present, only 5 percent of U.S. cropland receives any manure at all." Montgomery, *Growing a Revolution*, 263.

48. Mercola and Cummins, *The Truth About COVID-19*, 89, 157. See also Stephanie Seneff: "Health care is projected to account for nearly 20 percent of our gross domestic product by 2028. At the same time . . . our health outcomes lag behind most countries in the industrialized world." Seneff, *Toxic Legacy*, 144.

49. Leopold, *The River of the Mother of God*, 22–23.

50. Ohlson, *The Soil Will Save Us*, 183.

51. Jackson, *Nature as Measure*, 151. See also Berry, *What Are People For?*, 112: "The land and its human communities are not being thought about in places of study and leadership, and this failure to think is causing damage. But if one lives in a country place, and if one loves it, one must think about it."

52. "Shifting these expenditures towards those that encourage smaller-scale, diversified agriculture would help revitalize rural economies in both North and South, while promoting biodiversity, healthier soils, food security, balanced and diverse diets, and fresher food." Norberg-Hodge, *Local Is Our Future*, 52–53.

53. "Peasant farming remains more efficient than industrial farming. Were it given the kind of support that's been lent to industry-backed farming—research, subsidies, cheap or free land, and such—it could become better still. Instead those resources are siphoned away from the people who could build a real food system and instead used to ensure profits for industrial agriculture." Bittman, *Animal, Vegetable, Junk*, 291.

54. Carson, *Silent Spring*, 278.

55. "Research funded by big businesses doesn't tend to focus on low-cost preventative practices. But farmers increasingly do." Montgomery, *Growing a Revolution*, 176.

56. Coodley and Sarasohn, *The Green Years, 1964–1976*, 269.

57. Leopold, *The River of the Mother of God*, 22.

58. "To analyze the problem of action, the first thing to grasp is that government, no matter how good, can only do certain things. Government can't raise crops, maintain small scattered structures, or bring to bear on small local matters that combination of solicitude, foresight, and skill which we call husbandry. Husbandry watches no clock, knows no season of cessation, and for the most part is paid for in love, not dollars. Husbandry on somebody else's land is a contradiction in terms. Husbandry is the heart of conservation." Leopold, *The River of the Mother of God*, 298.

59. "Governments need to stop subsidizing environmentally and socially destructive activities and shift those same subsidies to activities that restore biotic communities and that promote

local food self-sufficiency. . . . The list of activities to be halted must include the manufacture of photovoltaic panels, windmills, hybrid cars, and so on." Jensen, Keith, and Wilbert, *Bright Green Lies*, 435, 443.

60. Bittman, *Animal, Vegetable, Junk*, 204.

61. "Two trillion dollars is more than three times the military budget, which is already enough to establish and nurture, for example, ten million new farmers—around enough to supply all Americans with real food." Bittman, *Animal, Vegetable, Junk*, 294.

62. See Philpott, *Perilous Bounty*, 176.

63. "Regenerative techniques can heal the Earth, arresting and even mitigating climate change by sequestering carbon in the soil. We can identify organic products that reduce weed growth without poisoning the Earth or the organisms that live in and on the soil. The human immune system functions best when the human it is protecting is well fed and toxicant-free. If food crops are well supplied with nutrients, they, too, are hardier, better able to withstand fungus growth and insect attacks. This creates a cycle of health, reducing the need for fungicides, insecticides, and herbicides." Seneff, *Toxic Legacy*, 162.

64. Philpott, *Perilous Bounty*, 177, 178.

65. "But in order for initiatives like these to spread more widely, localization also requires 'top down' policy change to reverse the structural forces that now promote the large and global. The aim of these policy shifts . . . is to promote 'small scale on a large scale.'" Norberg-Hodge, *Local Is Our Future*, 46. And Mark Bittman writes: "The true obstacle isn't necessarily discovering a sustainable farming method that mitigates the damage of industrial agriculture, but making the efforts more widespread so they become viable alternatives. People talk about 'scaling up,' but that really isn't the answer; it's more about scaling out, replicating small- and medium-scale sustainable systems in millions of places worldwide. In this way we can begin to transform and replace the industrial agriculture system." Bittman, *Animal, Vegetable, Junk*, 285.

Conclusion: A Beginning

1. 2016 Republican Policy Platform, 17. https://prod-cdn-static.gop.com/docs/Resolution _Platform_2020.pdf.

2. 2016 Republican Policy Platform, 18.

3. 2016 Republican Policy Platform, 18.

4. 2016 Republican Policy Platform, 21

5. "There you have it, the birth of Big Ag: The farming industrialized complex that the political left loves to hate was an unintended consequence of the Farm Bill, which is a bill that was enacted by the Democrats." McCullough, *Hands Off My Food!*, 72.

6. As Herbert Agar summarized, "Either we restore property, or we restore slavery through the communism found at the end of capitalism's work." Carlson, "Distributism: A Short History," 12–13.

7. McWilliams, *A Revolution in Eating*, 291.

INDEX

INDEX

INDEX

INDEX

INDEX

ABOUT THE AUTHOR

JOHN KLAR is a former tax attorney turned subsistence farmer follow-ing a debilitating battle with Lyme disease. From international corporate tax consultant to off-grid homesteader, John has crisscrossed the growing urban-rural divide. This odd combination of experiences has conditioned him to advocate for greater connection to land and food supply and for policies that will nurture them.

John lives in Vermont with his wife, Jackie, whose training as a reg-istered nurse has made her the ideal farming partner. The Klars hope to humbly encourage more people to take the leap into the priceless rewards of farming as rebellion against industrial alienation and for physical and spiritual rebirth.

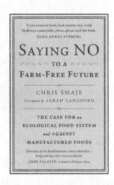

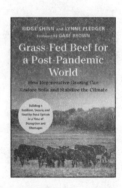